Watchdog

25 Years
of Muckraking and
Rabblerousing

BILL LUEDERS

JONES BOOKS • MADISON, WISCONSIN

Jones Books
3 Loon Lane
Madison, Wisconsin 53717
jonesbooks.com

First edition, first printing

All columns and articles in this collection were
originally published in *Isthmus*, except as otherwise noted.

Cover photo by Timothy Hughes
Book design by Ellen J. Meany

Library of Congress Cataloging-in-Publication Data

Lueders, Bill.
    Watchdog : 25 years of muckraking and rabblerousing / by Bill Lueders.
            p. cm.
    Selections of the author's previously published newspaper columns
from the weekly, *Isthmus*, (Madison, Wisconsin).
    ISBN 978-0-9790475-5-8 (alk. paper)
    I. Isthmus. II. Title.
    PN4874.L84A25 2010
    814'.54–dc22

                                                2010028705

Printed in the U.S.A.

For Linda, the love of my life

Contents

PART 3: GETTING PERSONAL

ABOUT THE AUTHOR

Foreword

IN AN INTRODUCTION TO A BOOK OF COLUMNS BY MIKE ROYKO, STUDS
Terkel noted that when Royko was trying to get to the bottom of the story
– to get to the truth – he appeared "possessed by a demon."

Terkel wrote: "Like a famished alley mutt, he digs away at the bone
of truth. Observers can point out scores of stories he has uncovered that
might otherwise have been safely interred. Usually they concerned the 'ordinary citizen' or the wholly dispossessed."

For the past 25 years in Madison, it has been our great good fortune to
have our own demon dog of print journalism, an alley mutt hungry for the
truth. Bill Lueders' splendid new collection could not have a better title. He
has been a "Watchdog," all right.

As an editor, reporter and columnist at *Isthmus*, Madison's highly
regarded weekly paper, Lueders has angered cops, prosecutors and powerful politicians with his opinions and investigations. He has been fearless
in the face of authority, and anyone who thinks that is easy is mistaken. It
is much easier to be liked. The relentless pursuit of truth makes people
uneasy.

Many in the journalism business in Madison weren't sure what to make
of Lueders when he first landed in town in 1986. He was admittedly green
– "a truck driver who edited and wrote in his spare time," as he notes in an
early column in this book – when *Isthmus* hired him away from the alternative paper in his native Milwaukee.

But young as he was, Lueders had a plum job – news editor of *Isthmus*
– in the landscape of Madison journalism. What he wrote got noticed. Some
of the early stuff – or so it says here – was a little shrill. In hindsight, it seems
the work of a passionate journalist looking to find his voice. What matters
is that Bill Lueders found that voice soon enough.

Even in the early columns collected here, Lueders' trademarks – an
affinity for the underdog, a distrust of conventional wisdom and the platitudes of elected officials – are in evidence. His distain for Bronson La

Follette – hiding, in Lueders' view, behind a revered name and refusing to answer reporters' questions – is as palpable as his admiration for Gene Parks, who for all his demerits was always front and center in the fight, open to a fault.

The opinion columns that comprise one of three sections of this book – the others are investigations and a shorter section titled "Getting Personal" – offer some surprises, at least to the reader who might know Lueders' work only casually. How can an editor of a good liberal paper in a good liberal city like Madison be against hate crime legislation? Lueders' position on the issue appears linked to his belief – it might be his core belief – in the absolute right in this country to freedom of expression. Much in the same vein, he has labored mightily to ensure the availability of public records to the public, a statement that would be comic except that so many officials seem to want to keep them private.

Lueders' best-known story, which is beyond the scope of this collection, is the "Patty" rape case. Reporting this tale to the end took the better part of a decade, and resulted in a fine book, *Cry Rape*, Lueders' second after a biography of the radical journalist Erwin Knoll.

The Patty story – in which local authorities not only refused to believe she'd been raped, but wound up charging her with filing a false report – took a toll on Lueders. It got personal. He became so convinced of her truthfulness that at one point he wrote a letter to Madison's mayor at the time, Sue Bauman, offering to quit his job if he was proved wrong. In the end, Lueders – and Patty – were proved right, but something had shifted in Bill, in terms of his bond with Madison.

"It has screwed up my relationship with my city," he told me in 2006, when the book was published. "I think the city of Madison was deeply implicated in the injustice that was done to Patty."

Occasionally in his work in *Isthmus*, Lueders gives his readers a peek into his personal life. It is both a smart and winning thing to do. People who read you, and some have been reading Bill Lueders for a quarter of a century now, appreciate a look behind the curtain. Some of those columns are presented in the concluding section of this book, and they are welcome after the sense of gravity that necessarily informs the investigative pieces.

Lueders takes us skydiving; in search of the perfect pet (he plants a garden instead); to the gym (good intentions, but he throws in the towel); to the dentist and to the cabin he and his wife had built in the woods.

Best of all is his ode to his late father, a hard-working route salesman for a Milwaukee laundry. It is unsentimental – Lueders acknowledges an awkwardness in the relationship – but it's clear the son learned much from the father, and more than that, loved him very much.

Writing a couple of months after his father died, of lung cancer, Bill wrote, "Goodbye, Dad. I'll miss you. I'll fight like hell for you until the end."

The rest of us, especially those of us in Madison, can be glad about that, and glad, too, for this lively and important book.

DOUG MOE

Preface

GROWING UP, I NEVER WANTED TO BE A JOURNALIST. WHEN SISTER JUDITH Ann predicted this would be my fate, in her annoyingly perfect penmanship on the back of a 47-page paper I wrote in 7th grade (it was about Milwaukee's own wannabe assassin Arthur Bremer and titled "In Lukewarm Blood"), I rebelled against it. If she wanted this future for me, I didn't.

The only journalism class I ever took was in high school, and the only thing I remember about it was that the teacher, Sister Michael, once grabbed me by the hair and banged my head on the desk for not paying attention, prompting my legendary rejoinder, "What's your bag, man?"

In my senior year of high school, I helped start an alternative newspaper called *Speak Easy* – which years later, in circumstances too involved to recount here, drew a mention in *The New Yorker*. That same passion for an alternative outlet drove me, when I was finishing up my English major at the University of Wisconsin – Milwaukee in 1982, to be part of the team that founded a paper called *The Crazy Shepherd*.

It was all downhill from there. An internship at *The Progressive* in 1984, during the summer I turned 25, introduced me to the craft of editing, which led to my anointment as editor of the *Shepherd* that fall (the first and only promotion of my journalistic career) and to freelance editing work for *Milwaukee Magazine*. Then, in March 1986, on the day after my son Jesse was born, I was hired as news editor at *Isthmus*, Madison's then-still-young alternative weekly.

And thus I became, against all odds and most logic, a professional journalist. It's a role I've grown into over time, as the pieces collected in this book attest. But some of my favorites are from those early days, when my style was uncorrupted by the dictates of convention, which in my best moments I manage still to avoid.

The book is called *Watchdog*, the current name of the biweekly news column I've written for more than two decades. But it includes no items from these columns, or any other short-form news reporting – which probably accounts for 80 percent of the work I've done over the last quarter century.

Instead, with a little help from some friends, I've selected a sampling of opinion columns, longer investigative stories and other, often more personal writing. These are pieces that seemed to best withstand the test of time, and cry out for preservation. I've made a few tweaks and trims, mostly trims, but for the most part this collection reflects what appeared in now-yellowing newsprint and stiffening magazine pages. Indeed, much of what was here was scanned in electronically from these archival sources.

I don't mean to date myself. I think I have a few years of living and writing left. But for various reasons, this feels like a good time to bring together some of the work that I've already done, in book form. I hope it finds a way into your homes and hearts.

Thanks to Joan Strasbaugh of Jones Books (yes, the name is a pun) for her efforts to enrich the world, one book at a time; I am proud to join her shelf of achievements. Thanks also to *Isthmus* newspaper for believing in me and putting up with me, especially to Vince O'Hern and Linda Baldwin for their support of this book, and my colleagues Dean Robbins and Michana Buchman for helping me prepare it. I'm grateful to the photographers who let me use their work and Timothy Hughes for taking the cover photo of me and my dog Bailey. Special thanks to Ellen Meany, *Isthmus'* extraordinary creative director, for designing the cover and doing the layout, and to Doug Moe, for his lovely Foreword.

Finally, and most importantly, I'd like to thank my wife, Linda Falkenstein, not just for all the help she's given me on my writing, but for being my best friend.

SUMMER 2010, MADISON, WISCONSIN

Part One

IN MY OPINION

Hello, Disneyland

The first time I saw Madison I was 9 years old and on vacation with my parents. We were making a quick detour on our way to Devil's Lake – which I had never seen before either and which sounded a lot more interesting. But then, suddenly, there it was, so majestic it almost took my breath away: the state Capitol. Wow, I thought, it looks just like the castle on "The Wonderful World of Disney."

It doesn't really, but it did to me then, and the association took hold. Madison is still a fantasy kind of place for me. Though I lived here for a few months in 1984, I've never been quite certain it's real. Moving to Madison to begin a new life is, for me, like charting a course for the Magic Kingdom.

Milwaukee is where my roots are. I've lived there for almost all of my 26 years. On the one hand, I don't think it's as nice a city as Madison, but on the other, I have no doubt it's real.

On a visit to Madison a few years back, I was taking in the sights downtown. There was a guy on the corner, screaming drunk, hanging on to a light pole. He seemed to be in a good mood. Just then a cop car pulled up. The officer behind the wheel rolled down his window and said something to the drunk, who in turn loudly compared the officer to a certain farm animal.

Uh-oh, I thought, now he's really going to get it.

To my astonishment, the officer behind the wheel stayed there. In fact, after calmly trading jibes with the man ("You're a pig!" "You're a drunk!" "Get lost!" "Sleep it off!"), he actually smiled and waved goodbye before driving off.

The incident baffles me. In Milwaukee, mouthing off to a police officer is ... well, it's just not the kind of thing you can reasonably expect to get away with. It makes me wonder: What's with this place, anyway, that even the cops are laid back?

OF ALL THE CITIES I'VE SEEN IN THE 38 STATES I'VE VISITED, MADISON IS the most atypical. Nothing (with the possible exception of Boulder, Colo.) compares with it. Sometimes, I think of Madison as an exception to reality.

The exciting thing about Madison, like Disneyland, is that there's always so much going on. There's a lecture here, an art show there, nightclubs and entertainment everywhere. As an occasional visitor, I often felt as though I should have to pay admission upon entering the city limits.

Before we were married, my wife, Marie, and I used to drive to Madison a couple of times each year. We'd hang out on State Street or at the university, go down to Lake Mendota for the sunset, stroll in the soft summer air. Something about this place took hold of us and found a place in our dreams.

When I heard that *Isthmus* was looking for a news editor, it took me about two seconds to decide to apply. Madison had a pull on me, as did the paper, and the thought of being a part of both had an immediate appeal.

I'm not entirely certain why I was selected for the job. It wasn't for lack of competition: The word is that more than three dozen applicants from here to West Jesus threw their hats into the ring. And it wasn't because I had the most impressive resume: I was the editor of an alternative Milwaukee paper called *The Crazy Shepherd* and had a few freelance credits to boot. Mostly, though, I was a truck driver who edited and wrote in his spare time.

What it was, I think, is that the people at *Isthmus* recognized in me a potential as great as the potential they see in their paper. For that, they have my gratitude; for that, I'll work very hard to prove them right.

A large part of what I hope to accomplish here, certainly, is to uphold the reputation for excellence *Isthmus* has earned during its first 10 years. Besides being one of the nation's best cities to live in, Madison has one of the nation's best weekly papers. I intend to help keep it that way.

But there is more. I also hope to bring to *Isthmus* my sense of urgency about the world. Madison is a nice town, but like every other place it could use a little shaking up. As a journalist, I'd rather be honest than safe, and I'd rather be provocative than popular.

For me, Madison is a new beginning – a new city, a new job, a new place to live. Best of all, Marie and I have a new baby, Jesse, who was born the day before I accepted this job. We are a family now, living in the city of our dreams.

Madison is still something of an enigma to me, and will be for some time. But now, it is also my home.

APRIL 4, 1986

Bronson La Follette with his grandfather's portrait.
Illustration by David Michael Miller

Fighting Bronson

Now that the Wisconsin Ethics Board, following the most extensive investigation in its history, has found state Attorney General Bronson La Follette guilty of only a trivial infraction of the state ethics code, we can all join Bronson in proclaiming victory and breathing a sigh of relief. One of Wisconsin's greatest treasures, the La Follette name, has been rescued from the jaws of disgrace.

For a while there, things were looking mighty grim. Bronson, the grandson of Robert ("Fighting Bob") La Follette, former Wisconsin governor and senator, stood accused of a host of indiscretions, ranging from abject crony-ism to apparent conflict of interest. All of the charges, assures La Follette, were partisan cheap shots from political enemies, parroted by a reckless and irre-sponsible press.

Consider, for instance, the allegation that there is some connection between a $35,000 loan from cemetery operator Dale Armstrong to a firm in which La Follette invested and La Follette's issuance of an opinion favor-able to Armstrong two months later.

"There's an appearance of relationship," La Follette explained. "There's so many things that are coincidental."

But of course. Coincidence. Just like it was a coincidence that La Follette abruptly decided to reverse a decision to take legal action against a company represented by his friend and business partner, Madison lobbyist James Boullion. Or that La Follette, completely unaware that Armstrong was under investigation for allegedly bilking Wisconsin residents out of $2.5 million for mausoleums that were sold but never built, provided Boullion with letters of introduction to promote Armstrong's mausoleum business in Minnesota and Texas.

Finally it dawned on La Follette, as the five-month Ethics Board inves-tigation neared its conclusion, that his presumed friend Boullion had "used" him and betrayed his trust. It must have come as quite a shock. Who would have guessed that a professional lobbyist would ever try to use his influence to win favors for his clients?

At least La Follette has been consistent. At first, he insisted there was no need for an Ethics Board probe; then he requested one to clear his name. When Boullion questioned the board's ability to render a fair verdict, La Follette denounced Boullion's comments as "appalling," "ludicrous" and indicative of a "total lack of any judgment or common sense whatsoever." Then last week La Follette's attorney, Gordon Baldwin, criticized the board's procedures and questioned its ability to return a fair verdict.

THE SADDEST ASPECT OF THIS WHOLE AFFAIR, CERTAINLY, IS THE WAY THE press has pounced on poor Bronson. It soon got so bad that La Follette, frustrated by his inability to get across his side of the story, quite logically refused to answer questions, walked out on interviews and ignored phone messages requesting comment.

Later, an aide remarked that La Follette was "hamstrung" by an "agree-ment" with the Ethics Board not to discuss the case, and could not even reply to charges made by state Sen. Donald Hanaway, his Republican rival for attorney general. The media then stabbed La Follette in the back again, by reporting that the board had imposed absolutely no restrictions on his ability to comment.

Most vicious of all, La Follette recently told the *Milwaukee Journal*, have been the Madison media. These hellhounds of journalism have been nipping at his heels with such ferocity that La Follette says he'll avoid campaigning in Dane County. As he so eloquently put it, "Why should I continue to answer questions in Madison when they'd just go and rehash the whole goddamn story?"

Outside county limits, La Follette believes he can still get a fair shake from journalists who care more about campaign "issues" than alleged conflicts. This same concern no doubt drives La Follette's refusal of numerous debate requests from Hanaway and Labor-Farm candidate Dennis Boyer: Everyone knows debates are not a forum where real issues can reasonably be discussed.

La Follette apparently believes he can secure reelection on the strength of the La Follette name. At heart is our state's enduring fondness for Bronson's grandpa. Fighting Bob, you'll recall, was an outspoken radical who repeatedly imperiled his political future by taking principled but unpopular stands; an insurgent who fought with all his might to curtail the power of such organized special interests as utilities and corporations; a man who was in his day widely branded a traitor.

Yes, Wisconsin's love for the La Follette name springs eternal. So long as the people in this state never reflect on what it stands for, Bronson may well be elected forever.

OCTOBER 17, 1986

On Nov. 4, 1986, Bronson La Follette was defeated by Republican Donald Hanaway. La Follette has never since sought political office.

Madison R.F.D.

Honest to goodness, old buddy, you are just not going to believe all the things that have been happening right here in your hometown, Madison R.F.D. I suppose now that you're in the Marines with all of them big-shot national heroes like Ollie North, you probably think little old Madison doesn't amount to a hill of beans. But what I have to tell you is going to turn your head around.

Where do I begin? Well, you know how for years here there was a law saying you couldn't buy beer to take home after 9 o'clock at night? That meant people getting tanked up at parties and such had to drive all the way to Sun Prairie or the town of Burke to buy more beer if they ran out. Well, now it seems some people on the city council want to fix it so you can buy beer – even Coors – clear up to 11 o'clock. Not only that, there's talk about letting bars stay open till 2 in the morning.

Sheriff Taylor is just sick about it – says he and Barney won't be able to handle all the trouble that'll get started if people who don't have sense to buy enough beer ahead of time are allowed to pick up six-packs after it's dark out and Opie is in bed and everything. Aunt Bea says it'll never pass, but folks around here are pretty riled anyway.

Then there's this flap over how the city spent $150 to buy a painting from the Madison Art Fair on the Square to hang in the Common Council office. The city said it was just doing its part to support Madison artists. But Larry Olson, the alderman, thought this was crackers. "That's like saying we should only buy our toilet paper from trees planted in the city," he said.

You remember Larry Olson. He's the same fellow who earlier this year said the committee that handles art for the city wasn't fair because it didn't include people who don't like art. Larry says he knows $150 doesn't sound like much out of a budget of $90 million. But he figures that since some of this money came from "elderly and low-income people," the city could find a better use.

The mayor seems to agree: His new budget won't include a penny for new arts projects. I guess that sort of thing is best left to really big cities, like Marshfield or Watertown.

BUT THE BIGGEST EXCITEMENT AROUND HERE — FLOYD THE BARBER SAYS it's a sign of the times — has to deal with bribes to county supervisors. It all started with a board meeting last month when Robert Anders — he's from Middleton — and Judy Rendall from Mazomanie 'fessed up about how they had been offered money in return for favors.

Bob said that 10 years ago someone offered him $20 in gratitude for all the work he'd done on a zoning issue ("Here is $20, take your wife out to lunch") and he turned it down. Judy said that during the last five years someone offered her $100 to vote a certain way, and she turned it down.

Well, as you can imagine, it caused quite a stir. The *Wisconsin State Journal* ran a banner headline. County supervisor Stu Levitan demanded that Bob and Judy finger the scoundrels who tried to make them do the devil's bidding. And Hal Harlowe, the district attorney, ordered a high-level probe.

Gollllllll-y!

As it turned out, though, Judy later admitted she'd made the whole thing up, and Hal found that no one had broken any laws. But Hal did say there should be some sort of rule that if someone offers a bribe it has to be reported. That way, he reckoned, "When those discussions begin, an official can say, 'Stop. If you're saying what I think you're trying to say, I'm going to have to report this.'"

Bob Anders had an even brighter idea. He said that every 90 days public officials should have to make a "public confession" to prove they are sticking to the straight and narrow: "We would raise our right hand before the County Board meeting and swear before God and the public that we have not been on the take nor have we received any monetary or sexual favors during the past 90 days. I believe this would be a good ordinance amendment, since money and sex is destroying so many elected officials."

I'll tell you one thing, Gomer: Madison R.F.D. sure ain't what it used to be. Why, I remember when it was just a simple place with simple folk.

YOUR COUSIN, GOOBER

JULY 17, 1987

Larry Olson, Robert Anders and Judy Rendall — whose quotes here are actual — all later left public office. Aunt Bea, Sheriff Taylor, Barney and Floyd remain at their posts.

The Media's Acid Test

"Is there ... any citizen of the United States who thinks that Dan Quayle is qualified to be the next drug czar?"

– MICHAEL DUKAKIS

A s a newspaper editor, I'm well aware that many potential stories never make the news – usually because they lack timeliness or relevance or substantiation. But I'm utterly baffled by the absence of coverage given one gem of a story I came across recently.

The story, first reported in the *Shepherd Express*, the alternative weekly newspaper of Milwaukee, is this: In the fall of 1968, vice presidential candidate Dan Quayle's Delta Kappa Epsilon fraternity at DePauw University in Indiana sponsored a party called "The Trip," described in the school yearbook as "a colorful psychedelic journey into the wild sights and sounds produced by LSD."

The *Shepherd Express* quotes Quayle's former college mate, who now lives in Milwaukee, as saying "LSD was not served directly by the fraternity, but it most certainly would have been taken by the members." He added that fraternity members would be expected to attend all such social functions.

At first I wondered if the article was some kind of joke. Back in the old days, when the *Shepherd* was monthly and I was its editor, the paper was known to do things like that. But the article's author, current *Shepherd Express* editor Doug Hissom, assures me that he saw the yearbook – called the *Mirage* – with his own eyes. And his source, knowledgeable and full of information, assured him that LSD had in fact been used.

When Hissom tried to get comment from a Bush-Quayle campaign official, the official hung up. When I tried to interest the mainstream media in the story, their reaction was practically the same.

A member of the state Associated Press seemed curious at first, but his superiors turned thumbs down. There was nothing in the *Shepherd Express* article, they said, to confirm that LSD was actually taken.

Wow. Here is the world's largest press organization, with thousands of reporters, unable to even conceive that it should interview some of the dozens of frat members whose names and photos appear alongside Quayle's in the yearbook. No wonder it took a Beirut weekly to break the Iran-Contra scandal.

I called the *Indianapolis Star*, which is within 40 miles of DePauw, and spoke with Tom Leyden, an assistant city editor, who subsequently assigned a reporter to check out the yearbook. Per my request, the reporter, Jo Ellen Sharp, later called back. She confirmed there was a reference to the frat's acid party above Dan Quayle's picture on page 154 of the 1968 *Mirage*. It said exactly what the *Shepherd* reported. And ... she wasn't really interested in the story.

Why in heaven's name not? Because although there "was no doubt ... this fraternity was known as a party place," the university as a whole was quite conservative. Thus, Sharp said, "I just can't imagine they would put something this blatant in the yearbook if it meant what you think it means."

Talk about a lack of imagination. Sharp also noted that other frat entries seemed tongue-in-cheek and pointed out that Quayle has elsewhere said he has never used marijuana or LSD.

SO HERE YOU HAVE A CANDIDATE FOR VICE PRESIDENT WHO – AS THE *Cleveland Plain Dealer* and other papers have documented – out-and-out lied about the circumstances of his induction into the National Guard, and who is now being taken at his word about drug use. This despite his membership as a C-plus student in a fraternity notorious for partying.

The *Shepherd Express* sent its article to a host of media outlets, and it was picked up by Alexander Cockburn in his *Nation* column. But others have maintained a peculiar silence. Jeff Cohen, executive director of Fairness and Accuracy in Reporting, a New York-based group that tracks the mainstream media's conservative bias, has no idea why.

"Frankly, I couldn't give a shit if he took acid, but I think it does raise a good hypocrisy angle," Cohen says. "I think it could be a potentially big story. Most people in his generation were doing that kind of thing. And I believe he's on record supporting the death penalty for crimes involving drugs. So ... I think it should be pursued as much as it can."

Hear, hear. There is no rational reason the press should rush into print with false accusations that Michael Dukakis received psychological counseling and then leave a story like this untouched. At the very least, Dan Quayle should have to give a public accounting. I'm waiting.

SEPTEMBER 23, 1988

I'm still waiting.

Gene Parks in his office, 1988. Photo by Brent Nicastro

A Time for Anger

It seems every time I walk past the City-County Building these days, Madison's embattled affirmative action officer, Gene Parks, is on the front steps, holding a press conference. Last Wednesday I watched him calmly read his prepared statement, which got almost no coverage, then launch into an extemporaneous fit, which did. Afterward, one spectator sized up the situation: "He's flipped his lid."

It's hard not to agree. The events leading to Parks' 30-day unpaid suspension suggested a man overcome with irrationality, heedless of inevitable consequences. He is becoming the Joe McCarthy of the Madison left ("I have here in my hand the names of 57 racists ..."), and his longtime paranoia has become a self-fulfilling prophecy: Now people really *are* out to get him.

The problem isn't that Parks called the mayor a racist and a coward, or alderpersons "whores" – others have said worse – but that he did so publicly, with nothing to gain. Madison's affirmative action officer is burning bridges, and coming across as a bit of a nutcase in the process.

Last week in an interview, I asked Parks about something a mayoral aide had told me. Enraged, he jumped up from his chair, hurled a sheaf of newspapers to the floor, and bellowed, "As God is my witness, I'm not a liar!" No one said he was. Clearly the guy is on edge.

The now-public charge that Parks drinks too much infuriates him, professedly because it comes from unnamed sources. But a few months ago Ed Durkin, Park's former boss at the Fire Department, told me on the record and without equivocation that Parks had "an incredible alcoholic problem" before going on the wagon a few years back. Parks is drinking again. You figure it out.

But booze alone cannot explain Parks' seeming decision to commit political suicide. A few months back he was drinking too, but when I asked him whether he thought Mayor Joe Sensenbrenner was racist, he said, "That's a simple question, but I cannot give you a simple answer. All of us are affected by racism to a certain degree, regardless of our color." Last week Parks called Sensenbrenner "racist to his soul."

What happened? "I was trying to be diplomatic," Parks says of his earlier remarks, "but they continued the assault, so now I've got to tell it like it is."

AT LEAST ONE OBSERVER AGREES PARKS WAS PUSHED INTO A NEW LEVEL of outspokenness.

"The mayor's office," says Ald. Joe Szwaja, "has acted illegally as well as unfairly in the way it has treated Gene." Szwaja notes, among other things, that the mayor and his staff fouled up Parks' receipt of budget documents, transferred compliance duties that by contract belonged to Parks to an employee who complained about him, solicited public feedback while contemplating disciplinary action, and twice disciplined Parks under an ordinance from which the affirmative action officer is specifically exempt.

Now the city is gearing up to come down on Parks like a ton of bricks. After years of praise for Parks' handling of the affirmative action office, suddenly the mayor has produced — at God knows how much city expense and staff time — a nine-page list of alleged incidents of misconduct, which will be the topic of a pre-disciplinary hearing on Oct. 24.

In contrast to this "pattern of harassment," as Szwaja calls it, Parks' assaults have been purely verbal, and no one has accused him of breaking any laws. What's more, most of the angry things he says are true.

City officials have engaged in fruitless trysting with wealthy developers while neglecting more worthy causes. The city's sponsorship of tax-exempt bonds that will enrich the owners of the Monona Shores Apartments, earlier implicated for housing discrimination, stinks to high heaven.

Even Parks' most outrageous remarks regarding gubernatorial infidelity were, in context, absolutely right on. His point was that the press won't print these rumors (unlike those about Parks' drinking), but "whisper them" among themselves. In fact, members of the media have fairly shouted these rumors to anyone who will listen, but hypocritically waited for Parks' utterance before putting them on the airwaves and front pages.

In the battle that's looming, Parks says, "I am David, and the giant is going to fall." I don't think so. Goliath is going to clobber him. Parks has broken the rules of discourse – rules that ensure nothing changes except in the tiniest increments. It is a transgression for which people in power know no forgiveness.

And yet these are times for anger. We need leaders unafraid to lose their jobs to say the things that must be said. Gene Parks' tragedy, and his redemption, may be that he loves Madison too much to shut up.

OCTOBER 14, 1988

Mayor Sensenbrenner fired Gene Parks in late October 1988. Parks sued, and his termination was eventually overturned; he wound up with a different city job and a $442,000 settlement, plus retirement benefits. Parks died on Feb. 28, 2005, at age 57.

Kill the Poor

Here in Wisconsin, we treat poor people like the miserable scum they really are. Not long ago, for instance, the Dane County Department of Social Services illegally denied General Assistance to a man so wracked with pain he filled out his application while lying on the Social Services floor. Apparently, one of the nine digits on his Social Security card (not a required form of ID) was illegible.

Recently Wisconsin has been breaking brave new ground in this kind of cruelty toward people on welfare. Gov. Tommy Thompson and the Democrat-controlled Legislature have slashed AFDC benefits by 6 percent (which, counting the loss due to inflation, makes for a total cut of 29 percent since 1980) and started withholding benefits from teen parents and parents of teens who miss too much school.

Thompson reckons these measures have already saved $5 million that otherwise would have gone to people in desperate need. The state also has one of the nation's toughest workfare programs, aimed at getting these loafers away from the TV set and into low-paying jobs. And, just to ensure that these people don't get jobs and like it, the Thompson team torpedoed funds for a pilot program advanced by Assembly Speaker Tom Loftus that would have removed some of the disincentives for people who leave the welfare rolls to go to work.

Now Thompson and state Senate Majority Leader Joe Strohl are pushing another excellent idea: a "two-tiered" welfare system, which would keep new arrivals at their former state's aid levels for six months.

Damn straight. If these cashless cretins come from a state like Illinois that pays $386 per month for a family of four, then by God they deserve $386 per month. What family of four needs more than $4,632 per year to live on, anyway?

Wisconsin's rush to a two-tier system was prompted by a study earlier this year by the Wisconsin Policy Research Institute – a think tank headed by men who realize, for instance, that opposition to the Nicaraguan Contras is "objectively anti-American." The group found that a whopping 29 percent of new welfare applicants were from states other than Wisconsin. Furthermore, 40 percent of these new arrivals were on the welfare rolls within 90 days.

That means a mere 88 percent of new welfare cases were either Wisconsin residents or people who did not immediately seek aid. But some of the remaining 12 percent, damn them, may have been attracted by the higher benefits.

Last week Thompson mined the whole ugly truth, telling Vice President Dan Quayle, "Because Wisconsin is so generous, we have attracted several people from other states." Whoa. Several. Talk about your welfare magnet.

Even one tired, poor Illinois family is one too many. Wisconsin has a hard enough time abusing its own poor people without having to abuse poor people from all over the country.

FOR A WHILE, THE STROHL-THOMPSON PLAN SEEMED TO BE THE PERFECT solution. It was cruel, discriminatory, probably even unconstitutional. Leave it to Tom Still to find a dark cloud.

In his column on Oct. 22, the *Wisconsin State Journal* associate editor questioned the effectiveness – not the goal – of the two-tier scheme. He noted that welfare mothers from other states who make the move to Wisconsin can still enjoy better schools, less crime, more affordable housing and the promise of higher benefits six months down the line.

Citing a Washington, D.C., group's study showing that urban rental housing for welfare recipients is more affordable in Wisconsin than anywhere in the continental United States, Still mused, "If someone knows that she can rent an apartment for less money in Wisconsin, why is a six-month wait for higher welfare benefits going to stop her?" (He immediately added, quite unnecessarily, "Please don't think I've given up welfare-bashing in my old age.")

Still neglected to mention one startling detail in the Washington group's study: The reason Wisconsin ranked so high for urban welfare dwellers is that here the average three-person family on AFDC must apply only 85 percent of its $517 monthly check to the cost of rent. Can you imagine? Being able to pay the rent and still have $77 per month for all other living expenses? No wonder poor people are flocking here in severals.

Clearly, Tom Still is on to something. Getting rid of welfare migration is going to take more than token gestures. If we truly are going to keep the welfare rats out, Wisconsin needs worse schools, more crime, higher rents and lower welfare payments for everyone, not just new arrivals.

Wisconsin's generosity has to have limits. For the good of all, we must pursue even harsher, crueler methods of punishing those who have the audacity to lack money. How about the death penalty?

NOVEMBER 3, 1989

This column won the Golden Quill, the top annual award for editorial writing from the International Society of Weekly Newspaper Editors, an honor I accepted in Reading, Penn.

Why People Hate Madison

As Bob Brennan sees it, people are just envious. They hate Madison for the same reason some sports types hate ball clubs that always seem to win. "Madison," he proclaims, "is a winning city." People elsewhere resent it for having things they don't.

Brennan, president of the Greater Madison Chamber of Commerce, is reflecting on the recent spate of Madison bashing by people in other places. People like Mike Royko, the besotted *Chicago Tribune* columnist, who characterized our fair city as a place where UW students call their parents "no-good gringo imperialists" and feminists wear buttons that say, "Male is a four-letter word."

Surpassing even Royko in its eagerness to tell casual lies is the *Tampa Tribune*, which last month ran an editorial (reprinted in the *Wisconsin State Journal*) about the now-infamous lesbian roommate case. The editorial, based largely on disproved allegations, suggested the now-tabled ordinance under which two Madison women were prosecuted for rejecting a roommate solely on the basis of sexual orientation is used in other cases to force Madisonians to room with convicted murderers.

This "university town of liberal repute," the paper declared, "is the scene of Big Brotherism so extreme [that] we'd better stop praying for democracy in Beijing and start working toward freedom in Madison."

I was in Tampa once. It's a suicide-inducing rat-trap of a city – strewn with used-car lots that boast of "clean" machines, restaurants called "Eat" and adult bookstores. No sane person, exposed to both cities, would prefer that one to this.

Still, I don't really accept Brennan's argument that people there are simply envious. I think they genuinely hate Madison – or rather, they hate the caricature of Madison they've concocted in their minds. They need the idea of Madison-as-Radical-Hotbed the way some religions need the concept of Hell – as a vision of utter terror to keep people in line.

This intellectually dishonest exercise of twisting the truth about Madison for the sake of ridiculing it is by no means limited to outsiders. David Blaska of *The Capital Times* does it all the time. Most recently, it was to attack the "couple dozen" people – out of a community of 350,000 – who turned out to protest the U.S. invasion of Panama.

"The marchers," wrote Blaska, "are people of great faith – that Marxism will yet succeed, somewhere in the world."

FROM WHAT I KNOW OF THE MADISON LEFT, I SINCERELY DOUBT ALL THESE "couple dozen" people share this goal; some probably just don't want their country behaving like an international outlaw. But I'll affirm Blaska's presumption to make a point:

The emergence of a humane, democratic state founded on socialist (Marxist, if you will) principles is something devoutly to be wished. I also think rich people should be taxed silly; military spending should be slashed; workers should have strong, progressive unions; everyone should have adequate housing and health care; marijuana should be legalized; women's reproductive rights should be absolute; nuclear weapons should be dismantled; handguns should be banned; ROTC should be kicked off campus; laws against overt anti-gay bias should apply even to roommate situations; alternative families should enjoy the same rights as traditional ones; and property magnate Jerome Mullins should return my phone calls.

There ... I said it. Did anything change? Of course not. The distinguishing thing about Madison is not that people who think like I do have any real power, but that we are occasionally permitted to join the debate. Bob Brennan sees this as a positive thing. So does Paul Soglin, who was reelected mayor amid musings, here and nationally, about Madison's resurgent leftist bent – only to make leaf collection his most pressing concern.

"We're proud," Soglin tells me, "to be the home of Eddie Ben Elson" – the late great loony lawyer who once announced his candidacy for district attorney in the nude – "and we're proud we've got the Festival of the Swamps, and we're proud of *Isthmus*."

I'm proud, too, of all these things. But none of them makes this the bastion of radicalism-run-amok that blowhards like Blaska make it out to be. You can still pick up the newspaper and read, for instance, school board member Earl Kielley's boneheaded remark that teaching students to "be accepting of" others' sexual orientation is really an effort "to advance the agenda of gays and lesbians."

Maybe the *Tampa Tribune* was accidentally right: We *do* need to start working toward freedom in Madison.

JANUARY 25, 1990

Many years later, a Madison resident who grew up in Tampa told me he showed this column to fellow Tampa native Hulk Hogan, the wrestler, who expressed a desire to impact my derrière. David Blaska is now a blogger for Isthmus | TheDailyPage.com.

High Pressure, Low Pay

I have never, to my credit, encouraged anyone to become a newspaper writer. But I confess to having aided and abetted young people en route to careers in the field.

Among such souls are my editorial interns – students trying to snag a few bylines to show they've learned, despite their university studies, how to write for publication. Working with them on stories, I feel like a bartender serving drinks to a drunk. All the usual arguments parade past my aching conscience: It's their choice, not mine. If I don't serve them, somebody else will. It's better that they get it from me than from the dailies.

But the bitter truth is that I need what they give me. I can't keep my business open without them. And the best customers of all are the ones who are the most addicted.

I once had an intern who drove to Iowa to cover the presidential primary for the *Daily Cardinal*, where he also worked. He transmitted his story by midnight, and then wrote another story for *Isthmus* on a laptop computer on his way back to town (someone else drove). He was at *Isthmus* in the early morn – eyes bloodshot, computer in hand. We tried to transfer the story and the whole thing got lost. It took several hours to rewrite the piece, just in time for him to go to class.

This sort of thing, mind you, was not an aberration. It was his lifestyle. The students who write for me are the hardest-working people I know.

They have to be if they want to get a real job in the field. Every opening draws dozens of applicants. Every paper is in a position to demand that minimal 110 percent.

Of course, there are lazy journalists, but chances are they have simply burned out. Like meat-packing plants with workers missing parts of fingers, newspapers are notorious for people who have lost their spark – not just for writing, but for living as well. Sometimes these people are shunted aside to attend to menial tasks. More often they are made editors.

NEWSPAPER WRITING IS GRUELING WORK. MEETING DEADLINES ON A regular basis has a similar effect on one's innards as drinking Drano now and then.

What's more, it's a ridiculously low-paying profession, considering the level of skill and commitment. I've seen bright-star former interns hired into full-time reporting jobs that paid $15,000 a year.

According to a 1987 survey by the Wisconsin Newspaper Association, the pay for reporters at weekly papers ranged from an average low of $5.41 per hour to an average high of $7.17. Only five of 36 papers surveyed paid reporters anything for overtime; three others gave comp time.

More telling still, the pay rates had little to do with the paper's revenues (and presumed profitability). One example: A paper with gross annual sales of $400,000 had a salary range for reporters of $5.63 to $8.75 per hour, while a paper with sales of $16 million paid $5.63 to $6.88. What does that add up to weekly? A lot of Hamburger Helper.

While the people who own newspapers rake in the dough, the people who write them are treated like barrels of ink – mere costs to be contained. George Hesselberg of the *Wisconsin State Journal* says that, in "a majority of cases" involving reporters at Madison Newspapers, Inc., "raises do not equal or exceed the cost of living." (*State Journal* editor Frank Denton disputes this, but won't discuss actual numbers.)

As best as I can determine, MNI's profits totaled about $11.5 million in 1989. Profit, honestly defined, is the difference between what workers earn and what they get paid. That means the company's 530 employees earned an average of $21,698 more than they were paid last year.

There are other crosses to bear. Newspaper writers, myself included, generally may not write for other area outlets – even if it's only to offer an opinion on the issues of the day.

The *State Journal* prohibits even its part-time reporters from contributing to "competing" publications. Such a deal: First the paper decides it will exploit the hell out of these people (low wages, no benefits), then it prevents them from making money elsewhere in the local market. Don't like it? Don't work here.

Still, addiction is a powerful thing; it allows us to tolerate things we otherwise would not. The thrill of a story – and the occasional feeling that what we write matters – makes all that Hamburger Helper a little easier to swallow.

JULY 6, 1990

Snuff Out the Collusion

My father died of lung cancer on Oct. 28, 1985. I was smoking a cigarette when a phone call brought the news. I snuffed it out and haven't had another since.

I hadn't planned on quitting, and certainly hadn't lost the urge. But I simply couldn't stand giving more money to companies who caused my dad to suffer so – robbing him of his breath, and finally his life.

In the year my father died, according to a report prepared for Congress by the U.S. Department of Health and Human Services, smoking caused 5,636 deaths and cost $1.1 billion in Wisconsin alone. Nationally, smoking is the leading preventable cause of death and disease, each year claiming an estimated 390,000 lives – 195 times as many as the current demon drug, cocaine.

Yet the state of Wisconsin, like the nation as a whole, still openly colludes with the pushers of this deadly and addictive drug. The State of Wisconsin Investment Board, which has previously shown its moral turpitude by refusing to divest its holdings in companies doing business in South Africa, has $330 million locked up in four of the world's largest tobacco companies – Lorillard, Philip Morris, RJR Nabisco and Hanson PLC. Meanwhile, the University of Wisconsin System owns more than $580,000 of Philip Morris stock.

In June, a Board of Regents committee swiftly rejected grad student Ira Sharenow's suggestion that it unload its holdings in tobacco companies, as Harvard University and City University of New York did earlier this year. The state Investment Board seems similarly insistent on its right to make money off these corporate killers.

"Only 20 percent of Lorillard's revenues, 50 percent of Philip Morris' revenues and less than 40 percent of Hanson's revenues come from the sale of tobacco products," wrote Jacqueline Doeler, the board's investment services manager, responding to a query from Democratic state Sen. Lynn Adelman. She cited the companies' Wisconsin ties – Philip Morris, for instance, owns Oscar Mayer and Miller Brewery – and noted that the board's tobacco company holdings make up just 2 percent of its portfolio.

Investment Board executive director Patricia Lipton has promised a review of the "fiscal impacts" of Adelman's call for tobacco divestment. But the topic is not on the agenda for the board's next meeting. And Lipton has wearily suggested such divestment is yet another attempt to get the board to tailor its holdings to suit "everyone's concerns."

How can the Wisconsin Investment Board, which handles retirement plans for public employees, in good conscience profit from a product that prevents so many people from enjoying retirement?

The answer probably isn't, as an *Isthmus* columnist recently suggested, that the state wants workers to die before they can become a drain on the fund. The answer is that the board has no conscience and no principles beyond its desire to attain the best possible return.

UNFORTUNATELY, SEN. ADELMAN STANDS VIRTUALLY ALONE AMONG Wisconsin public officials in challenging the state's willingness to profit from these murderers of millions.

"It is neither profitable nor moral for states, which bear the brunt of tobacco's runaway health-care and insurance costs, to contribute to this deadly industry," he asserted earlier this month. "Divestment will help strip away the veneer of respectability and end the silent collusion of states that allows tobacco to flourish."

Stripping away this veneer will not be easy. Last year in Wisconsin, some 2,500 farmers harvested 4,700 acres of tobacco. Dane County, according to a 1987 agricultural census, produces half the state's crop. Last weekend the community of Edgerton, home to a huge tobacco warehouse, celebrated its annual "Tobacco Days" extravaganza, complete with "Pride in Tobacco" signs strung about the downtown.

"Tobacco companies are still regarded as relatively normal members of the business establishment," writes Michael Kinsley in the *New Republic*. But in just a few years, he predicts, "the relative absence of stigma associated with the production and peddling of tobacco products" will seem "incredible."

My father smoked Camel straights – for which, like many an addict, he would have not only walked a mile but crawled through broken glass. It wasn't until his lung collapsed, two years to the day before he died, that he finally stopped lighting up. That was also his last day of work.

Not even Lynn Adelman (whose father ran the company, Adelman Laundry and Dry Cleaners in Milwaukee, at which my father worked for more than three decades) is suggesting that tobacco be banned. He just wants the state to stop profiting from its sale to addicts.

"While Wisconsin divestment will not solve all tobacco-related problems, it may spark a significant national trend," he says, noting that New York, Massachusetts and Rhode Island are considering similar action. "Wisconsin has the opportunity to take a clear leadership role."

I say let's do it. Profiting from the tobacco industry is the moral equivalent of stealing jewelry from genocide victims in a mass grave. The fact that it is not yet recognized as such shows the industry's continued success turning profits into respectability – like a pimp prancing in a $500 suit.

"Respectability," writes Kinsley, "is a fragile flower. Start pulling petals and it quickly wilts. And without respectability, the tobacco purveyors stand naked. People and institutions not deterred by their own consciences will be deterred by the stigma."

There was, strictly speaking, little reason my father did not live to enjoy his own retirement. In fact, there was no reason at all ... except that he was addicted to a dangerous drug whose respectability, more so than any smoker's life, deserves to come to an end.

JULY 27, 1990

The State of Wisconsin Investment Board and UW System have continued to reject calls for policy constraints on tobacco-related investments. As of September 2009, the investment board had $250 million in tobacco-related holdings. The UW System, meanwhile, has about $1.5 million invested in tobacco companies. In 1997 Lynn Adelman was tapped by President Bill Clinton to become a federal judge for the Eastern District of Wisconsin.

Radicalism and Regret

I n the early morning hours of Aug. 24, 1970, an explosion ripped through the Army Mathematics Research Center at the UW–Madison's Sterling Hall. It broke windows for miles, collapsed an entire side of the six-story building, wrecked cars and uprooted trees, and killed a 33-year-old physics researcher named Robert Fassnacht.

The bombing, carried out by four young radicals known as the New Year's Gang, was a calculated domestic response to the war in Vietnam. Fassnacht's death, which traumatized the antiwar movement in Madison and throughout the nation, was not. Twenty years later, the explosion's aftershocks are still being felt.

"The Wisconsin media wrote about the story for 10 years and never got below the surface," asserts Tom Bates, a nationally known writer whose long-awaited book on the bombing, due out next spring, will professedly contain many surprises, and much of the subtext others never bothered to mine. His goal: "To put it together in such a way as to make sense to people who thought they already knew."

Bates' book – titled *Rads* – is one of several thrusting Madison into the national limelight. Earlier this year, historian Paul Buhle published a collection of essays on the intellectual radicalism of the UW–Madison in the 1950s and 1960s. Soon to be released: local activist Sam Day's autobiography, including the most complete account ever written of the federal government's efforts to suppress *The Progressive* magazine's 1979 article about the hydrogen bomb.

Madison history is pounding at the door, demanding to be let into the nation's consciousness. It is a knock many people will prefer to ignore, hoping that it goes away. It is, after all, a history filled with pain and regret.

"It was a terrible mistake; it was a foolish, foolish act," says former Madison radical journalist Dave Wagner of the bombing of Army Math. "But that was nothing I could say publicly at the time. Then I had to defend it – at least the people who did it – and I did."

Wagner, now a newspaper editor in Arizona, passed up an invitation to write a retrospective on the case: "I resist the tyranny of having the bombing define that period. Why should it?" Karl Armstrong, the only New Year's Gang member to remain in Madison, declined to be interviewed – not just by *Isthmus* but by a plethora of national media. He has served his time in prison; now he just wants to get on with his life, selling lemonade from his cart to college students who haven't the foggiest notion who he is.

STILL, WHAT HAPPENED 20 YEARS AGO DESERVES EXAMINATION. THE bombing, says Wagner, probably was more instrumental in convincing Nixon of the need to step up domestic political repression – COINTELPRO and the like – than of the need to end the war. Worse, it demolished the hope for revolutionary transformation that in those days hung in the air like Che Guevara posters on dormitory walls.

Wagner, once energized by visions of a better world, now reflects glumly on that time and this: "I don't see that much has changed, really."

A look at the newspaper confirms it. The exercise of power by the United States in the world is just as immoral today as when soldiers were gunning down women and babies at My Lai. Uncle Sam has achieved successes in Panama and Nicaragua. In the Persian Gulf, thousands of U.S. troops prepare to defend this country's right to cheap oil, while oil companies jack up prices at home.

Now Bush wants to send another $85 million in military aid to the murderous government of El Salvador, and the best the Democrats who control Congress can muster in the way of opposition is to propose "controls" on how this money is spent.

Rep. Joe Moakley (D-Mass.) recently explained El Salvador's failure to bring to justice the murderers of six Jesuit priests (not to mention more than 60,000 Salvadoran civilians) thus: "Salvadoran military officers have withheld evidence, destroyed evidence, falsified evidence and repeatedly perjured themselves in testimony" – incidentally the exact same things that made Oliver North a national hero.

The need for revolutionary transformation is as great as ever. Sam Day and *The Progressive* shout what truth they can from their respective mountaintops. Intellectual radicals, perhaps not so numerous or bold as in the past, sow seeds of dissent on the UW campus.

But for the most part, as the world prepares to drink in the details of its often anguished past, Madison sits contentedly in the calm of the moment, sipping lemonade.

AUGUST 24, 1990

Remembering
Whom to Thank

Like all Americans, I can hardly contain my euphoria over the success of the United States and its allies in the Persian Gulf. When I reflect on how quickly and absolutely we kicked the ass of the aggressor, Saddam Hussein, with so little loss of American life, my heart nearly bursts with pride.

In recent weeks, our great nation has united around a common purpose. To eliminate poverty, hunger, bigotry, homelessness or AIDS? To provide health care for children or rescue the environment from near-certain disaster? To build the foundations of a more just society? No, it was a cause worth dying for: to make sure no one ever calls George Bush a wimp again.

To this noble end – oh yes, and to keep down the price of gasoline – we sent our brave men and women to bomb Iraq to smithereens. With this higher goal in mind, we collectively countenanced the collateral damage willfully inflicted on thousands of Iraqi women, children and babies. Now it's time to celebrate.

Last week, after Saddam Hussein announced he would accept terms he appeared willing to negotiate toward before the war began, President Bush noted the "wonderful sense of patriotism" sweeping the nation. "There isn't any antiwar movement out there," he crowed. "A handful of voices, but you can't hear them."

For that we should remember to thank those good Christians who spontaneously sang "God Bless America" to drown out a man who complained in President Bush's church about the bombing of Iraqi civilians. And the patriotic souls who brandished flags and yellow ribbons, tore up "It's Time for Peace" signs on people's lawns and shouted "U.S.A., U.S.A.!" at antiwar demonstrations.

Laughably, the so-called peace movement badly misjudged both the war and the strategy behind it. U.S. officials, meanwhile, more accurately assessed the content of our nation's character.

On Dec. 28, the *Los Angeles Times* reported that two of the president's top war advisers "said Bush assumes that the American public will be mainly concerned about the number of U.S. casualties, not the tens of thousands of Iraqis who stand to die or be maimed in a massive air assault, and that even the killing of thousands of civilians – including women and children – probably would not undermine support for the war effort."

Bush and the military turned this sunny forecast into happy reality. All it took was for us to kill tens of thousands of Iraqis (most of them soldiers in retreat, the cowards), unleash environmental havoc, and sow enough instability to ensure our need to maintain a huge military presence in the Middle East until the end of time.

AS AMERICANS REJOICE OVER THE OUTCOME OF THIS WAR, WE CAN LOOK forward to more such adventures – other bad guys to conquer, other civilizations to destroy, other monarchies to defend. As the president himself has proclaimed: "By God, we've kicked the Vietnam syndrome once and for all." Never again will we hesitate to use brutal force to get another nation to see things our way.

Bush remembered to thank God, to whom he and Dan Rather so often directed our prayers during this war effort. God, of course, came through with flying colors: red, white and blue. Indeed, God's role in bringing Iraq to its knees rivaled that of Stormin' Norman Schwartzkopf.

In times like these, we should be grateful that God is an American who shares our disregard for the lives of foreigners. In times like these – and rest assured there will be more of them – we as a nation should pray together in the words that Mark Twain left us:

"Oh Lord our God, help us to tear their soldiers to bloody shreds with our shells; help us to cover their smiling fields with the pale forms of their patriot dead; help us to drown the thunder of the guns with the shrieks of their wounded, writhing in pain; help us to lay waste their humble homes with a hurricane of fire; help us to wring the hearts of their unoffending widows with unavailing grief; help us to turn them out roofless with their little children to wander unfriended the wastes of their desolate land in rags and hunger and thirst...."

This we ask in the name of our Lord Jesus Christ.

MARCH 8, 1991

A Nation of Cowards

Not long ago I got a call from a woman worried about her new furnace, which due to a design flaw leaked fumes into her home. The woman thought someone ought to raise a fuss about this public health hazard, but said it couldn't be her. Why not? "My son works for the state."

Can't you just hear it? "Sorry, Tom, your work here has been outstanding, but we just have to let you go now that your mother has gone public with this furnace thing...."

Then there's the guy who wanted to make an issue out of the state's ruthless exploitation of limited-term employees, but backed down so as not to risk offending his ruthless exploiters. And tenants afraid to take on landlords who rip off their security deposits. And workers who obligingly pee into bottles or otherwise let their bosses abuse them, all the while turning pale at the mention of the word "union."

The system has created real dangers – unemployment, ostracism, imprisonment – for people who step out of line. And most people, predictably, have inflated their fears about these dangers into credos of craven conduct.

We proclaim ourselves to be the land of the free and the home of the brave, but in truth we have become a nation of cowards, the land of the meek and the home of the 'fraid. We pledge allegiance not to freedom but to a flag, and rush on cue to join the patriotic mobs.

Perhaps the greatest threat to our liberty comes not from a Supreme Court stacked with reactionaries but from people who have freedom, and consciences, but lack the courage to use them.

WHERE IS THE LEADERSHIP THAT DOESN'T PUT CAUTION BEFORE candor? How our leaders' backbones bend when the pull of conscience meets the push for consensus; it's a wonder they can even walk upright!

Years from now, when it has become even more apparent that the

Gulf War was a terrible failure, I bet our local politicians claim they were against it all along. Yet in every way that mattered they supported it – from the yellow ribbon state Rep. David Clarenbach hung from his home to the cheerful presence of Mayor Paul Soglin and Dane County Executive Rick Phelps at last month's gala pro-war parade.

"The mass of men [P.C. interruptus: and women] serve the state ... not as men mainly, but as machines," wrote Henry David Thoreau in *Civil Disobedience*. "In most cases there is no free exercise whatever of the judgment or of the moral sense; but they put themselves on a level with wood and earth and stones; and wooden men can perhaps be manufactured that will serve the purpose as well."

But there were, Thoreau continued, a very few heroes, patriots, martyrs and reformers who "serve the state with their consciences also, and so necessarily resist it for the most part; and they are commonly treated as enemies by it."

Thoreau, who wrote these words after being jailed for refusing to pay taxes supporting the Mexican-American War, goes on to say that men (and women) of conscience "cannot without disgrace be associated with" the U.S. government, which at that time (1849) sanctioned slavery.

Our government and institutions have not become more moral since. Slavery has merely diversified: People still feel bound by shackles on what they do and think. Meanwhile, Uncle Sam's global behavior has grown steadily more depraved. Ecological catastrophe and economic collapse seem inevitable. Americans are living in bus shelters and dying for want of medical care.

Now is not the time to let fear oppress us. Now is the time to serve the state with our conscience – that is, to become its enemy.

AUGUST 23, 1991

Scouting for Bigotry

Kathy Kennedy-Steffen thought it might be a good experience for Carly to join the Girl Scouts. So early this month she signed her daughter up with the troop at Crestwood Elementary, where 8-year-old Carly is in the third grade. She told the troop leader, Gail Longworth, that Carly has autism.

Otherwise, Longworth might never have known. Carly Steffen is among the roughly 25 percent of people with autism classified as high-functioning, meaning she's not intellectually impaired. Her disability manifests itself mainly as a lack of social skills, a case of extreme shyness.

"When kids talk to her," says Carly's mom, "sometimes she doesn't answer them. It's not because she doesn't want to but because she can't."

Like some other people with autism, Carly has special abilities. She can remember phone numbers months after hearing them. She can tell you that Nickelodeon's "Ren and Stimpy" show first aired on Aug. 11, 1991.

But for the most part, Carly is an ordinary 8-year-old. She gets a charge out of Disney cartoons and draws pictures of animals with strange shapes and happy faces. Although she's in a special-education program, Carly spends most of her time at Crestwood in the regular class. She's well-behaved and has no trouble following directions. If anything, she's a bit too rule-conscious; she watches the clock to make sure she's in bed by 8:30 every night.

To the Girl Scouts, however, Carly is first and foremost a freak – a problem the local troop didn't want on its hands.

Kennedy-Steffen gives this account: On Tuesday, Sept. 15, she got a call from Longworth, who said that for Carly to become a Girl Scout, one of her parents or another adult supervisor would have to accompany her to every meeting.

Kennedy-Steffen explained that this wasn't necessary. Carly, she noted, didn't require special supervision at school or in religious-education classes. But Longworth, says Carly's mom, insisted this was scout policy, as conveyed to her by Jan Stolz, membership director of the nine-county Girl Scouts Black Hawk Council. (Both Stolz and Longworth refused to discuss the matter with *Isthmus*.)

During the next 48 hours, Kathy and her husband, Gary Steffen, spoke to Stolz and another official at the Black Hawk Council, which oversees 9,300 girls and 2,200 volunteers in nearly 900 scout troops in and around Dane County. The Steffens say both officials, while disclaiming any set policy, backed up Longworth on her demand that Carly be accompanied, and hotly denied there was anything discriminatory about this.

But singling out Carly for special treatment that her disability does not require sure seemed like discrimination to the Steffens. It also seemed clear that the scout leaders were prejudiced – they had, after all, prejudged that Carly would be too much to handle before even giving her a chance.

"We're not trying to cause trouble," says Kennedy-Steffen. "I never would have registered Carly for the Girl Scouts in the first place unless I thought she could do it."

AT FIRST, THE STEFFENS CONSIDERED FINDING AN ADULT SUPERVISOR. BUT
a local human-service agency that had worked with Carly was reluctant to commit resources to helping meet what it felt was an unnecessary demand. And Marcy Kreisler, Carly's special-education teacher at Crestwood, called the Girl Scouts' position "ridiculous."

Kennedy-Steffen related this assessment to Longworth, whom she says shot back about Kreisler, "She's not the volunteer who has to deal with Carly." Recalls Steffen, "I can't tell you how much that hurt, to have someone say that about my child."

The Steffens decided they no longer wanted Carly to join the Girl Scouts. "To push Carly on people who do not want her is an affront to her dignity," says Kennedy-Steffen. "I don't think there's a chance in the world that she'd be treated fairly."

Glenis Benson, a UW grad student in educational psychology who knows Carly through her work with high-functioning people with autism, agrees with the Steffens' decision not to subject their daughter to a prejudicial environment. But she believes that being a scout might have aided Carly's struggle to develop social skills.

Perhaps more important, Benson says Carly could help broaden the horizons of the other girls: "If the people who are now denying Carly equal access had been exposed to someone with autism when they were young, they might be a lot more tolerant."

An hour after Stolz refused to talk with me, I got a call from Diane Schnitzer, executive director of the Black Hawk Council. So did Kennedy-Steffen.

Schnitzer told Carly's mom that the family had been treated unfairly, and that she was eager to meet with them to work things out. The Steffens declined. Schnitzer chalked the whole thing up to "miscommunication" – that Longworth had wrongly presented the option of supervision as an absolute. But she could not explain why high-ranking scout officials then backed Longworth up.

Finally, Schnitzer urged me to "consider the long-term implications" of writing about how shabbily the Steffens were treated. Perhaps she fears that Girl Scout cookies might sell less briskly this year.

But I prefer to consider the long-term implications of letting bigotry go unchallenged, of letting people make judgments based on fear and ignorance. The costs are just too great – including, in this case, the Girl Scouts' missed opportunity to recruit Carly Steffen.

SEPTEMBER 25, 1992

Carly Steffen graduated from Madison Area Technical College in the spring of 2009 with a degree in medical transcription.

King Soglin: A Farce in One Act

SCENE: THE CITY-COUNTY FORUM

CHORUS: We are the people of Madison,
behold our drama, hear our rhymes.
We're a bunch of rads in Bates' book,
"a boutique of flower power" in *The New York Times*.
A bed of hot radicalism
we are called from sea to sea.
How came us to this reputation?
It is Greek to we.

CITIZEN NO. 1: Hark, our leader approaches.

CITIZEN NO. 2: Great Caesar's Ghost!

CITIZEN NO. 1: Nay, you idiot. 'Tis only King Soglin.

SOGLIN (entering, in robes, accompanied by an aide): Wow, that was some toga party last night. I couldn't believe that guy drank his own vomit! *

AIDE: Quiet, sire, the press will hear you.

SOGLIN: Screw the ... oh, it's you.

SCRIBE: Aye, your highness.

SOGLIN: What is it you wish to ask me?

SCRIBE: Sire, the merchants are restless. They say they cannot live with the new rule protecting eatery workers and other diners from cigarette smoke.

SOGLIN: But it was the council's will. The citizens strongly back it. The measure, I have signed it. Am I not king? Is this not my kingdom?

SCRIBE: But Philip Morris, who pushes this addictive drug, is also displeased. Phil is paying lobbyists to twist the council members' arms. Now a measure to reconsider the restrictions has been introduced by Napoleon ...

SOGLIN: Napoleon!

AIDE: Sire, he means Napoleon Smith, a member of the council.

At a U.S. Conference of Mayors event in San Diego in mid-1991, Soglin reminisced in conversation about his first experience with peyote buttons, saying, "We smeared them with peanut butter. One guy threw up, and when I looked again, he was drinking his vomit. He didn't want to waste it." Unfortunately, the person he was reminiscing to was a reporter for the weekly San Diego Reader. Soglin later claimed he was misquoted: "I didn't say 'vomit,' I said 'puke.'"

SOGLIN: And what would this measure accomplish?

SCRIBE: It would ask that the restrictions be softened, and give the lobbyists another chance to kill the whole idea, along with their customers.

SOGLIN: And the merchants, they favor this?

AIDE: Aye, my Lord.

SOGLIN: Then I applaud this measure.

SCRIBE: But your wonderfulness, doesn't this mean the kingdom is capitulating to the will of saucy killers?

SOGLIN: Of course not, you idiot. Write that down!

SCRIBE: As you wish. How do you spell "idiot"?

CHORUS: Groan!

In rushes a messenger.

MESSENGER: My Lord, I have terrible news.

SOGLIN: Off with his head!

MESSENGER: I haven't even told you yet!

SOGLIN: Why should I wait to hear bad news?

MESSENGER: But my Lord, the fault is not mine. It is with your own staff. They've leaked a copy of your secret plan to take away a small fraction of the people's guns.

SOGLIN: Leaked? My secret plan was leaked? But it was a draft. Sure, it's eight pages single-spaced and it occupied many hours of the kingdom council's time. But the people whose lives it would affect weren't supposed to know of it. Boy, am I miffed.

MESSENGER: Your deceit was justified, oh wise one. Already, the pro-gun lobby is going berserk. And, as you know, they're crazy to begin with.

SOGLIN: I will not stand for this. I am too busy making sure the merchants get their Frank Lloyd Wright meeting palace and trying to come up with a kingdom budget that doesn't stir an uprising. I withdraw the gun plan. It no longer exists.

SCRIBE: What would this plan accomplish?

SOGLIN: There is no plan!

SCRIBE: Is this the one that would prohibit possession of any weapons that are not legal for hunting, but would still allow people to blow each other away left and right with any weapon you can hunt with, whether or not they hunt?

SOGLIN: What are you, dumb? There is no plan!

SCRIBE: But, your slyness, do not the polls show that a clear majority of citizens – even those who own guns for sport – favor gun control? Have we not had enough senseless carnage because our leaders won't take a stand against a few crazy people?

SOGLIN: Silence! Write this down: I, King Soglin of Madison, rule in my own way, by my own rhythms. I will bring back this gun plan in good time, maybe, because I believe it is best for my beloved kingdom. What do the merchants think?

CHORUS: Woe are we in Madison,
Behold, our hippie king.
The whole nation calls us leftist,
but he hasn't done a leftist thing.
Our wilted flowers know no power,
our bed's hot with radicalism ... not!
Merchants and landowners write the script,
what a tragedy we've got.

NOVEMBER 20, 1992

Why Hate
Shouldn't Be
Illegal

Bad public policy often comes from good intentions, especially when what's at issue are the thoughts in people's heads.

This is certainly true of the ill-fated bans on bigoted speech enacted by the University of Wisconsin and other institutions of higher learning. And it's true, I believe, of Wisconsin's law hiking penalties for crimes driven by hate, the constitutionality of which was argued before the U.S. Supreme Court last week.

I say this not just as a surveyor of legal contention, but as one of the few people on whose behalf Wisconsin's hate crimes statute has been invoked. Just after midnight on the morning of Aug. 22, 1990, my girlfriend and I were walking home in Madison, just blocks from where Wisconsin's 1988 law was deliberated and passed. Two young males passed us on the sidewalk. Obviously drug-zonked, they turned on us. One struck me in the face. He referred to himself as "Satan" and called my girlfriend "Jew girl." When bystanders took notice the pair backed off. They were arrested a short while later; "Satan's" resistance sent one officer to the hospital.

This assault occurred amid a spate of highly publicized anti-Semitic incidents in Madison, including the severing of brake lines on a bus used to take Jewish kids to camp. In this charged atmosphere, the district attorney prosecuted 17-year-old "Satan" for a hate crime, which allows adding up to five years to the sentence of criminals who select their victims based on race, religion, ancestry, national origin, disability or sexual orientation.

Some 30 states have passed similar laws. Wisconsin Attorney General James Doyle, in his Supreme Court brief, says it is fair game to consider motive in gauging the severity of crime and that crimes motivated by bigotry are "doubly depraved."

Wisconsin's position is backed by the U.S. Justice Department, the attorneys general of all 50 states, the Anti-Defamation League, the NAACP and even the ACLU. But count me among the dissenters – notably including the Center for Constitutional Rights and journalist Nat Hentoff – who see bad public policy in efforts to punish people for having the "wrong" ideas.

THE CASE UNDER REVIEW CONCERNS THE PROSECUTION OF TODD MITCHELL,
one of 10 black males who left an apartment complex in Kenosha, Wis., on the evening of Oct. 7, 1989. The group was talking about a scene from the movie *Mississippi Burning* in which white men beat a praying black child. Mr. Mitchell, then 19, pointed to the other side of the street and said, "There goes a white boy. Go get him."

Group members, not including Mitchell, severely beat 14-year-old Greg Reddick, leaving him in a coma for four days. Mitchell, who sought to call off the attackers and summoned help for Mr. Reddick, received the maximum two-year prison sentence for instigating the assault – plus two years under the hate crimes statute.

Last June the Wisconsin Supreme Court struck down the statute on First Amendment grounds. The U.S. Supreme Court agreed to hear the case; its decision is expected by early summer. Observers say the court could rule either way. I hope it strikes a blow for common sense and the First Amendment and keeps this bad law down.

The conduct for which Mitchell, and "Satan," were convicted is already illegal. The additional penalties secured through a hate crimes statute merely punish defendants for having said the wrong thing: Beat a man and it's battery. Utter an ethnic slur during the beating and it's a hate crime.

Laws against bigotry are political, and subject to the vagaries of politics. In Wisconsin, you can't get extra penalties for deliberately victimizing a woman, or someone who is anti-abortion – or a Yankees fan. Don't these people deserve full legal protection?

What happens when a criminal hates *everyone*? Are these crimes less serious? Prosecutors don't need a bigger book to throw at young blacks – or anti-Semites. (FBI statistics show that hate crimes are disproportionately enforced against minority-group members.) These laws do nothing to deter crime, and may ultimately teach people that certain forms of expression – "white boy," "Jew girl" – are not just offensive but illegal.

As state Sen. Lynn Adelman, counsel for respondent Mitchell, argued: "Wisconsin will not cure bigotry by punishing it, nor teach tolerance by being intolerant. Locking up or silencing the bigots among us will only bring about the illusion of mutual acceptance and respect, and reliance upon illusions is dangerous."

It's a lesson I hope "Satan" has learned.

APRIL 26, 1993, CHRISTIAN SCIENCE MONITOR

In June 1993, the U.S. Supreme Court unanimously upheld the constitutionality of Wisconsin's hate crimes law.

The Scourge of Ethics

[IN THE SPRING OF 1993, DEVELOPER MARTY RIFKEN AND HIS ARCHITECT made a presentation for a project to the Madison Landmarks Commission, on which they both served. They did not vote but remained present for the commission's discussion. The Madison Ethics Board, acting on a complaint from Ald. Bert Zipperer, recommended that both men resign. They did. This drew cries of protest from Landmarks Commission chair Mary Mohs, prompted the preemptive resignation of Jesse Ishikawa from the Madison Park Commission, and led to calls from Ald. Wayne Bigelow and others that the city should rescind the ethics rules that Rifken allegedly violated.]

There once was a city, Madison was its name,
whose leaders ne'er acted for personal gain.
They colluded in back rooms and cut deals with friends,
but always they acted for the noblest of ends.

The leaders were joyous, their skids were all greased,
but suddenly all of their happiness ceased.
A disaster hit Madison, hard as a twister,
'twas ethics that caused all their hinders to blister!

Ethics, oh Ethics, what a terrible thing.
It strikes without pity, and man, does it sting.

Poor developer Rifken was the first to be stricken.
He brought his own project before the Landmarks Commission.
Now he served on this body, as did his designer.
They said that their project couldn't be any finer.

"We just need permission to tear an old landmark down.
While you folks decide, we'll just stick around."
They were warned not to do this, but what did they care?
Their plan was approved as though Ethics weren't there.

Ethics, oh Ethics, it's a plague worse than boils,
even the best schemes it trips up and spoils.

Ald. Zipperer was outraged, he lodged a complaint.
The Ethics Board agreed what was done wasn't quaint.
They lost their seats on the body, and Chairperson Mohs cried,
"Look out, everybody, Ethics' after our hide.

"And oh, how we've suffered, because of this trash.
We've had to pay lawyers, and they insisted on cash!
This will ruin our committees, all the best folks will flee.
By the way, Mr. Mayor, please reappoint me."

Ethics, oh Ethics, it stings and it burns,
and the people it hurts most are members of firms!

Just when these leaders could stand it no longer,
the city attorney said, "Let's make our Ethics stronger."
Some Wisconsin state lawmakers pushed new Ethics too,
more things that our leaders should and shouldn't do.

The Park Commission's Ishikawa, whose name doesn't rhyme,
said "Before I get in trouble, I'd better resign."
Urban Design members likewise threatened to quit,
so the city eased its rules, their Ethics to fit.

Ethics, oh Ethics, it burns and it sickens,
away from it these leaders ran like the Dickens!

The *State Journal* howled and Ald. Bigelow blurted,
"Let us join now and work to get Ethics diverted.
Let's go back to the start, to poor Rifken's plight.
Maybe there's some way to make his behavior all right."

Others joined this chorus, they were sick to the core:
"Ethics, oh Ethics, we don't want you no more."
Alas, for these leaders, there's no happy end.
They just pray for the day they can be unethical again!

JULY 2, 1993

New Proof: Guns Cause Nuttiness

In yet another stunning display of investigative prowess, *Isthmus* has learned that a proposal to pass four city gun-control measures is part of an experiment being conducted by a renowned University of Vienna psychologist.

Prof. Wolfgang Von Schmartass, the world's foremost authority on Firearm-Induced Insecurity Syndrome, has been working behind the scenes to monitor reaction to the ordinances, which he helped draft.

"Vat ve vere looking for vas a zet of meazures zo zensible no zane person could oppose zem," explains Schmartass. "Zen ve would zee vether my zientific hypothezis ist correct."

And vat ist zis zientific hypothezis? "Zat having guns makes people crazy and stupit."

The four measures, co-sponsored by Mayor Paul Soglin and nine members of the Common Council, would ban assault weapons, snub-nosed pistols, expanding bullets and carrying loaded weapons in public, in the city of Madison. Schmartass says the reaction thus far supports his theory.

"Zese people are convinced zey need veapons to protect zemselves, but ze more veapons zey have, ze more insecure zey become," notes Schmartass, who agreed to speak to *Isthmus* after word of his experiment was leaked by Deep Chamber, an inside source. "Also, it zeems zese weapons und zis constant worrying ist a drain on ze brain."

Schmartass, author of *I'm Okay, You're a Gun Nut*, observed recent city hearings on the proposed ordinance changes on closed-circuit TV. As speaker after speaker took the microphone, most to register vehement opposition to the proposed controls, Schmartass excitedly scribbled notes and uttered gleeful affirmations. [All quotes, except those of Dr. Schmartass, are actual.]

"Yez, yez," exclaimed Schmartass as Bob Syring testified at the May 16 hearing. "I'm really pissed to be here," declared Syring, noting that a proposed city handgun ban was beaten back last year. "And I'm not even sure I'm opposed to the ordinances."

"Zis ist exactly vat my rezearch has found," says Schmartass. "Even ven zese people realize, intellectually, zat zertain controls make zense, zey oppose zem, because zat ist how zey have been programmed."

Schmartass also reacted excitedly to testimony from Ross Walcott of Edgerton, who drew a parallel between the proposed ordinances and Nazi Germany. "It's definitely a national conspiracy for removing guns from law-abiding citizens," said Walcott. He also referred to a recent shoes-for-guns swap program as "psychological conditioning" for gun confiscation, and he ended his address with a Nazi-style salute: "Heil Soglin!"

"You zee!" exclaimed Schmartass, nearly falling off his chair. "He's zo insecure he zinks his rights to blow his own head off or shoot people in his own family are threatened by shoes! Und zis fellow doesn't even live in Madison. He's just an outzide agitator sticking his big nose vere it has no business belonging."

ALL ACROSS AMERICA, SCHMARTASS SAYS, GUN NUTS LIKE THESE ARE encouraging the mass possession of deadly weapons. In Arizona, which boasts having more guns than people, the NRA last year shot down local ordinances requiring children under 18 who carry guns to have a permission slip from their parents. And in Franklintown, Penn., the repeal of an ordinance requiring every head of household to have a gun caused Mayor Robert Wolfe to lament, "This pretty country of ours isn't free anymore."

"Vat ist meant by zis kind of freedom?" asks Schmartass. "It zeems to me zuch freedom ist, how do I zay, just another word for ... nothing left to shoot."

Individuals who suffer from Firearm-Induced Insecurity Syndrome, Schmartass says, are right to be afraid: Having guns in the home vastly increases their risk of robbery, accidental shooting or spur-of-the-moment homicide. But instead, gun owners mainly fear the loss of the weapons that threaten them. Often they become obsessed.

Schmartass points to a letter to the NRA from Richard Carone, a member of a pro-gun group called Californians Against Corruption. "What brings us great pleasure and satisfaction is producing political pain by bleeding our targets," Carone wrote. "Our methods make it extremely expensive, difficult and unpleasant for the target to remain in office.... [We never back off] until the target has either resigned, has been destroyed, or has otherwise been effectively neutralized. Only then do we move on to another Prime Target."

"Vat ve have here ist a policy of group terrorism, fed by Firearm-Induced Inzecurity Zyndrome," says Schmartass. "It's no wonder zome of your Common Council members have been rezeiving threats. Zat ist ze form zis madness takes."

Will threats and coercion keep Madison from banning weapons only a crazy person could defend? "Possibly," says Schmartass. "But you zee, it doezn't matter. Vether zese meazures pass or not, zere will always be plenty of deadly veapons left in America to kill wit. Zat's why I'm going back to Vienna. Your country is too zick in ze head."

JUNE 3, 1994

The Madison Common Council approved the four measures in December 1994, but they were struck down within a year when the state Legislature preempted the ability of local governments to establish stricter gun rules than for the state as whole. When the U.S. Supreme Court in July 2010 undercut the ability of local governments to enact gun control laws, Madison's were already shot down.

Take a Stand Against Bad Cops

When I was a boy, I watched three cops assault a black youth in the alley behind my home on Milwaukee's north side. They pulled the kid, who was perhaps 16, from the fringes of an open-housing march, and beat him with clubs.

The cops of my hometown routinely did things like this because they knew they would get away with it. In 1981, Milwaukee's Finest brutalized to death a young black man named Ernest Lacey whom they suspected of rape (it turned out he was innocent). A decade later, they returned a naked, bleeding, incoherent Laotian child to Jeffrey Dahmer, who killed him, rather than heed a black woman who tried to intervene on the boy's behalf.

But the real problem, I now see, is not misbehavin' officers but police departments, city bureaucracies and courts that wink at obvious abuses. (The Dahmer cops were last month ordered reinstated with back pay.) Indeed, today's bad cops are not only tolerated but glorified.

Witness "NYPD Blue," in which police regularly con and threaten suspects into giving up their right to an attorney. In one episode, hero-Detective John Kelly explains to a rookie under what circumstances it's okay to beat a suspect into spilling his guts: when you know he's guilty.

Madison once had some pretty bad boys in blue too, to judge from all the footage of cops beating antiwar protesters in the famed documentary *The War at Home*. In fact, I suspect the natural inclination of all cops – or anyone to whom society grants as much power as cops – is to abuse. Madison's police force is today relatively unbrutal because people in power here have sent clear messages about what will not be permitted.

Sadly, there is reason to believe those messages are being diluted, and the standards of permissible behavior loosened. Just ask John Steele.

ON NOV. 3, 1991, STEELE WAS ARRESTED ON HIS MIDDLETON FARM FOR selling marijuana. He later testified that one of the arresting officers, Sgt.

Mark Bradley of the Madison PD, placed his gun to Steele's temple. And then, as Steele went into a fit of trembling and heart palpitations, Bradley continued to terrorize him, saying he would go to prison and never see his family again unless he cooperated. Steele agreed to call up people to whom he'd sold marijuana; police nabbed them as they came to the farm.

Of course, the judge believed the officer and slapped Steele with an eight-year prison term – considerably longer than he would have gotten had he not insisted on making "false" allegations of police misconduct.

But then, in April 1993, the assistant U.S. attorney who prosecuted Steele drove to Chicago with one of the Madison police officers who was present during the arrest. The prosecutor, Chris Van Wagner, subsequently produced a memorandum about what the officer, Madison Det. Linda Draeger of the Madison PD, told him along the way.

According to the memo, which *The Capital Times* last month managed to get released, Draeger was disgusted with the conduct she observed, which substantiated Steele's version. The interrogations at the farmhouse, Draeger purportedly told Van Wagner, were done with guns drawn, and Bradley threatened Steele with automatic prison and loss of his family. The memo says Draeger saw another arrestee at the farmhouse interrogated "with threats, intimidation and with guns out and pointed to his head" – a technique she said Bradley used routinely, much to her dismay.

The memo was made available, as the law requires, to Steele's Madison attorney, David Lasker, and its allegations were the subject of a hearing last Dec. 6 in U.S. District Court. Draeger, called to the stand as an adverse witness, denied telling Van Wagner (the only person in this drama with no motive to lie) much of what his memo recounts – for instance, that she had seen drawn guns during Steele's interrogation. U.S. Magistrate Stephen Crocker dismissed the conflicting testimony as inconclusive.

"I believe Det. Draeger told the truth to Van Wagner and then lied to the court under oath," says Lasker, who is still seeking to have Steele's sentence dismissed due to "outrageous police conduct." Why would Draeger lie to protect Bradley? Because, Lasker notes, she depends on other cops to back her up in a pinch: "I believe she did it possibly to save her own life."

In the past, says Lasker, the courts made it their business to protect individual liberties. Now officials like Crocker, confronted with evidence of police misconduct, instead heed another imperative: to insulate and protect police. "This case shows there is very little if any regulation of the behavior of police officers in this district," says Lasker. "It's really frightening."

So is the apparent lack of vigilance by the Madison PD. In response to the allegations in Van Wagner's memo, the department's Professional Standards Unit launched a formal probe – to determine whether Det. Draeger ought to be disciplined for spreading lies about Bradley! The unit head, Lt. Steve Sheets, says the case against Draeger could not be sustained. He and Madison Police Chief Richard Williams both say they see nothing to indicate that an investigation of Sgt. Bradley is in order.

Whoa. Draeger disputed much of the content of Van Wagner's memo, but not all of it. In fact, she repeatedly affirmed that Bradley often put his gun to the head of people he arrested, and that she disagreed with this method: "I thought it was too dangerous."

But when I asked Williams about Bradley allegedly holding his gun to suspects' heads, the chief corrected me: "What would be more accurate would be *pointing* a loaded gun."

Draeger's testimony on this score was crystal clear, and when a questioner used the term "pointing" she set him straight: "I don't think I said [to Van Wagner that] I disagreed with [Bradley] pointing the gun at somebody's head. I think I said I disagreed with him putting a gun to somebody's head. There is a difference."

It is a difference Sheets and Williams have decided to fudge, presumably to protect Bradley. At another point during the hearing, Draeger recounts telling Sheets that Bradley, despite his own sworn testimony to the contrary, put guns to heads. But this practice – the mark of a terrorist – arouses no concern among the Madison Police Department's current leadership.

This whole sorry episode cries out for the involvement of city officials – including Mayor Paul Soglin, who in his student-activist days was himself brutalized by police. Someone outside the department should order a probe – and see to it that Lt. Sheets and Chief Williams are not involved, except possibly as subjects.

The bottom line is that we should respect police, but not trust them to police themselves. That's a beat the community as a whole must be prepared to walk.

JULY 1, 1994

Prompted by the Steele case, Isthmus *made a request for complaints against Madison police under the state's open records law; it was denied. That led to two lawsuits by* Isthmus, *the* Wisconsin State Journal *and* The Capital Times; *Mayor Soglin and his successor, Sue Bauman, sided with police. The papers eventually won both lawsuits and were awarded legal costs totaling $96,000. John Steele served his full sentence.*

Erwin Knoll, 1986. Photo by Zane Williams

In Remembrance of Erwin Knoll

The first thing Erwin Knoll taught me was never be mawkish.

It was May 1984, soon after I began an editorial internship at *The Progressive*. We were discussing the headline of a piece I'd written about the magazine's founder, "Fighting Bob" La Follette, for a special 75th anniversary issue. Erwin wanted to call it "The Fighting Founder." I suggested "The Founding Fighter."

"No!" he exclaimed, as though in horror. "That would make it *mawkish.*"

Erwin's rebuke – and a few other things he imparted – helped launch a journalistic career in which, I'm proud to say, I've never again been accused of being mawkish. And the terribly sad occasion of Erwin's death, in his sleep last Wednesday at age 63, is no time to regress.

For all his gentleness and good humor, Erwin was not a sentimental man. He would probably be embarrassed that so many people – in Madison and throughout the land – are remembering him fondly and grieving his loss. Yet that is what we are moved to by his extraordinary life.

He fled Nazi terror as a young Jewish child in his native Austria to become a journalist who covered the exploits of presidents he loathed for news outlets including the *Washington Post*. In 1973, he became editor of *The Progressive*, the nation's oldest and most venerable monthly political magazine. In 1979, he successfully resisted the federal government's efforts to suppress publication of an article exploding the myth of H-bomb secrecy. He was a great editor who became, in recent years, the most radical commentator allowed on prime-time TV.

Erwin celebrated his own past in the anecdotes he was forever telling. My favorite: how when he and his wife, Doris, were entertaining dinner guests including a speech writer for President Johnson, their young son David inquired from the top of the stairs, "Which one's the bloody war criminal?"

Out of the maelstrom of his own experience, Erwin Knoll became a man with a mission: to change the way people thought about politics; to champion an absolute commitment to nonviolence and freedom of speech; and to lock horns, through his own life and intellect, with the seemingly endless capacity of human beings to inflict suffering on one another.

Erwin believed deeply in the power of language – for educating, for agitating, for fashioning a politics that is at once radical and compelling and capable of making a positive difference in people's lives. He wrote sparkling prose and spoke with great style and eloquence, yet he understood the aptness of such a fine word as "bullshit."

He also understood the need for conflict to bring about change. His politics, ultimately, were of the street.

THAT SUMMER OF 1984, I JOINED ERWIN AND OTHER AGITATORS IN handing out copies of the Bill of Rights at East Towne mall, whose owners decided to suspend the First Amendment on their private property. A beefy security guard snuck up behind Erwin and tried to snatch away his copies of the Bill of Rights. Erwin turned on him and unleashed a tongue-lashing unlike any I've heard since. It contained no pejoratives or threats, yet seethed with indignation so hot it's a wonder the guard's walkie-talkie didn't melt in his hand.

When it came to things that mattered, Erwin Knoll stood on principle, and he didn't budge. He welcomed the clash of ideas because he believed his ideas were sound enough to withstand scrutiny and the test of time. And, just about always, Erwin and his magazine were on the mark.

In the 10 years since my *Progressive* internship, I've come to see that, even in the areas where we once disagreed, Erwin was right.

He was right to be absolute in defending freedom of speech, because any authority granted the state to curb the sleaziest pornographer or most vile hate group is power that will in the end be used to suppress threats to the state.

He was right to insist on nonviolent civil disobedience as being always the best response to oppression. He was right to oppose militarism in all its forms, to quarrel with leftists who decried tyranny but not the bloodshed committed by those who sought its overthrow.

He was right to brand the two-party system "the enemy of democracy in America" and right to underscore – in part by refusing to vote in presidential elections – that true reform will come only from a mass movement of the people built over decades from the grassroots up.

As the left's most prominent spokesperson, Erwin Knoll touched many people, and his influence extends in more directions than anyone can tell. Each of us is left with a sense of emptiness, a void we need to fill. There is no doubt how Erwin would have wanted us to fill it.

In September 1984, *The Progressive* celebrated its 75th anniversary at Bob La Follette's former home in Maple Bluff. Erwin, taking the microphone, distanced himself from the celebratory tone of other speakers and importuned the crowd to turn its energy to activism – "to educate, to agitate" for progressive change. And he meant *right away*, as in *put down that fizzy water*.

That is, of course, the same challenging message Erwin Knoll would impart to those who mourn him: There's a world of change that still needs agitating for. Get to work. *Now.*

NOVEMBER 11, 1994

Just Say No, Stupid

What would Bill Foust do if local drug cops showed up at his door asking to search his home and belongings? "I'd say no," he answers without hesitation.

Of course he would. Because Foust, the district attorney for Dane County, knows that police have no legal right to search his home without a warrant, or stop him on the street and dig into his pockets. And yet cops in Dane County are, with his knowledge and consent, doing this to other people, he says, "all the time."

Worse still, Foust has no sympathy for people who are too scared of armed officers or too ignorant of their legal rights to resist such brazen assaults on their civil liberties. "Don't punish us for stupidity," he says, referring not to the stupidity of a society that sacrifices its most important freedoms in order to bust people for often minor drug offenses, but to the stupidity of the citizens who tolerate this.

"I don't know how much education you need to say no to somebody's request to put their hands in your pockets," says Foust, who defends warrantless searches of people and their homes as "good police work."

Foust's idea of good police work is implemented routinely by the Dane County Narcotics and Gang Task Force.

Madison Police Sgt. Jay Lengfeld, a task force member, says he and his fellows conduct 30 to 40 warrantless searches each month, based on tips about possible illegal drug activity. As he puts it, "Why go through the trouble of getting a search warrant when you can just knock on the door?" Most of the time, the cops couldn't get a warrant anyway because they don't have enough evidence.

Foust says these warrantless searches don't trouble him because they are consensual: "I have not heard accounts that the contacts have been coercive."

But local attorneys who handle drug cases say the task-force cops use extremely aggressive tactics. As many as eight narcs at a time appear on doorsteps and badger their way inside. People don't understand they have the right to tell the cops to get lost, and the cops don't enlighten them. Neither does Bill Foust.

Local defense attorney Jack Priester tells of one case in which a woman answered the door to task-force cops, refused them entry and turned to walk away. One of the cops ordered her to stop and grabbed her arm. When she tried to free herself, the cops threw her against a wall, arrested her for obstructing an officer, handcuffed her and dug through her pockets, turning up a small quantity of drugs.

Critics say police single out poor people and minorities, who are less likely to assert their rights. "I've had numerous black young clients who think that if a cop asks to search your car you have to let them because they're going to do it anyway," says attorney Mark Borns.

Rest assured, there are a lot of white people smoking pot and using cocaine in University Heights who don't have to worry about that knock on their door. Neither does Bill Foust, a longtime addict whose dangerous drug of choice – nicotine – happens to be legal.

IN ADDITION TO WINKING AT GESTAPO POLICE TACTICS, FOUST HAS embraced a policy of excessively punishing people for illegal drug use. Even simple possession of marijuana is criminally prosecuted in cases where a person has prior convictions or is simultaneously charged with another crime, like drunk driving. In one case being prosecuted by Foust's office, a man caught with half a joint in his pocket stands to lose his license, his job and thousands of dollars in fines and attorneys fees. He should have smoked the whole joint, and spared himself a lot of harm.

To his credit, Foust backs a Dane County drug court program that will allow drug offenders to receive treatment rather than jail terms and criminal records. He says a first batch of test cases will be processed soon.

But I for one think people who use illegal drugs like marijuana pose a far less serious threat to society than do the members of the Dane County Narcotics and Gang Task Force. The county's citizenry, and especially its elected leaders, ought to be resisting the war on civil liberties that masquerades as a war on drugs.

Bill Foust is an honorable man and an able district attorney. But he should defend the right of citizens besides himself to be free from warrantless intrusions, and he should stop ruining people's lives through idiotic prosecutions. Otherwise, one of the county's gazillion attorneys ought to run against him this November, vowing a more sensible approach.

In the meantime, be prepared to defend your rights. If the cops ask "permission" to dig through your pockets or search your home or car, just say no, adding, "What do you think I am, stupid?"

APRIL 5, 1996

Foust was reelected without opposition in the fall election and a year later appointed Dane County judge, a position he still holds.

Get Rid of Regulators

H aving no marketable skills of any sort, I gravitated to journalism. But the career I've always dreamed of is to be a regulator.

Ah, to be a government-employed consumer advocate, dispensing swift justice to companies that make bogus claims or unsafe products! To be vested with the power to purge incompetent doctors or sleazy lawyers! To fearlessly champion fair elections and honest government! That's the job of my dreams.

Over the years, though, I've come to the heartbreaking realization that regulators are perhaps every bit as powerless as journalists when it comes to these worthy pursuits. In fact, regulators accomplish so little that I wonder whether we should do away with them altogether.

Take the state Elections Board ... please. Charged with protecting Wisconsin's reputation for clean elections, this body of eight political appointees has actually served to undermine the state's campaign-finance laws.

Recently, the board was faced with what many observers felt was a clear and deliberate violation of the law. State Rep. Scott Jensen, the Assembly Majority leader, circumvented a $6,000 limit on campaign contributions by claiming that the Republican Party in each of the state's 72 counties was a separate entity. The board's staff attorney recommended a hefty fine, but its four Republican members dismissed the case. Thus the $6,000 limit has been torpedoed: Political action committees can henceforth pour hundreds of thousands of dollars into the coffers of their favorite political party.

Such corrupt and ineffective regulation may be worse than no regulation at all, because it helps sustain the illusion that special-interest influence is being kept in check, when in fact the opposite is true. The state should terminate the Election Board's regulatory function and admit that elections in this state are now openly for sale.

Similarly, we ought to subject other regulatory agencies to a sober assessment, to see whether they serve any useful purpose. My suspicion is that most of these agencies do less to protect the public than they do to delude it into thinking it's being protected.

Last year I filed a complaint with the Board of Attorneys Professional Responsibility, part of the Wisconsin Supreme Court, against a local attorney who made false representations to me regarding a house for sale. The attorney, in his written response, admitted he knew within hours of making them that his representations were false, yet did nothing to set the record straight. As a result, a friend and I lost hundreds of dollars.

The complaint I filed was put on the back burner for months, then dismissed without even the pretense of an investigation. There was, so far as I could tell, no application of intellect by any board employee, merely the application of a process that had exoneration of this sleazy lawyer as its foregone conclusion. I later learned that this attorney went on to make similar false representations to the next people who tried to buy this house. The board's authority is, from this attorney's point of view, a joke.

He's right. The Board of Attorneys Professional Responsibility in 1995–96 received 1,316 complaints, according to its annual report. The vast majority (1,128) were dismissed, including cases where the attorney's conduct was deemed "close to the line." Of the remaining cases, 42 led to private reprimands – meaning the board finds evidence of bad behavior but decides to keep it secret. Public discipline was imposed in just 33 cases, about 2.5 percent of the total.

Interestingly, the board's $1.4 million annual budget comes from an assessment on state attorneys. In return, they get a regulatory apparatus whose primary function is to cover up and ignore misconduct.

I COULD GO ON. MOST OF THE MORE THAN 100,000 CONSUMER complaints filed in Wisconsin each year are just that – filed, as in out of sight and out of mind.

This summer, I alerted the Department of Agriculture, Trade and

Consumer Protection to a scam operation that called me, only to hang up when I began asking questions. The department responded by sending the scam operation a polite letter, followed by another polite letter when this was ignored, then another. That's where it stands now: Unless this scam operation belatedly admits – in writing – that its purpose is to rip people off, nothing will be done.

Stuart Engerman, a supervisor with the state Department of Regulation and Licensing, explains that tight budgets force regulators to focus on the most serious cases, and those where the evidence is strongest. But this means most complaints are not pursued.

Regulators, by and large, are sincerely committed to righting wrongs. But their good intentions should not blind us to their poor performance. Even when the will is there, the might is not.

Consider the case of Dr. Jose Kanshepolsky, a Racine-based physician and surgeon. The Medical Examining Board in 1985 charged him with unprofessional conduct and incompetence in three cases dating from 1977, 1978 and 1981. It took until 1989 for the board to revoke his license. Then Kanshepolsky was able to drag the issue through the courts until November 1992. During this whole time, he continued to practice medicine on unsuspecting patients.

"It kind of defeats the whole purpose of the board," admits Deanna Zychowski, its administrative assistant. She'd like license revocations to take effect while the appeal process plays out. I suggest another response: Shut down the Medical Examining Board and admit that the state doesn't do much of anything to protect the public from incompetent doctors.

At least that would be honest.

DECEMBER 6, 1996

Donn Eithun, 1987. Photo by Brent Nicastro

A Star Burning Bright

Awhile back, when we went out to lunch, Donn Eithun bought two egg salad sandwiches, one to eat and one to go. Afterward, as we walked back to our respective offices, he dropped the extra sandwich into the outstretched hands of a nearly toothless panhandler – an obvious alcoholic – he had spotted on the street. He addressed the man by name, asked how he was doing.

Eithun, who died last week in a tragic rafting accident in California, was a former Madison alderperson, card-carrying Republican and successful stockbroker. But taking care of the needy was always among his chief concerns; one of his pet projects, which never came to pass, was to open a soup kitchen in the heart of Madison's downtown.

It wasn't upper-class guilt or some sense of religious obligation that made Eithun try to make life a little better for the less fortunate. He did it because he knew that, but for a few simple twists of fate, the man on the street with the outstretched hand could very well be him.

As I wrote in an *Isthmus* cover story in 1987, Donn Eithun was a chronic alcoholic and substance abuser who'd found enough love in his life to embrace living as passionately as he once embraced drinking.

"These things are not supposed to be happening to me," Eithun said of his family, his career, his work on the Common Council. "I'm supposed to be like the guy I saw lying on a bench who really needs 10 bucks to eat for a day or two."

Eithun, who was only 39 when he died, spent much of the first part of his life in an alcoholic haze. He dropped out of high school, got kicked out of the Navy, and repeatedly drank himself into unconsciousness on the streets of Madison. When he was 18, he drank so much his heart stopped, and he had to be revived using emergency procedures. Afterward, he was furious with the doctor for suggesting he was an alcoholic.

Denial gave way to acceptance: Donn drank hard because he was a drunk, and he knew it. But when his wife, Kim, became pregnant with the first of the couple's two children, Donn pulled himself together with the help of AA. He accepted that he was powerless over alcohol, "and it no longer meant that I could never drink again, but that I didn't have to. And I knew a new freedom and a new happiness."

DONN EITHUN, ONE OF HIS OLD FRIENDS TOLD ME, WAS "A STAR BURNING bright. There was never any sense that he was just going along for the ride. He always provided the transportation."

As I wrote 10 years ago, "[Eithun's] politics are hopelessly iconoclastic and his manner often brash. There is an almost manic intensity about him, and a compulsion toward uniqueness that is sometimes at war with his yearning to be liked. But he's certainly not someone you can meet and soon forget." The memory of his presence still burns bright in the minds of those who knew him.

Throughout his life, Eithun put some of his bountiful energy at the service of the community. He worked as a sales rep and reporter for the *Madison Press Connection*, served two terms on the Common Council, wrote columns for *The Capital Times* and *Wisconsin State Journal*, hosted television shows for the city's government cable channel, and served as chair of the Madison chapter of the March of Dimes.

What I admired most about Eithun was his zest for life. He did it all: parasailing, scuba diving, skydiving, bungee jumping. "People who go to a salad bar and load their plate with lettuce," he once told me, "are *missing the point!*" I can still hear his voice, booming and emphatic.

Let us give thanks to people like Donn Eithun for making Madison a community of which we can be proud. It's a debt of gratitude we repay every time we treat a person who's down and out with kindness and respect.

JUNE 27, 1997

To this day, I never visit a salad bar without thinking about Donn.

You Pay, I'll Play

Fifteen years ago, when I got my start in journalism, I used to say that my primary ambition was to never sell out. Times change, and I have too. Looking back on my career, I confess I've grown weary of fighting the good fight, accomplishing little. I've decided to put out the "For Sale" sign.

Let's face it: Most of what journalists do is simply irrelevant. Just ask Rick Fetherston, the former local TV anchor who's now a mouthpiece for American Family Insurance. "I have learned that press coverage has very little lasting impact, positive or negative, on anything or anyone," Fetherston said in a deposition regarding his company's purging of dissidents. "That's just a personal opinion after years in the media."

It's getting to be my opinion, too. In my job at *Isthmus*, I get contacted all the time by people seeking to call attention to some or another injustice. Even if I pursue a story, I always tell them not to expect that it will make any difference. And often, I decline to get involved because media attention is more likely to hurt than help.

Take the Madison woman who has called and written me about her son, a drug addict who sought but could not afford treatment. He began to steal to support his habit and eventually drew a huge prison term for burglarizing an empty house while unarmed. Now he's been banished to solitary confinement in prison for what is arguably a trumped-up infraction of a minor rule. He receives no treatment for his addiction. He has nothing to read. He is slowly losing his mind.

I tell this woman that I cannot help. The state prison system, callous to the core, isn't going to bend in response to a newspaper article, and no politician will spend the slightest bit of political capital on her son's behalf. Most of the public won't give a damn, and a good portion of the rest will be outraged – absolutely outraged – that anyone is seeking sympathy for this, this ... criminal. It's good that he's suffering, they'll say; let's hope and pray he suffers more.

Even when the plight of a prisoner – or person on welfare – indisputably intersects with public-policy issues, it's nearly impossible to get anyone to care.

In recent years, I've written a slew of articles and columns about John Steele, a Madison man sentenced to 87 months in prison for being a bit player in a marijuana ring. Steele believes that records of an internal police probe involving Madison Police Sgt. Mark Bradley and Det. Linda Draeger may support his claims of police misconduct during his 1991 arrest. The Police Department, backed by the city attorney's office, is still fighting to keep these records secret.

My suspicion, and I could be wrong on this, is that the cops are engaged in a deliberate cover-up. What I'm sure of is that all of the attention I've brought to this matter has had no effect. Mayor Soglin didn't care. Mayor Bauman doesn't care. The Common Council doesn't care. The public doesn't care. The State Bar of Wisconsin gave me an award for my reporting on this case, yet there is not a single attorney in the state of Wisconsin willing to help Steele press his open-records claim on a pro bono basis.

Why? As much as I hate to generalize, I think it's because attorneys are people who care when they get paid to care. Maybe I should take the same approach.

I MEAN, EVERYONE ELSE IS DOING IT. THE UW-MADISON ENTERED AN agreement with Reebok that bars it from uttering a discouraging word about that company's use of virtual slave labor in Southeast Asia. (A contract clause to this effect was dropped, but UW officials have maintained their utter silence.)

The Madison school district has agreed to sell only Coca-Cola products (motto: "Sugar Helps You Learn") in city schools. Naming rights for public buildings – even buildings like the Brewers Stadium, which will be mostly paid for with public funds – are now routinely offered for sale to corporations. And plans have been revived to turn Madison buses into giant advertisements on wheels.

I want to be a giant advertisement on wheels, too. Just cut me a big check and tell me what to say. I'm ready.

Maybe I could go to law school and get a job in the city attorney's office, where I could work to ensure that police misconduct in this community is covered up. Or I could go into politics, picking only those fights that promise an electoral payoff.

Better yet, there's the booming field of public relations. I could work for American Family, defending purges and profiteering. Or for tobacco companies, which already pay part of my salary through ads in *Isthmus*. Or Janesville's Accudyne Corp., a manufacturer of land mines for which Gov. Tommy Thompson last year helped snare $1 million in tax credits and a $250,000 loan. The company says its land mines are safer for civilians than those produced by China, Russia or Italy. That's not much consolation to kids who have their legs blown off, but it certainly is the essence of good PR.

Count me in. I'm willing to tell any lie, suppress any truth, twist any reality to suit my bosses' depraved world view, so long as I get paid for it. I'll be here as always, waiting for the phone to ring.

SEPTEMBER 19, 1997

Without a Remedy

Patricia L. Davis of Madison was a single mom working two jobs, as a nurse's aide at St. Mary's Care Center and as a taxi-cab driver for Madison Metro. In April 1997, a same-shift coworker named Deanise Hollingsworth snatched Davis' driver's license to cash a forged check. Hollingsworth around this time committed a spate of similar crimes, for which she is now serving a six-year prison term. But police and prosecutors did not go after Hollingsworth for this forgery; instead, they went after Davis.

When Davis, who has no criminal record, said she didn't know anything about the check, police asked her for a handwriting sample, which she provided. Madison Police Det. Rick Miller, who has received some training in handwriting analysis, concluded that Davis forged the check.

Amazingly, Miller was never shown samples of Hollingsworth's handwriting; apparently she wasn't even a suspect. Yet on the basis of Miller's review, Davis was this spring charged with a felony, arrested and thrown in jail overnight. The state of Wisconsin yanked her nurse's aide license; the city pulled her taxi-driver's permit. Davis had to find two new jobs to support herself. Plus she incurred thousands of dollars in legal bills to avoid being convicted of a crime in which she was actually the victim.

Throughout the year, in various pleadings and motion hearings, Davis' attorney, Dan Stein, argued that Hollingsworth was the most likely culprit. Asst. District Attorney Ann Sayles, who also prosecuted Hollingsworth, objected to this on grounds of relevance. Two weeks ago, just before Davis was set to go on trial, handwriting samples obtained by Stein and analyzed by the State Crime Lab confirmed that the check was forged by Hollingsworth. The charges against Davis were dismissed.

Afterward, I asked Sayles whether the DA's office owed Davis an apology. She said it was an interesting question. Later that day, when I ran into her in court, Sayles volunteered, "The answer to the question, 'Is an apology owed to Ms. Davis?' is yes."

Davis is still waiting to hear it. "Nobody has told me anything," she says. "Nobody has apologized. They were so willing to prosecute me, but now that they've found out I'm not guilty, they're like, 'Oh well, we're through with her.'"

Worse, Davis is learning there's not much she can do about it. Although she suffered actual monetary losses as well as extreme emotional pain, for no good reason, she's left without recourse.

"Vindicated criminal targets or defendants generally are without a remedy in our system," reported the *Wisconsin Lawyer* in its September 1998 issue. "The immunity doctrines and the very high bar for any civil remedy historically have made recovery for even the most abusive prosecution virtually impossible."

Sayles, to her credit, has taken steps to help clear Davis' name. Her boss, District Attorney Diane Nicks, defends her office's handling of the case while noting it has, as a matter of law, "no civil or financial obligation" to Davis.

SOMEHOW OR OTHER, PEOPLE IN THIS COUNTRY GOT SOLD ON THE IDEA that the more power we give to police and prosecutors, the safer we'll be. Instead, we've allowed police and prosecutors to become so powerful they're potentially more dangerous than criminals.

Think of it: Hollingsworth used Davis' name to forge a check, but it was police and prosecutors who turned Davis' life upside down.

What happened to Davis may be extreme, but it has elements in common with other cases that have attracted *Isthmus'* attention in 1998:

• In January, the Dane County DA's Office dropped charges it brought against Wieslaw Kasmarek of Madison for allegedly stealing $11.35 of packaged meat from a supermarket. Kasmarek, a Polish immigrant with a European sense of honor, held out for an apology, noting that a store clerk had practically told police she intended to plant evidence. He went on a 40-day hunger strike, which he abandoned only after being persuaded that he would surely die before the DA's office admitted error, which it never did.

• Patty, a Madison woman, was criminally charged by the DA's office for allegedly fabricating a reported rape. This despite the fact that Patty's confession was, as she charged, obtained through the use of lies and deception. Ten days before Patty's trial, the office moved to dismiss, citing belatedly analyzed semen stains that showed Patty had maybe been raped after all. There was no admission of error, and no apology. The prosecutor, Deputy DA Jill Karofsky, declared that the officers who deceived Patty "ought to be proud of what they did." *

• Last April Nicks, citing new medical evidence, dropped felony child-abuse charges against Susan Pankow, accused of breaking the leg of an infant in her care. Pankow speculatively confessed ("My God, if I did this....") to the same detective who secured a confession from Patty. Police were told that the scenario Pankow confessed to – a sharp movement during diaper changing – could not have caused the infant's injuries. But the DA's office filed charges anyway, and now refuses to disclose what medical evidence led to the dismissal of charges.

Nicks insists prosecutors are mindful of their capacity for error. "I think everybody in this office worries about the decisions we make, the possibility we can make a mistake," she says. "Nobody wields the power cavalierly and without concern."

Yet Nicks can't think of any cases in which prosecutorial error has clearly occurred. Even in the Davis case, she says, police had not just a forged check but a detective's analysis of the handwriting: "I don't know if there was an error in charging."

Tell that to Patty Davis.

NOVEMBER 13, 1998

* *Patty's ordeal is the subject of my 2006 book,* Cry Rape: The True Story of One Woman's Harrowing Quest for Justice

On, Wisconsin!

I t's about time someone had the guts to stand up for God and country and against all of this freedom. I applaud the Wisconsin Legislature for leading the way.

Take Assembly Speaker Scott Jensen. At a time when the state's working families are struggling to afford health coverage, child care and housing, he's devoting his energy to something really important: passing a law requiring that an American flag be displayed in every classroom, and that every school day begin with the Pledge of Allegiance or National Anthem.

Jensen says this would "refocus our society on things that unify our nation instead of the things that tear our social fabric apart."

Great idea. When kids come to school hungry because Dad got downsized out of a job and Mom's bedridden with an illness her HMO won't cover, what they really need is to mouth platitudes about the land of the free and liberty and justice for all. After years of such conditioning, these young men and women will do whatever their government asks without a second thought. Or even a first.

Meanwhile, state Sen. David Zien and Rep. Mark Pettis are pushing legislation to prohibit anyone from damaging a flag "under circumstances in which the actor knows his or her conduct is likely to cause violence or a breach of the peace." In practice, this means that if a) some punk burns a flag to protest some immoral act committed by the U.S. government, and b) some true-blue, love-it-or-leave-it patriots beat the punk to a bloody pulp, then c) the punk can be arrested and charged with a serious crime for having incited violence.

In other respects, this is a glorious time to be a Cheesehead. Wisconsin is recognized nationally for our leadership in kicking poor people off welfare, making it difficult for women to make reproductive choices and keeping taxes low for fat cats and corporations. We've gotten so tough on crime that our prisons are overflowing.

Even in liberal Madison, we have a criminal justice system that eats raw meat for breakfast. The Dane County District Attorney's Office recently charged a barely 13-year-old boy as an adult for shooting a classmate. To date, no charges have been brought against the store owner who left loaded guns within the lad's reach. Here in Wisconsin, we're not too keen on the First Amendment, but we love the Second.

That's why state voters last fall overwhelmingly approved a constitutional amendment affirming our right to bear arms. People here were sick and tired of all those constraints. Why, it was getting to where you almost couldn't give loaded guns to school kids without getting in trouble.

YES, WE LIVE IN A GRAND STATE, WHERE GOVERNMENT IS BOLDLY endeavoring to be more self-consciously righteous and moral.

Last week the state Department of Natural Resources announced that it will ban overnight camping on a popular stretch of the Wisconsin River near Mazomanie. The road to the beach, where people have been known to go naked (something God never intended), will be closed, except from September to February, so that hunters can still have easy access.

If there's anything we Cheeseheads can't stand, it's the notion that nature serves some purpose other than providing things to shoot at.

The state also deserves kudos for passing a law that restricts people with certain criminal convictions from working in nursing homes or programs for people with disabilities. It went into effect for new hires in October 1998; this coming October, it will apply to existing employees.

Sure, it's already difficult to find people willing to do these grueling, low-paying jobs. But it's far better to let the elderly and disabled go without help than to expose them to someone who was once convicted of a crime. Even those former convicts who have worked as conscientious caregivers for many years deserve to be fired, because that's the way we do things in Wisconsin: We're stupid, and proud of it.

Why, just look at the outpouring of community reaction to the story about the Madison school bus driver who slapped a 7-year-old girl in the face. The driver was arrested and later fired, but callers to *The Capital Times'* Sound Off line were ready to give him a medal.

"Kudos to the bus driver who slapped that child," declared one pleased parent. "If any bus driver or teacher needs to discipline my child in the same manner, go right ahead. When they get home, there'll be another slap coming."

Several other callers sounded off in complete agreement. That's the kind of society we Cheeseheads want: where 7-year-olds (practically adults!) are slapped in the face for acting like children, then pointed to an American flag and told to pledge allegiance.

FEBRUARY 19, 1999

Madison's Grand Illusion

A few years ago I drove Flea, the bass player for the Red Hot Chili Peppers, from the Dane County airport to the Concourse Hotel. An old friend of mine who worked for the promoter asked me to come along and bring my car, in case the whole band couldn't fit into his. Flea ended up riding with me. Along the way, I assured him that Madison was a fine place to live – *progressive* was the word I used.

I didn't know much about Flea and his band, other than that it did a great cover of Stevie Wonder's "Higher Ground." But somehow I assumed he would be heartened to hear Madison was a progressive place.

The next night, I got a backstage view of the Chili Peppers' show at the Madison Civic Center. A bunch of guys playing in their underwear while fans charging the stage are tossed back like rag dolls by beefy security guards. The lead singer having violent simulated sex with an inflatable love doll. And Flea, as a birthday treat, licking whipped cream off the breasts of a stripper lowered from the rafters.

At the time, I felt foolish to have presumed Flea would care whether Madison is progressive. But my real mistake was in harboring the illusion that there is anything progressive about Madison. We like to bandy about the term but do little to live up to it.

This is a town where people who resist the UW–Madison's ties to sweatshops are dragged off in handcuffs by cops in full riot gear. Where people who smoke pot are routinely prosecuted as serious criminals. Where people in power see injustice and do what's expected: Keep their mouths shut.

Last month, I was among a panel of journalists invited to a forum on the topic of media and race. Mayor Sue Bauman was present, as were representatives from the media and the African American community.

The discussion was soon hijacked by audience members voicing their gripes about how the media portray people of color. Kirbie Mack, the city's affirmative action officer, held up a copy of the newspaper picturing four young men, all African American, charged with the shooting death of 13-year-old Adrian Gonzalez. Her objections were utter nonsense: Does anyone really think that if four white men were charged with killing a 13-year-old boy, their photos would *not* be in the paper?

A more salient issue, I noted at the meeting, is the role of race in the criminal justice system. It affects who becomes a target of police suspicion, how aggressively prosecutors press charges, the quality of representation, and the length of sentences.

In the Gonzalez shooting, the Dane County District Attorney's Office recently heaped additional charges against these young men. They now collectively face more than 1,000 years in prison. Would the justice system be as intent on erasing four lives to pay for one if the alleged perpetrators were white? Mack and other African American leaders don't seem to be asking.

Another example: In separate incidents last year, two young boys got their hands on guns and killed playmates. Both said it was accidental. The cops believed the white boy, age 11, and no charges were filed. The African American boy, age 12, was assumed to be lying and charged as an adult. Then he was forced to actually lie — by pleading guilty to first-degree intentional homicide, which contradicted his version of events, because that was the only way prosecutors would agree to handle the case in juvenile court.

So far as I know, no elected official or African American leader in Madison has raised concerns about this boy's treatment. That would mean fighting the power, instead of mere posturing.

IT'S TRUE MADISON HAS ITS SHARE OF PROGRESSIVE VOICES. CERTAIN people here do speak out in favor of a fairer and more just society. But that has not translated into progressive leadership.

Take Mayor Bauman. See how she reflexively blames others — the Common Council, the media, you name it — for her own lack of vision and failure to lead. There is no evidence she cares about anything except her own political fortunes.

Recently I sent Bauman an e-mail regarding the UW–Madison's arrest of 54 people protesting the university's ties to sweatshops. Does she think the arrests were justified? Does she join local activists in asking that no charges be brought?

Bauman, predictably, ignored the message. She's not about to expend political capital on behalf of people fighting for justice, because she doesn't care. At least County Supv. David Blaska has the courage of his reactionary convictions in publicly asking prosecutors to reject requests for leniency.

Bauman, in contrast, comes up empty in both departments: courage *and* convictions. Her inclination is always to do nothing – unless or until her failure to act becomes a political liability. Some progressive.

On a recent episode of Madison City Channel 12's "The Mayor's Report," Bauman said she was "shocked" over the jury verdict exonerating the New York police officers who fired 41 times to kill an innocent, unarmed man. "How can that not be some kind of violation?" she asked, quickly suggesting that such a thing could not happen in Madison.

Of course it could – especially now that the city is outfitting Madison police with semiautomatic assault rifles. And if the resulting controversy pitted protesters against police, is there any question whose side Bauman would be on?

MARCH 24, 2000

In April 2003, Mayor Bauman was defeated in the primary in her bid for reelection, coming in fourth among four contenders.

Cruel Zealotry

Whenever I try to understand the Dane County District Attorney's Office, I think of Helen Gamble. The prosecutor on the hit TV show "The Practice," Gamble exercises power like an angry god hurling lightning bolts from Mount Olympus.

She orders a cop to commit perjury, tells a judge who rules against her to shove a pole up her ass, and berates a jury who reach a not-guilty verdict as "12 people too stupid to get out of jury duty." When she wants a store clerk to detain a suspect, she barks, "I don't care what your policy is – do it or I'll charge you with obstruction of justice."

On a recent episode, Gamble tricks a 15-year-old girl who stabbed herself in the abdomen as a method of late-term abortion into making incriminating statements. She assures the girl that her intention is to help, and lies about having had an abortion herself. "Trust me," she urges, only to betray the girl, without contrition.

What a monster.

I realize, of course, that "The Practice" is just a TV show. But, based on what I know about the legal system, the character of Helen Gamble rings true. In the show, as in real life, her cruel zealotry never brings negative consequences (except, in some cases, not getting the convictions she seeks). For instance, a judge upholds the 15-year-old girl's confession, agreeing with Gamble that the justice system "isn't a moral arena, it's a legal one" and noting that courts have consistently allowed the use of trickery and deceit to con suspects out of their rights.

The show also seems credible in that Gamble, for all her excesses, is driven by an overarching sense of responsibility and concern for the victims of crime. If she has become a monster, it is in part because society has made her one to do its dirty work.

PROSECUTORS HAVE ALWAYS BEEN THE JUSTICE SYSTEM'S MOST powerful and least accountable players. But in recent years their clout has grown as tough-on-crime lawmakers and hang-'em-high judges have enshrined vengeance as the justice system's main ethic. At the same time, burgeoning caseloads have reduced the level of supervision they receive.

In such an environment, it's hardly surprising – indeed, it's predictable – that some prosecutors abuse their authority.

Two weeks ago I wrote about Thomas Champion, a mentally ill man who has spent nine months in jail, charged with multiple felony counts for not paying child support. Mental health experts say it would difficult if not impossible for him to work. To undercut this legitimate defense, Assistant District Attorney Robert Kaiser concocted a bizarre argument that if Champion couldn't pay because he's mentally disabled, he had to plead that he was insane. Judge Robert DeChambeau, shamelessly acquiescing to prosecutorial whim, agreed.

Champion's attorney tried to get him released pending appeal, so he could pursue additional disability payments that would go directly to support his children. But Kaiser strenuously objected. "My job is to punish people for crimes," he fulminated. "This is not about collecting money for children."

Thus Kaiser laid bare a prosecutorial philosophy predicated on meanness. Never mind the intent of the child support law; focus only on how good it feels when you can use it to hurt someone.

What a monster.

And yet I remember a 1993 *Isthmus* article in which Kaiser talked about how he wept for a two-month-old baby boy whose parents he prosecuted for beating him to death. How many cases like this can a man handle before he becomes hardened and starts inflicting harm?

We give prosecutors a button and tell them to deliver shocks every time a test subject screws up. Whose fault is it when they don't exercise reasonable restraint?

IN TOM CHAMPION'S CASE, THE DA'S OFFICE BEAT A FULL RETREAT. AFTER investing countless hours and wasting thousands of taxpayer dollars, it stopped trying to undermine Champion's defense and agreed to terms that may free him from jail.

District Attorney Diane Nicks, in an April 6 letter to *Isthmus*, took responsibility for pulling the plug on Kaiser's cruel experiment. Nicks said that while she understood the argument Kaiser made and the court accepted, "I believe the correct interpretation of [the child-support law] is that mental illness may constitute the 'inability' defense, and that an [insanity] plea is not a prerequisite for raising this defense." She also disagreed with the "implication that some may draw from ADA Kaiser's remarks that punishment is the only proper goal of a criminal prosecution."

Nicks, who is accountable to voters and vulnerable to public opinion, did the right thing, at some risk to herself. In this and other cases, she has shown courage and integrity. Yet the office she heads is still mired in moral muck.

Nicks needs to set clearer and higher standards about what kinds of prosecutions have merit, and to provide better oversight. And she needs to reexamine cases in which overzealous prosecutors may have managed to convict the innocent.

But Nicks is not likely to do these things unless there is public pressure, just as she didn't intervene in the Champion case until it became a source of public embarrassment. It goes to show that the whole community – the media, citizens and elected officials – has a role to play in making sure our prosecutors do not act like Helen Gamble.

APRIL 14, 2000

Diane Nicks left the DA's office to become a Dane County judge, retiring in 2009.

Justice Explained

Careful readers of *Isthmus* may have noticed that I sometimes write about the criminal justice system. One colleague jokingly calls me the "people's tribune," an advocate of last resort for folks who have bad experiences with prosecutors and police.

As a result, I often hear from people with stories to tell. Most of the time, I end up explaining that I am unable to write about their particular tale of woe, for reasons that may bear stating publicly. I also find myself dispensing advice on how the system works, if that's the right word for it.

Therefore, and in hopes of curtailing the volume of contacts, here is a list of some commonly asked questions and the answers I would give.

Question: I am being prosecuted unfairly. What can I do? Answer: Get an attorney and do what he or she tells you to do. Generally speaking, I won't write about your case or situation unless your attorney agrees to cooperate.

Why is that? Because chances are that your attorney will think it's a bad idea, and will be upset to learn that you've spoken to the press. Then you'll call back begging me not to write the story.

Why do attorneys not want clients to talk to the media? They worry that the judge will see it as an attempt to leverage the outcome, or that the prosecutor – who has enormous discretionary power and virtually no checks on its abuse – will get mad and seek revenge.

But you do write about cases sometimes, so there must be exceptions, right? There are. Sometimes attorneys will talk when they feel the judge or prosecutor has behaved so badly that a client's interest – or the public interest – is served by calling attention to it. And they may speak more freely *after* the conclusion of a case, when their clients can no longer be punished for it.

Don't prosecutors understand that they are fallible and make mistakes? As a general theoretical construct, sure. With regard to any given case, not bloody likely.

What if I agreed to plead guilty or no contest to something and now regret it? You're screwed. Every day defendants sign off on plea agreements. Judges ask whether they understand that they are forfeiting certain rights, such as making the state prove its charges. Defendants are also asked whether they were threatened or promised anything in return. They always answer "No, your Honor," and they are always lying, because in every case they were threatened with harsher penalties and promised lighter ones. But once you utter this lie in court, you really do forfeit your rights and are stuck with the consequences.

The police report is full of lies. What can I do about it? Usually, nothing. It's what the officer will testify to in court, whether or not it's the truth, and the officer's word will have much more weight than yours. Police skew their reports to make defendants look bad. One attorney told me he always advises people against talking to police "not because of what they might say but because of what the police might say they said."

Speaking of that, I was never read my rights. What's up with that? Most criminal defendants never are. Only on TV do people regularly get Miranda warnings. That's because the law says two factors must be simultaneously present: the person must be in custody, and the police must be asking questions intended to elicit an incriminating response. Cops get around this by questioning people *before* placing them under arrest. And afterward, they can and will use any statements, so long as they are not pried loose with questions.

I want to complain about the way I was treated by Madison police. What can I do? You can file a complaint with the Madison Police Department. There are complaint forms available.

What will happen then? The office will look into your complaint and in almost every case conclude that police did nothing wrong. Then they'll advise you that if you aren't happy with this outcome you can file a complaint with the Madison Police and Fire Commission.

What if I complain to the PFC? You will be crushed. The city will hire a lawyer to defend the accused officer and beat back your complaint by any means necessary. You'll have to hire an attorney at your own expense or personally take charge of marshaling evidence, subpoenaing and questioning witnesses, writing legal briefs, etc. In fact, no citizen has ever brought a successful PFC complaint against a Madison police officer, and it's unlikely that any ever will. The PFC, by design, is useless to citizens as an instrument of police accountability.

Aren't there political players I can turn to? Doesn't Mayor Bauman care? No.

Will you tell my story? Maybe. But you must understand that I am not your advocate. I will try to get the other side of the story, and sometimes it's pretty compelling. Most situations involving the justice system are complicated, and media attention may not help resolve anything. And even if the injustice you identify is egregious and clear, there's no guarantee anything will change simply because it gets media attention.

Okay, but can you write about my situation without using my name? [Click!]
AUGUST 11, 2000

Just Gotta Be Free

As usual, there were a lot of speeches this week commemorating the birthday of Dr. Martin Luther King, Jr. Speeches about the ability of ordinary people to make a difference. Speeches about King's courage and eloquence. Speeches about how speaking out is a fundamental American right.

But my thoughts turn to another speech and another example of courage – that of a homeless, odiferous, mentally ill man named Joseph Stockett.

Stockett, 54, stopped by the *Isthmus* office last week to talk about his experience of being detained and questioned by Madison police due to the content of a speech he gave last fall at the UW–Madison.

I heard Stockett out, and gathered a few details about his circumstance. He says – and I've no reason to doubt him – that he lives in a storage shed and can be contacted only through the shelter at Grace Episcopal. He moved to Madison (from California) last summer, having lived here for a while in the late 1980s when he was following the Grateful Dead.

He calls himself a hippie, and he's a rebel to the core. He's been diagnosed as paranoid schizophrenic, which along with his six heart attacks qualifies him for a $540 monthly federal disability check. He boasts about getting kicked out of the Navy and serving 18 months in military prison for organizing a mutiny in 1966. According to an article I found online, in 1988 he helped lead 19 homeless advocates arrested for storming then-Sen. Dan Quayle's office in Washington, D.C., holding candles to mock George Bush I's campaign claptrap about "a thousand points of light."

Stockett, smart and articulate, talks about reading Noam Chomsky and has a sophisticated understanding of how the right to free speech is preserved through its vigorous exercise. He knows the First Amendment isn't needed to protect popular speech, the sort people make in honor of King. It's needed for speech that affronts and offends, speech that other people and the government would stamp out if only they could.

It was this sort of speech that Stockett delivered Oct. 16 from the elevated concrete podium on Library Mall. "I intentionally tried to push the envelope," he told me. And how.

Stockett's impromptu address, which he helpfully recorded, was an angry screed against the U.S. government and its allies occasioned by the terrorist bombing of the U.S.S. Cole in Yemen a few days before.

"How does it feel, America?" he shouted, comparing the deaths of 17 Americans to those of countless Palestinians. "You got your ass kicked by a little rubber raft, Mr. Almighty America, Mr. Policeman of the World." Stockett made one reference to "Jewish terrorism" and used variations of the F-word twice, including: "You stood by in your American arrogance. Now the body bags are coming home. You should all be ashamed of your fucking selves."

NOT EXACTLY "I HAVE A DREAM," BUT THE VULGARITY WAS PROBABLY something passersby have heard before, and the political perspective was likely not too different from what some students and professors were expressing in class. Stockett, in conclusion, urged his audience to "call your congressman" to urge that U.S. soldiers be brought home from entanglements throughout the world.

Stockett had barely finished and was apparently starting to walk away when a voice is captured on his still-running hidden recorder: "Hey, partner, can I have a moment of your valuable time?"

It was the police – three from the Madison Police Department and one from the UW. The person who addressed Stockett was Madison Officer Phillip Yahnke. "No," replied Stockett, who continued walking.

A few seconds later, Yahnke can be heard saying, "Hey, do not blow me off like that." According to Yahnke's report, he grabbed Stockett by the sleeve as he said this. "You're assaulting me," Stockett asserted, repeatedly. "I haven't broken any law. I demand that you let loose, officer."

"I'm detaining you pending an investigation," said Yahnke, twice, asking Stockett to produce some ID. Stockett continued to protest, and to demand that he be let go. "I was exercising my right to free speech."

Said Yahnke, "We have some concerns expressed by some of the mall vendors about some of your rhetoric." (Actually, according to Yahnke's report, it was a single vendor, who asked to not be identified.) "They thought it was a little over the top, in terms of Jews and so forth."

Compared to Bull Connor with his fire hoses and attack dogs, it was a gentle intervention, and the police remained courteous throughout. Stockett, for his part, sought to turn the encounter into a civics lesson.

"If they [the vendors] didn't like the content of my speech, they should get up and make their own speech," Stockett told the police. "The fact that they complained shows how little they actually believe in freedom of speech."

Stockett noted that he never incited anyone to violence or urged anyone to break the law and that "everything I said was said in public from a podium which was designed for that purpose." His speech had a political point – that unless something is done about Israel killing Palestinians, "we're going to see more and more of this."

Before long, Stockett had his questioners on the ropes, and he knew it. "The next time I speak – I'm going to be speaking again – should I call you first?" he asked the cops.

"I don't think that's necessary," one of them replied. It was soon over, with both sides exchanging thank-yous. As Yahnke wrote in his report, "Stockett was allowed to go about his business, whatever it may be."

There may not be any clear heroes here, or villains. The point is that the right to speak freely reigned supreme, as it should, because a homeless man understood the First Amendment better than his campus audience, or even the police.

JANUARY 19, 2001

Sam Day. Photo by Joseph Blough

A Font of Moral Courage

Just before the last election, Sam Day called *Isthmus* to propose writing an opinion column taking presidential contender Ralph Nader to task for not being outspoken enough on issues of progressive concern. We weren't able to fit it in, but the pitch was quintessential Sam: forthright, uncompromising, perhaps more principled than politic.

Day, who died last Friday at age 74 after suffering a massive stroke in his home, was a font of moral courage the likes of which Madison may not see again. Time and again, as a journalist and activist, he put himself on the line fighting social injustice and the insanity of nuclear weapons. He was, in the best sense of the word, a patriot, serving not a nation but a notion – that we can, and therefore must, create a world that's fairer and less dangerous.

In 1979, as managing editor of *The Progressive*, Day helped conceive an audacious article that challenged nuclear secrecy by revealing what was considered to be a secret of H-bomb design. For six months, the U.S. government tried to block publication, until it was forced to abandon its case.

Day went on to found the anti-nuclear group Nukewatch; to fight the owners of East Towne, unsuccessfully, for free-speech rights in shopping malls; to chase after and report on trucks that surreptitiously transport nuclear bomb materials on the nation's highways; and to participate in direct actions against nuclear weapons sites, in one case drawing a six-month prison term. In recent years, Day has led the effort to secure the release from prison of Mordechai Vanunu, an Israeli nuclear technician who blew the whistle on that country's secret nuclear weapons program.

The son of an American diplomat, Day lived in South Africa until he was 12. (In 1982, he returned to write a superb investigative piece on that nation's secret campaign to build and test a nuclear bomb.) After graduating from Swarthmore College, he embarked on a career in journalism by taking an entry-level job at the *Washington Evening Star*, which he chose over another option – a State Department position in Asia – with the flip of a coin. Much of his middle years were spent as a reporter in Idaho, where he met Kathleen, his wife of more than four decades, and eventually became editor of the *Intermountain Observer*, a feisty weekly in Boise.

Unlike the usual life trajectory, in which advancing age tends to instill caution, Day grew more radical and daring as his life went on. His first venture into direct political action, a human traffic blockade in Boise to protest a U.S. nuclear weapons test in Alaska, took place in 1971, when Day was 45 and the father of three sons. As he recalled in his 1991 autobiography, *Crossing the Line*, the succession of emotions he experienced – inner struggle, deep fear, calm during the action itself and then exhilaration – would recur with each confrontation with authority.

DAY'S DECISION TO CROSS THE LINE PRECIPITATED THE DEMISE OF HIS paper and launched him on a new path, beginning with his editorship of *The Bulletin of the Atomic Scientists* from 1974 to 1978 and continuing with his years (1978–80) at *The Progressive*, where he helped make the magazine a national leader in reporting on nuclear issues, and subsequent work for Nukewatch.

Beginning in 1984, Day contributed regular opinion columns to *Isthmus* – writing, sometimes from jail and prison, on everything from Gov. Tommy

Thompson's harsh anti-welfare agenda to why moms should be able to bring their babies to work. The loss of much of his eyesight while in prison in 1989 broadened the focus of his activism to include the rights of the blind.

Part of Sam Day's peculiar courage was that he valued truth above personal consequences. It was Day who leaked to the press a memo of grievances written by long-suffering women staffers at *The Progressive* and, more consequentially, a letter from a civilian nuclear weapons buff whose publication in the *Madison Press Connection* prompted the U.S. government to drop its attempt to block publication of the H-bomb story.

But Day never wore his courage as a badge of honor. Gracious and unassuming, he inspired others by his example, not his insistence that he was correct. He was, above all, a kind man. He left his mark on the world, and his death leaves a void the rest of us will be hard-pressed to fill. But his life and his legacy instruct us to try.

FEBRUARY 2, 2001

Like Father, Like Son

Scott McCallum is right about one thing: If he weren't governor, the prosecution of his 19-year-old son, Zachary, for allegedly beating a girl at a graduation party last June would not be statewide news. And maybe that's unfair to Zach and other family members, as the governor has repeatedly asserted.

But part of the reason the case has gotten attention is that statements made by McCallum – Scott, not Zach – raise troubling questions about his fidelity to truth.

Late last month, as charges were about to be filed, Gov. McCallum declared his son was "not involved" in what he described as "fights" at a Memorial High graduation party/beer bash in Adams County. He claimed Zach was singled out for prosecution because he was the governor's son, that he was "being held to a different standard."

All Zach did wrong, the governor said, was underage drinking: "The upside is that nobody was killed. The downside is there was drinking."

Jeannie Retelle, the mother of the girl Zach is accused of repeatedly kicking in the head as she lay on the ground, is aghast, telling *Isthmus*, "That's my daughter he's talking about." The girl, Cecilia Retelle, adds that if others hadn't pulled off Zach and a second youth who allegedly participated in her beating (not "a fight" by any stretch), "who's to say where it would have stopped?"

As for Scott McCallum's claim that Zach was not involved, Cecilia, who suffered injuries to the head, neck, jaw, legs and hands, has this to say: "I was lying on the ground. I could see him. I know who he is."

Gary Silka, an investigator with the Adams County Sheriff's Department, says witnesses "saw Zach in a kicking posture and Cecilia on the ground." The criminal complaint names one witness who purportedly saw Zach kick Cecilia "at least three to five times," another who says he pulled Zach off Cecilia, and others who placed him at the scene.

If Zach McCallum really were innocent of involvement in Cecilia's beating, the honorable thing would have been to plead not guilty and fight the charges. Especially if, as Scott McCallum claims, they were politically motivated. But that's not what happened, and, indeed, the overwhelming weight of evidence suggests that Zach got favorable treatment from the justice system.

Last fall, Adams County District Attorney Mark Thibodeau asked the state Attorney General's Office to take the case off his hands, explaining that Retelle "was assaulted by the Lt. Governor's son, Zachary S. McCallum." He gave no reason for this request, other than his peculiar identification of the assailant by his father's job title at that time. [McCallum became governor in February 2001.] The AG's Office declined, and this year Adams County worked out a deal to charge Zach with disorderly conduct, instead of the felony physical-abuse-of-a-child charge Thibodeau asked the state to bring, or a charge of battery, as the facts seem to support.

"If it wouldn't have been a McCallum who did this, it wouldn't have been pleaded down to disorderly conduct," says Cecilia.

Last week, Zach was sentenced to six months' probation and ordered to undergo substance-abuse and anger-management counseling. If he keeps out of trouble for six months, the conviction will be expunged from his record.

IN A STATEMENT, GOV. MCCALLUM PROCLAIMS "THE MATTER IS OVER,"

seeing how his son "has accepted responsibility." Say what? Zach McCallum has never admitted to attacking Retelle, never apologized to her and never accepted responsibility on any level, beyond agreeing to the sweetheart deal his high-priced lawyer worked out. Given a chance to address the court last week, Zach declined.

He didn't have to say anything. His dad, the governor, was still arguing against the evidence that Zach did nothing wrong, other than tip a few brewskis at an underage party. (By the way, according to the criminal complaint, there were eight to 10 half-barrels for about 90 young people.)

Investigator Silka charitably assesses Scott McCallum's role: "The governor's being a father, and he's protecting his son." Jeannie Retelle takes a harsher view, noting that when her kids have gotten into trouble she's made them own up to it. "As a parent, I can't believe he did not make his kid accountable for what he did," she says of Scott. "It shows poor moral character."

Cecilia, now a student in Minnesota, agrees: "Obviously, his father has the same problem Zach does in not taking responsibility, and I think it reflects on both their characters."

Actually, the governor's handling of this matter is not atypical. When his proposed state budget drew criticism, McCallum blamed his predecessor, Tommy Thompson, falsely claiming he had "four hours to make changes." One recurring theme in that budget is how it would undercut the quality of criminal justice, especially for folks who can't afford pricey lawyers. The state Public Defender's Office is slated to take a $3.2 million hit, which it says will mean laying off 50 attorneys and hiring out work to private lawyers at a cost of $5.9 million per year. Office head Nicholas Chiarkas says the McCallum team is holding firm, with Department of Administration chief George Lightbourn conveying to him that "the people we represent aren't a priority."

The governor's budget also cuts funding to the state court system and state law library, and fails to provide requested funds to create a statewide program of interpreters for Hispanic and Asian defendants. Meanwhile, funding for the prison system and state prosecutors is virtually untouched. Will Scott McCallum take responsibility for that?

APRIL 27, 2001

Zach McCallum successfully completed his probation and had his record expunged. Scott McCallum was defeated in the 2002 election.

Surviving the New McCarthyism

L ike many Americans, I've been living in fear since Sept. 11. What frightens me most is not the remote possibility of being attacked by bombs or anthrax, or the slightly greater possibility that government agents will eavesdrop on my conversations. It's the very real possibility that I might say or do the wrong thing, incurring the wrath of a volatile public.

Witness what's happened to the Madison school board. Faced with a new state law requiring schools to begin each day with either the Pledge of Allegiance or the National Anthem, the board decided that Madison schools should simply play an instrumental rendition of the anthem. This action, falsely reported as a "ban" on the pledge, ignited a firestorm of controversy, from local residents threatening to stop paying school taxes, to Gov. Scott McCallum deriding board members as "oddballs who place politics above patriotism," to Rush Limbaugh and other talk-show jocks whipping up national vilification.

The board had to eat heaping plates of crow, repealing this policy early Tuesday after a raucous, jam-packed, nine-and-a-half-hour meeting at which speakers who questioned U.S. policies were booed and shouted down. Despite buckling under, several board members still face recall attempts, and there is talk of diminishing state support for Madison schools. It's not clear how punishing students for having a board that momentarily deviates from Taliban-like dogmatism serves the interests of a vital democracy, but who am I to argue?

A similar controversy ensued when the Madison Common Council voted to remove a reference to "prayers" from a resolution condemning the Sept. 11 attacks. The *Wisconsin State Journal* – Command Central for the local "Love It or Leave It" movement – reacted with furious indignation, as did an angry public. The alderpersons who supported this outrage against God and country have been targeted for electoral termination.

It's all part of a push toward unthinking conformity, enforced with the blunt instrument of American intolerance, wielded in the name of national unity. Columnists have been fired for presenting dissenting views. Bill Maher saw his politically incorrect career flash before his eyes for stating the obvious – that it takes more courage to fly a plane into a building than to lob missiles from afar.

Bush spokesperson Ari Fleischer applauded the backlash against these individuals, saying it served to remind "all Americans that they need to watch what they say, watch what they do." It's no wonder the television networks promptly agreed to self-censor footage of Osama bin Laden from U.S. airwaves, ostensibly to prevent him from relaying secret hidden messages – a preposterous claim given that his followers have ample access to these images.

OOPS, DID I USE THE WORD PREPOSTEROUS? I MEANT PERPLEXING. I'M sure it makes sense somehow, if only I were blindly patriotic enough to see it.

I for one am not about to point fingers at a time when the American public is on the verge of chopping off hands. I intend to be a survivor of the new McCarthyism, a dutiful citizen who shares our nation's common values, or at least pretends to. Let's all say it together:

"I pledge allegiance to the flag of the United States of America and to the republic for which it stands, one nation, under God – not the God to whom the terrorists prayed before their wildly successful mission, but the American God who did such a swell job protecting all those innocent people in the towers and Pentagon – indivisible, with liberty and justice for all."

At some other time I might quibble with the notion that the United States, which has more than two million citizens behind bars – some innocent, many there because of the absurd war on drugs – offers liberty and justice for all. But now is not that time.

Nor will you catch me among the "Blame America First" crowd that suggests there is some historical and political basis for the fact that much of the rest of the world hates our guts. That they hate us because we don't even know why they hate us is no reason to educate ourselves about anything.

The truth of the matter, at least the only truth it's safe to state right now, is that we are good and they are evil. Forget the images of the wounded children and babies – alleged victims of U.S. bombing raids on Afghanistan – that have briefly flashed across our TV screens. Let us agree that if these victims exist at all, they are evil children and babies.

And let us join with our fellow Americans in waving flags and mouthing platitudes. We need to gag those who present us with unpopular points of view and demonize anyone who interferes with our wonderful new ortho-doxy of patriotic conformity. And if that means throwing dissidents out of work or running them out of office, so be it. That's the price we pay to live in a free country.

OCTOBER 19, 2001

Abolish the Legislature!

Marty Reynolds did the right thing. In June, this Democratic state representative from Ladysmith, disgusted with the Legislature in which he has served with distinction for the past 12 years, decided to walk away from the job.

"I'm fed up with it," said Reynolds, explaining why he would not seek reelection. He said the Legislature had become "more partisan" and less willing to cooperate on major issues. The egos of his colleagues had gotten "bigger" (the mind reels, as when contemplating infinity) and he was "embarrassed" by rampant allegations of improper and illegal conduct.

"This has to change," declared Reynolds, who is now running for lieutenant governor on the Libertarian ticket headed by Ed Thompson. "We cannot continue along the same path."

Actually, we can and probably will, because few legislators want to change the status quo. Noted Reynolds, "The fact that neither house is willing to elect new leaders" – even though Senate Majority Leader Chuck Chvala and Assembly Speaker Scott Jensen are both mired in scandal – "is a negative reflection on both houses."

And there's no reason to believe the next Legislature will be an improvement. This year, 116 of 132 seats are supposedly up for grabs. But even with the shake-up caused by redistricting, 49 of the legislative candidates on the Nov. 5 general election ballot are unopposed, the highest number in at least a decade. Another eight candidates face only minor-party opposition and most of the rest are shoo-ins.

Shameful. Given the Legislature's performance during the last few sessions – especially the most recent one – the honorable thing would be for everyone to resign. Equally appropriate would be if voters, instead of sometimes having a say about who represents them, instead got to decide whether the Legislature should represent them at all.

Certainly, the Legislature in recent years has not justified its existence. During its current biennial session, it considered about 1,500 bills, 109 of which it passed into law, by far the fewest since Wisconsin became a state in 1848. This for an entity that will have cost taxpayers about $120 million during this two-year period. That averages out to $1.1 million per new law!

What, exactly, did we get for this investment? Lawmakers, to their credit, plugged a loophole that put the state's wetlands at risk. They also ... well, that's about it in terms of consequential single-item legislation. The only others worth mentioning are the budget bill and the budget repair bill.

NOW, IT'S A DEAD GIVEAWAY THAT SOMETHING ISN'T RIGHT WITH ANY bill that requires a follow-up repair bill, but the problems go much deeper than that. Both were completed past due, after many months of partisan wrangling. The final product was so stuffed with perks and breaks that the nonpartisan watchdog group Wisconsin Democracy Campaign dubbed it a "Special Interest Protection Plan." (Gov. Scott McCallum vetoed many of the most egregious items, raising doubts as to whether even special interests got their money's worth.)

Lawmakers irresponsibly failed to solve the state's billion-dollar deficit, preferring a short-term fix designed to get them past the next election. Perhaps worst of all, they included a campaign-finance reform plan that proponents of true reform have labeled a cynical "sham," one intended to fail, leaving the corrupt system intact.

Does anyone seriously doubt that a select group of 12 seasoned administrators could put together a budget more effectively than Chuck Chvala, Scott Jensen and their minions? How about 12 monkeys picked randomly from the zoo?

"There's no question that this Legislature is dysfunctional," says Mike McCabe, executive director of Wisconsin Democracy Campaign. "They are not earning their paychecks, and they're not managing the state's affairs." Heck, he says, they can't even live within their own generous budget.

It wasn't always this way. When McCabe was a legislative aide 20 years ago, he recalls that many lawmakers still fit the "citizen legislator" ideal. "They were lathe operators, merchants and farmers, people who had real jobs, real lives." Now, "the place is infested with career politicians. They've lost their connection to the communities they're supposed to serve."

McCabe argues in favor of returning to a truly part-time Legislature, as in South Dakota. This could be done simply by paying people "considerably less" – that is, more in line with what they deserve – and cutting back on staff. He also suggests a unicameral legislature, as in Nebraska, to avoid the problems posed by perpetually warring houses.

But McCabe's most radical proposal is to do away with elected lawmakers. Instead, people in various areas of the state could be picked to represent their fellow citizens through some sort of draft, like jury duty. Wouldn't this cause the quality of representation to decline? McCabe doubts it: "I'm not sure it could decline any more. I don't think many members of the Legislature are even trying to represent their constituents. They're so busy trying to service their campaign contributors."

Of course, any such change would probably require legislative approval. Taxpayers, can you spare a few million bucks?

OCTOBER 2002, MILWAUKEE MAGAZINE

Taxes: We Want the Fairy Tale

O nce upon a time, there was a village called Madison, known far and wide as one of the best places to live in all the land. Madison was part of a province called Wisconsin in a kingdom called the United States, and its status as a great place hinged mainly on one thing: taxes.

It was taxes that allowed the people of Madison to have good schools and safe streets. It was taxes that allowed them to toss their wretched belongings onto curbs, as students often did, and have garbage fairies haul it all away, free of charge.

But then a terrible thing happened. The people fell under a spell in which they came to regard taxes, the lifeblood of Madison's prosperity, as evil and unnecessary. This was the fault of politicians, who for years advanced their fortunes by promising to lower taxes. They never did, of course, but their proclamations got people to view taxes as more terrible than tigers.

The village elders shook their heads sadly. They saw that the people had become enchanted with the anti-tax beliefs of the men and women who set the terms of their oppression. The rich, driven mad by their love of money (never did it come to pass that those who had a lot of it felt they had enough), hated taxes and devised all manner of devious ways to avoid paying them.

King Bush II slashed taxes for the well-to-do. He got the kingdom's ruling council to pass a $350 billion tax cut that would, over four years, deliver an average of $104,000 worth of tax breaks to people in the top 1 percent income bracket, and just $45 to the bottom 20 percent. The king, who if he were in a different fairy tale would have a very long nose, told the people the average dwelling would see a $1,000 yearly break. But as one elder pointed out, this was like saying that if a man worth $200 billion joined a colony of 200 penniless lepers, the average colony dweller would be a billionaire.

The king, by the way, could cut taxes for the rich without worrying whether the kingdom had enough money to manage its affairs. He simply spent money he did not have, on things like wars, ordaining that future generations should pay for his lack of responsibility. His father had done the same thing.

For Madison, and villages across the land, the king's reckless and profligate ways caused much suffering, as less money was available to meet the needs of ordinary folk. But an even greater peril was posed by the leaders of the province of Wisconsin, who went hog wild in their rejection of taxes.

The province's leader, Sir Doyle, pandered to the people's disdain for taxes, vowing not to impose any new ones. But since, unlike the king, he was not allowed to spend money he did not have, this vow compelled him to pursue policies that spelled bitter woe for villages like Madison.

SIR DOYLE COULD HAVE RAISED TAXES ON CORPORATIONS AND THE RICH,
or on a popular drug called tobacco that caused horrible addiction and disease. Instead, he cut deals to let the land's Ancient Inhabitants bleed more money from citizens through palaces called casinos. And he decreed that less of the province's money would go back to the villages from whence it came.

The knights who served on the province's governing body hated Sir Doyle, and cleverly conspired against him. They proposed a freeze on village tax levies, knowing this would bring disaster to villages throughout the province. They knew Sir Doyle would have no choice but to veto it. And then, when the people's village taxes shot up, as everyone knew would happen, the knights could blame Sir Doyle.

Some knights went further, calling for a freeze on province spending. This was more rank hypocrisy, since the province's money troubles traced to the vast growth in spending that occurred when their hero, Tommy the Untouchable, was in charge. Much of this spending was on roads and dungeons, each of which acquired legions of supporters more powerful than dragons. Even Sir Doyle was afraid to go near.

And so Madison was forced to contemplate a future in which it could not depend on taxes to preserve the things that made it great. Oh, how its leaders wailed and gnashed their teeth!

"Taxes, we need more taxes!" they cried. "Or at least our fair share of the taxes the province collects." The village leader, Dave the Green-Hearted, spent his energies seeking ways to save a penny here, or a dollar there. He said he would look into why people in big-ass houses paid far less in taxes than they should based on what their homes could fetch at market, making people in more modest dwellings shoulder a greater share of the load. But politicians say a lot of things.

"Taxes, we need more taxes!" screamed the schools, begging citizens to pass a plebiscite, as the province's knights had ordained they must. And the people, frightened half to death with tales of how the schools would be thrown back into the Dark Ages unless taxes were raised, narrowly approved the plebiscite, raising their own taxes. Some elders said the spell was broken. Others saw it as a fluke. Still others said, "D'oh! Looks like we'll have to do this all over again next year!"

But no one expected the village or its people to live happily ever after.

JUNE 6, 2003

Protecting Readers from Ideas

I t was not supposed to happen. In fact, it was the very thing the *Wisconsin State Journal* assured its readers in 2001 would never happen again.

On Sunday, Aug. 17, a political point of view escaped from the mind of a cartoonist and made it into the *State Journal*'s pages. Not on the editorial page, mind you, where people are paid to have opinions, but on the comics page.

By the time the authorities were alerted, it was too late. The comics section for that Sunday's paper had already been printed. It contained a "Pearls Before Swine" comic with an overtly political theme.

One of the comic's regular characters, a rat named Rat, types out a letter to President Bush noting that he's bombed only two of the world's 192 countries so far, meaning he'll have to bomb three per month to hit them all before the end of his second term. The strip ends with the president taking this suggestion to heart and ordering attacks on Mexico, Canada and Hawaii, not realizing that Hawaii is actually part of the U.S.

I know. It's pretty lame humor. The real joke was that the *State Journal* felt the need to apologize to its readers for allowing this content to see print. The comic, it declared in a notice published that day, "violated the *State Journal*'s standards against partisan advocacy in our news and features pages." The cartoonist and his syndicate were given stern warnings.

The cartoonist, Stephan Pastis, is the second in recent years to be on the receiving end of the *State Journal*'s finger-wagging. In April 2001, the paper expressed its regret for publishing a Johnny Hart "B.C." strip that showed a Jewish menorah being transformed into a Christian cross. Hart said he was trying to pay tribute to both religions, but *State Journal* editor Frank Denton felt he was promoting one over the other.

At the time, the paper assured its readers that comics would henceforth be reviewed prior to publication "well in advance." Denton thought this meant the review would occur before the section was printed, but learned through the "Pearls Before Swine" imbroglio that this was not the case.

Of course, the paper could have reprinted the section, but this would have cost money. And so it simply apologized to readers and renewed its commitment to ensuring that future offending strips are spiked in time.

FOR DENTON, THE QUESTION OF WHAT'S APPROPRIATE IS A BRIGHT RED LINE.

"The purpose of the comics page is to make people laugh and perhaps to poke fun at humanity," he says. "It is not a license for cartoonists to get up on a soap box and inflict their political views." Stephan Pastis is paid to produce a lighthearted strip that "anthropomorphizes animals" and cracks wise about the human condition, not to mouth off about world events. Asserts Denton, "If he wants his political opinions published, he's welcome to write a letter to the editor."

Denton's objections assume there's a rigid distinction between his paper's editorial page and its news and features content. Indeed, he says, in reference to Pastis' plunge into political commentary, "Can you imagine if everyone who worked for our newspaper did that?" The *State Journal* would be shorn of its credibility, with "opinions flying in" from all over.

But the bright red line that Denton imagines does not exist. All reporters and editors have opinions that influence how they cover stories. This is rarely perceived as a problem, so long as a journalist's bias is comfortably within the mainstream, and congruent with that of the paper's owners and publishers. When was the last time a *State Journal* reporter got in trouble for being too pro-business?

More to the point, cartoonists generally have license to unleash their opinions upon the world. Again, it's not a problem, so long as the topics are sufficiently inconsequential.

What's sad about the *State Journal*'s commitment to prior restraint is that it robs readers of the chance to make up their own minds. If Denton feels that Pastis went too far in having his talking animals suggest the president of the United States is a warmonger and not terribly bright – both demonstrably true statements – why not use some of that ink he buys by the barrel to advance a contrary view?

Instead he rushes to assure readers that steps are being taken to prevent them from ever again encountering "partisan advocacy" on the comics page. And Denton dismisses those readers who have protested this stance as "people who agree with the cartoonist's political view."

Perhaps. But apparently no one has written in to say, "Way to go, Frank. Thanks for protecting me from those sassy talking animals." And, really, at a time when American soldiers are dying daily in Iraq, in an unending war predicated on official lies, disregard for international law and contempt for world opinion, why shouldn't cartoonists be allowed to stray from the trivial? The *State Journal*'s readers can take it, even if they disagree.

Erwin Knoll, the late editor of *The Progressive*, used to say that there were two kinds of censors – the ignorant censor and the arrogant censor. He would elaborate:

"The ignorant censor says, 'I haven't read this, or listened to it, or seen it, but I know it's just terrible, so I can't allow you to see it or say it or read it or write it or listen to it.' And the arrogant censor says, 'I have read or seen or heard this, and it hasn't hurt me because I'm a very good person, but you're not nearly so good as I am, so I must make sure that you can't have access to this dangerous or filthy stuff.'"

Denton and the *State Journal* are not ignorant censors.

AUGUST 29, 2003

America the Beautiful. No, Really

I n mulling the concept behind this week's cover story, in which we ask folks in Madison, "What is the quintessential American trait?," members of *Isthmus*' editorial staff tried the question out on ourselves. Our answers were not pretty:

"Arrogance." "Hypocrisy." "Racism." "Obesity." "Excess." "Cognitive dissonance." "Crankiness." "Intolerance." "Immaturity." "Dishonesty." "Materialism." "Contrariness." "Freedom."

Aside from freedom, and perhaps contrariness, it's a uniformly grim list, befitting the essentially sour disposition of the brain trust at Madison's weekly newspaper. But when we asked a different question, "Do you love your country?," all but one person answered yes.

This might seem, at first glance, to reflect another quintessential American trait: contradiction. "Do I contradict myself?" asked Whitman. "Very well then I contradict myself."

There is no reason the multitudes we contain cannot both find fault with our nation and at the same time hold it dear. Most of us have similarly complicated relationships with our families and friends. But let's face it: The nation we love has never been less likable.

We have an incompetent, disengaged president who lies like some people breathe, a man who has dragged the nation into an unwise and unnecessary war while exacerbating the nation's vulnerabilities to terrorism. We have a national media that lets him get away with it, to where Jon Stewart of Comedy Central does a far better job than *The New York Times* of exposing the Bush administration's folly and moral corruption.

In Afghanistan and Iraq, we have replaced old authoritarian regimes with new ones, subjecting scores of people who have not been convicted of any crime to horrifying abuse. The most significant consequence of the Abu Ghraib prison scandal has been an edict from Defense Secretary Donald Rumsfeld banning cameras from U.S. military installations. Rumsfeld and others at the highest levels of the Bush administration who authorized this abuse have not been punished and show no remorse.

A few days ago, *The Capital Times* ran a small wire-service story about Sean Baker, a 37-year-old Gulf War veteran who, after the events of Sept. 11, volunteered for an additional tour of duty in the Kentucky National Guard. He was assigned to the U.S. military prison in Guantanamo Bay, Cuba, where he volunteered again, this time to put on an orange jumpsuit for a training exercise.

Unfortunately, the five-member military police team being trained was not told that Baker was a fake prisoner, so he got treated like a real one. They slammed him down, choked and beat him, pounding his head into the concrete floor.

"I'm a U.S. soldier! I'm a U.S. soldier!" Baker pleaded. The trainees ignored him until, in the course of this pummeling, they ripped through his jumpsuit and saw his military uniform beneath. The beating left Baker with a traumatic brain injury, leading to his honorable discharge from the military. Now, more than a year later, he is unable to work due to seizures and severe headaches, for which he takes nine prescription drugs.

The military has, of course, abandoned Baker. He has yet to receive disability payments.

THIS IS THE CONDUCT OF THE NATION WE ARE ASKED THIS JULY 4TH TO celebrate – barbarous and amoral, capable of great injustice even to those who risk their lives to defend it.

And yet, I would be willing to bet my complete set of Benjamin Franklin half-dollars that, if you asked him, Sean Baker would tell you he loves his country, no matter how badly the people who run it have betrayed him. In like vein, those of us living the good life in Madison can grasp the full foulness of our nation's political leadership and still tear up to hear Ray Charles belt out "America the Beautiful."

What we love is not our nation's politics or policies but its ideals. That all men (and women) are created equal. That we have an inalienable right to life, liberty and the pursuit of happiness. That government is not to intrude on the free expression of speech, or imprison people without due process. That in response to "a long train of abuses and usurpations," it is the people's right and duty to overthrow it. To the barricades!

This is a nation founded on revolution, in resistance to oppression, in the assertion of the rights of the individual over the power of the state. It is a nation that boasts a vast bounty of natural beauty, from the Redwood Forest to the Gulf Stream waters, from the mountains to the prairies, to the oceans white with foam from industrial pollutants.

This is a nation built by people drawn here by the promise of freedom, and their descendants. That is not to minimize the crimes they committed in stealing land from native inhabitants and exploiting resources with reckless abandon. But there is, at the heart of the American experience, something strong and noble and worthy of admiration.

The reflections in this issue about the quintessential American trait underscore that point. We see the bad as well as the good, but at the end of the day we care about the struggle to make this a better place. It is a cause worth fighting for, even if we always fall short.

JULY 2, 2004

This column won my second Golden Quill, the top annual award for editorial writing from the International Society of Weekly Newspaper Editors, an honor I accepted in Edmonton, Canada.

It's Time to Panic

TO: GROUP MEMBERS
FROM: I.M. FLIPPENOUT, PRESIDENT,
SUFFERING & ORNERY BUSINESSFOLK (S.O.B.)
RE: YOUR CONSTANT STATE OF AGITATION
MESSAGE: GOOD WORK, KEEP IT UP!

DEAR S.O.B.S,

Just a note to thank you all for the great work you've been doing to convey that the city of Madison is a terrible place to do business. Over the last several months, we have worked together to peg every challenge as an unparalleled catastrophe. You think businesses in New Orleans are having a tough time? Hah! What they're going through is nothing compared to what we claim to endure.

Take the minimum-wage ordinance. Those namby-pamby liberals in Madison tried to force us to pay workers $7.75 an hour by the year 2008. Think of it: seven dollars and 75 cents an hour! With wages like that, what would we have left for our vacations, pensions, bonuses and dream homes?

We cried so loud that the Legislature passed and Gov. Jim Doyle signed a bill barring any municipality from setting a minimum wage higher than the state's ever again. The moral of the story: Whining works!

Next came this absolutely outrageous Madison ban on indoor smoking, even in bars. It's the kind of thing you expect in New York City and Ireland – not to mention Flagstaff, Ariz.; Bloomington, Ind.; Lawrence, Kan.; Lincoln, Neb.; Columbus, Ohio; Eugene, Ore.; El Paso, Texas and dozens of other U.S. cities. But this is Wisconsin, where killing oneself with addictive substances is practically a birthright.

I mean, where does our government get off coming into our businesses and telling us – with only 14 months' notice – that we can't subject our employees and customers to known carcinogens that will predictably cause the premature deaths of some of them? Is this communist Russia or what?

The only bright spot is how uniformly you S.O.B.s have responded. No attempt to make the new system work. No effort to attract customers who have avoided bars because they don't like reeking like ashtrays. (Tavern owners, bless them, have even responded coolly to an offer of city and anti-tobacco money to promote smoke-free bars.) Nothing but sour gripes tossed in the face of the 85 percent of Madison residents who don't smoke, and potential customers from surrounding areas. Way to go!

I'd like thank all of you who've worked to portray this as the death knell of local business. Special mention goes to Dave Wiganowsky, the owner of Wiggies' bar and a local elected official.

In mid-August, he told *The Capital Times* that a "good" night at his bar once put $2,500 in the register; now a "good" night was just $700. Yet the numbers he presented this month to the city's Economic Development Commission show that combined daily food and drink sales passed the $2,000 mark only three times in all of July and August of 2004, and never reached $2,500. So, by his definition, he had no good nights in either month, before the ban.

In July and August of 2005, Wiggie's had 28 nights in which bar and food sales topped $700, including 12 above the $1,000 mark. So lots of "good" nights now, but clearly nothing to celebrate. At least not publicly.

OTHERS HAVE ALSO RUSHED TO PUT THE GLOOMIEST POSSIBLE SPIN ON what could be a temporary downturn, or a consequence of bar owners' resounding bitterness. Bob Reuter, president of the 72-member North Side Business Association, calls the ban "just a terrible thing" that's "putting a lot of businesses out of business."

Really, like which ones? Reuter can't name any, but says it's just a matter of time: "How long can you go with probably a 50 percent reduction in your revenue? I've been to a couple of these bars. It's like Death Valley."

Reuter, an American Family agent who sells health insurance and other policies, says "nonsmokers don't give a hoot" about smoke-free environments and are avoiding places they used to go when smoking was allowed, which makes a lot of sense if you don't think about it. He says city officials should stay out of such matters: "They're here to run the city, not make health policy."

Right on, Bob. If we don't put a stop to this now, the next thing you know the city will be telling businesses with rats and roaches and broken refrigerators that they can't sell food.

These developments are all to the good, you S.O.B.s, but let's take it to the next level. Since we're making stuff up to suit our level of indignation, why not say revenue in many bars is down 90 percent and it's like the surface of Uranus? A little more imagination, please.

Take Barb Mercer. When local leaders asked downtown bars to voluntarily close their doors 90 minutes early on the Saturday before Halloween, the head of the Dane County Tavern League went ballistic.

"This is not going to happen," thundered Mercer, noting the city's past efforts to curb drink specials and hike the minimum wage. "This is an industry that has been beaten up, sat on, chewed up and spit out. I'm angry."

You go, girl. Why on earth should tavern owners miss out on 90 minutes of income pumping drunks full of alcohol just to help avoid the property damage and clashes with police that this precipitates? Where is the logic in that?

The fact is, hysterical overreactions like these are working. When some meddling do-gooders wanted Madisonians who seek favors from the city to register as lobbyists, we raised a hue and cry and secured an exemption for business owners. Now there's a call to ram mandatory sick days for workers down our throats. Madison Mayor Dave Cieslewicz says he's against it – not because he thinks it's a bad idea, but out of concern that Madison businesses feel "put upon." Score another one for us whiners!

It is critical that the S.O.B.s among us continue to send the message loud and clear that this community is a stinking, fetid swamp of contagion. Pretty soon, everyone will stay away. We'll have no customers, no employees, no income and no future. Then we'll really have something to complain about. We can hardly wait.

SEPTEMBER 23, 2005

Learning Not to Harass

NEWS ITEM: *In the wake of accusations against former Overture Center president Bob D'Angelo, Madison Mayor Dave Cieslewicz has ordered all 2,700 city employees to undergo training on the city's sexual harassment policy.*

"**G**ood morning, ladies and gentleman – er, members of the female and male genders. And by this, I certainly do not mean to call attention to what kind of sex organs you have. Welcome to this city of Madison training session.

"Our purpose is to educate you regarding appropriate workplace behavior. This has become a devilishly complicated area, one in which conduct once considered collegial is now often a big hairy deal.

"For instance, did you know that it is probably not a good idea to make unsolicited sexual advances to subordinates or even peer employees? As strange as it may seem, this can now be seen as creating a hostile work environment.

"You may also want to avoid making references to disrobing and speculating about, say, the color of others' pubic hair, as Bob D'Angelo is said to have done. Sure, it seems harmless, but in today's hypersensitive workplace environment, this sort of thing is frowned upon.

"Groping of body parts, even through clothing, is another no-no. Yes, this is counterintuitive, and it's hard to fault someone who can't keep a rule like this in mind, but that's the climate in which we now operate.

"Oh, and fellows, you should at all times refrain from taking 'it' out. As natural as the impulse may be whip out Mr. Happy in a workplace situation, doing so could end up causing you a world of grief.

"I see we have a question. Yes?

"Ah, no, you don't have to urinate in your pants. In a proper restroom setting, it is okay to take 'it' out for this limited purpose. I agree this is all very confusing, which is why we are holding these sessions.

"Anyone else? Yes, the man with the — hey, put that thing away!

"In response to your question, sir, my feeling — and you should know my impulse is always to err on the side of caution — is that grabbing a co-worker, pushing her against a wall and kissing her would probably be considered inappropriate.

"Yes, over there.

"Right. No matter how scrumptious she happens to look.

"A basic rule of thumb: If something constitutes third- or fourth-degree sexual assault, you ought to think twice before doing it at work. And even mere comments about sexual intercourse, oral sex, infidelity, bestiality and necrophilia may be problematic.

"Any other questions? Okay then. We hope this training will prove useful in helping you navigate the perilous terrain of today's politically correct workplace. On behalf of the city of Madison, thanks for coming. No double entendre intended."

OCTOBER 7, 2005

Bob D'Angelo served 10½ months in prison after pleading guilty to charges that he misused his public office; the city of Madison in January 2010 agreed to pay $235,000 to settle a sexual harassment lawsuit filed by a former Overture employee.

Let's Talk About the Animals

L ast week, the national group People for the Ethical Treatment of Animals put out a list of the top 10 "worst offenders of abuse of animals" among U.S. universities. Number one on the list: the UW–Madison.

PETA rips the UW for federal Animal Welfare Act violations, the large number of animals it kills and/or subjects to painful and invasive experiments, and its "unwillingness to make humane improvements."

No one who knows how and why such lists are put together would regard this ranking as authoritative. But neither is it arbitrary. The UW–Madison, which currently uses about 2,000 monkeys, 400 dogs, 500 rabbits and thousands of other animals as research subjects, has indeed distinguished itself in this area, in troubling ways:

- In 2003, the state agreed to pay $260,000 to settle a lawsuit by a former assistant research veterinarian at the UW's National Primate Research Laboratory who alleged she was fired for raising concerns about the "cruel and inhumane" treatment of monkeys.

- In 2004, the university imposed a two-year animal-use suspension on researcher Ei Terasawa following the deaths of three monkeys, one of whom died in a restraint chair while a technician took an unapproved break.

- In July 2004, three marmoset monkeys were scalded to death when staff failed to remove the animals before cleaning their cages. Six months later, the same thing happened to a New Zealand white rabbit.

- In early 2005, 10 cows died from neglect at a UW–Madison research farm. The researcher's animal-use privileges were temporarily revoked.

- Last November, UW–Madison faculty member Goran Hellekant sued Chancellor John Wiley, challenging the UW's enforcement of animal welfare rules. Hellekant, who cuts into monkeys to study artificial sweeteners, claims he's been disciplined for past violations; the UW denies this.

- UW Prof. John Webster is now studying the lethality of Taser stun guns, using pigs as subjects. One of the study's consultants was booted for having an undisclosed role as top medical officer to a Taser manufacturer.

EVEN WITHOUT THESE PROBLEMS – SOME OF WHICH, IT SHOULD BE NOTED, came to light because UW officials took corrective action – there is ample reason to examine and debate the use of animals as research subjects.

How animals are treated says something about our values as a society, our moral character. Serious questions have been raised about the usefulness of this research and the conditions animals endure. The issue merits constant review and debate.

The problem: The UW seems far more interested in demonizing its critics than in having an open and honest exchange of ideas.

Recently, I attended an information session sponsored by the Alliance for Animals' Primate Freedom Project. Part of the program consisted of activist Rick Marolt recounting failed efforts to get UW research advocates to debate. His conclusion: UW officials are afraid, realizing that an informed public would reject the university's animal research. As he put it, "They have nothing to gain, and they have a lot to lose and a lot to hide."

Maybe. But the proponents of UW research I've spoken to – including Primate Center director Joe Kemnitz and Dr. Eric Sandgren, who chairs the UW's All-Campus Animal Care and Use Committee – strike me as thoughtful and persuasive. They could more than hold their own in a debate, which makes their reluctance to agree to one perplexing.

A FEW MONTHS BACK, A UW RESEARCHER PUBLICLY CITED WILEY'S "OFFER of open discussion regarding the current necessity of animal research." Local primate activist Rick Bogle sought to take him up on this, asking for a debate. Wiley shot this down: "There was never an offer on my part, nor anyone else from the university that I am aware of, to debate the issue publicly with you or anyone."

Does Wiley not realize how small-minded this makes him seem? Is he not ashamed at what it says about his own lack of confidence in the ability of his institution to face criticism and defend its actions?

Sandgren, too, stepped back from discussions he had begun toward a series of debates with research critics. Like Wiley, he blames activists including Bogle, who last fall broadcast footage of monkey mistreatment outside the homes of a half-dozen UW researchers, an action intended to embarrass and stigmatize.

"That caused us to lose interest," says Sandgren, who does not want to be seen as condoning or rewarding extreme behavior that caused considerable anger.

On the other hand, Sandgren has not foreclosed the possibility of a debate. Indeed, he feels his attendance at some Alliance meetings has helped him better understand how opponents view the university's ethical obligations regarding animal use.

That is the essence of a free exchange of ideas. It's also the reason both sides need to stop viewing each other as evil and start having an honest discussion.

The confrontational tactics embraced by Bogle and others do not help their cause, although I understand why people who feel ignored do desperate things. Equally distasteful are the persistent efforts of UW officials to peg research critics as violent extremists, as when primate center spokesperson Jordana Lenon last summer decried "the illegal acts Mr. Rick Bogle, in particular, has been associated with." This was outright slander: Bogle has never been charged with any crime.

Both sides need to dial it down. Maybe all of the research now being done is justified because of the benefits it brings to humans and animals.

Maybe much of it is pointless and cruel. Maybe some could be eliminated, or conducted more humanely.

These are matters worth exploring, and the public has a role to play. We must not avert our eyes. We must not accept assertion as fact. And we must not let the UW–Madison shirk its responsibility to disclose and discuss what it is doing to defenseless creatures.

FEBRUARY 10, 2006

Shortly after this column appeared, I helped organize and co-moderated a campus debate on animal research between Rick Bogle and Eric Sandgren. Other debates have since taken place. In January 2010, the UW internally discussed the ethics of primate research, giving itself a clean bill of health. Around this same time, the university was cited by federal authorities for serious new violations of the Animal Welfare Act.

Playing Politics with Death

Brian Blanchard does not question the sincerity of those who "want with due process to end the life of a person who without any due process took the life of someone they loved." As district attorney of Dane County, he's met with people in the throes of such grief, and deems their desire for the ultimate penalty "a human impulse, not an evil impulse."

But Blanchard is nonetheless working with the Wisconsin Coalition Against the Death Penalty to defeat an advisory referendum on the Nov. 7 ballot that would permit the state to execute convicted first-degree killers in cases "supported by DNA evidence."

He's against the death penalty because he's convinced "human beings don't have the wisdom or the tools to ensure fairness in this arena." He notes that, historically, people who are poor and nonwhite are much more likely to be executed. And he doesn't think any system can preclude the possibility that innocent people will die.

Certainly, the language regarding DNA evidence offers no such protection. As Blanchard puts it, "DNA does not mean guilt." There can be weak cases backed by DNA and rock-solid cases that aren't. A man could murder an entire gymnasium full of schoolchildren in a crime caught on tape and confess to it afterward and not face the death penalty if he somehow manages to not implicate himself through DNA.

The DNA clause, added to make the referendum more appealing, attests to its bastard birth as an act of pure political calculation. The impetus for asking citizens whether Wisconsin should end its 153-year ban on capital punishment came not from law enforcement or even grieving families. It came from Republican politicians, looking ahead to an election in which GOP candidates for governor, attorney general and other offices need all the help they can get.

Says Blanchard, "It feels like it's on the ballot really just to get out voters." But that doesn't mean the only consequence will be helping elect pro-death Republicans.

Blanchard thinks the referendum will probably pass, perhaps by a wide enough margin that state lawmakers will indeed restore the death penalty. (A new statewide poll shows 58 percent support for capital punishment and only 36 percent opposition.) The referendum's proponents, meanwhile, are doing everything they can to pave the way for Wisconsin to start killing people again.

THE CURRENT ISSUE OF WISCONSIN INTEREST, A JOURNAL PRODUCED BY the Wisconsin Policy Research Institute, contains a polemic entitled "Wisconsin Should Have the Death Penalty" by John McAdams, a professor at Marquette. McAdams seeks to lay waste to the various anti-death arguments.

He begins by accusing death penalty foes of being hypocrites, since they don't object to all killing, just when it's done by government to convicted criminals. Also, they don't seem to mind that the justice system "does nasty things to people other than killing them." Anyone who's ever gotten a bogus parking ticket can relate.

McAdams then attacks arguments against killing the innocent, saying not all of the more than 120 people freed after being on death row unquestionably fit this category. (How does that old saying go: "'Tis better that a hundred innocent people be executed than one guilty person go free"?) Indeed, says McAdams, the system works so well that "death penalty opponents have apparently given up claiming solid evidence of any innocent person executed in the modern era." Here's yet another area in which the state of Wisconsin could lead.

The death penalty is needed, insists McAdams, because there's no way to ensure that even a "life without parole" sentence will mean what it says.

"If a liberal legislature, or a liberal governor with the power of commutation, or a liberal activist court decides that life in prison is 'inhumane,' or that some 'disorder' or 'psychosis' caused the crime, the murderer will go free," he warns. "And indeed, if some executive feels it politically expedient to let violent criminals go, a 'life without parole' sentence is worthless."

Further, in states without the death penalty, inmates sentenced to life in prison — blithely ignoring their good chances of being sprung by wild-eyed liberals — can kill other inmates, says McAdams, and have it count as a "freebie." Gosh, how huge a problem is this?

"We haven't had any cases of inmates killing other inmates in the Wisconsin prison system at all since Christopher Scarver [killed Jeffrey Dahmer and another man] back in 1994," says John Dipko, a spokesperson for the state Department of Corrections. That means the DOC has managed to keep even Scarver, diagnosed as "a schizophrenic psychopath with messianic delusions," from killing again, without having to kill him.

Prof. McAdams' self-described "strongest argument" is that the death penalty serves as a deterrent. He cites discredited studies that concoct hypothetical homicide rates to conclude, for instance, that the decision of Illinois Gov. George Ryan to rescind the death penalty in his state "produced about 150 additional murders." From this, he pegs people opposed to the death penalty as not just misguided but heartless, "willing to sacrifice the lives of innocent victims." For shame!

There's no need to pick apart such absurd reasoning. The overwhelming weight of scientific evidence shows the death penalty has absolutely no deterrent effect. Plus it imposes major new costs on the criminal justice system.

Blanchard cites yet another reason for his opposition: He doesn't want himself or other prosecutors to have the power to seek to put people to death. "The death penalty is not only about victim's rights and justice," he says. "The death penalty is about ourselves and what powers we should have."

JUNE 30, 2006

The advisory referendum favoring the death penalty passed overwhelmingly, but the state has not yet reversed its ban on capital punishment.

Family photo of Vairin Meesouk and his daughter, included in a court filing

The End of Mercy

I met Vairin Meesouk for the first time last week, just before he was sentenced. Several years ago, I wrote about one of his earlier run-ins with the law. I referred to him by his initials, V.M., because he was a juvenile. Now he's all of 21.

We spoke briefly. Vairin thanked me for my interest, as did the family members around him. He seemed like a nice young man. It's a common impression.

"He's a good kid," a family friend wrote the judge. "I can recall many times, when I was over at their house, seeing him care for his [2-year-old] daughter. He comforted her when she was crying and fed her and changed her diapers while her mother was busy cooking." The friend said Vairin was doing all he could to "make life better for himself and his family."

Vairin Meesouk was born in a refugee camp in Laos and spent his early years in another camp in Thailand. His family moved to Madison in

1991, when Vairin was 6. His father, a CIA operative, was a drunk who "chronically beat him for no apparent reason," according to a state Department of Corrections (DOC) pre-sentencing report. The father eventually abandoned his family.

In 2000, when Vairin was 15, he was charged with multiple felonies as an adult in connection with a series of break-ins, including gas station/convenience stores. He and other youths stole items like cigarettes, and started a small fire at one location.

I wrote about how a local couple – including one of Vairin's former teachers – were pushing the Dane County District Attorney's Office to reduce the charges. An adult felony conviction, they noted, likely meant that Vairin, as a legal resident without U.S. citizenship, would be deported to Laos, where he knows no one, or held indefinitely in an Immigration and Naturalization Service prison.

The DA's office called these possible outcomes a "collateral consequence," which, while "unfortunate," was not a proper concern for the justice system. It opposed Circuit Court Judge Diane Nicks' move to amend the charge to avoid this consequence. The underlying issues came before the Wisconsin Supreme Court, which agreed Nicks could not change the charge but suggested other relief. In 2003, the DA's office reduced the counts to misdemeanors, and Vairin drew four years of probation. But by the time he got this second chance, he'd already blown it.

In the early morning hours of Sept. 15, 2002, Vairin, then 17, was one of four youths who broke into a residence on Madison's east side. The 77-year-old man who lived there was beaten and smothered until he lost consciousness. Four rifles were taken and purportedly later tossed.

More than three years later, in January 2006, one of the perpetrators confessed. He claimed Vairin took part in the beating, punching the elderly man in the testicles. Vairin denied this, and the victim did not recall being struck in this fashion. Vairin was charged with four felonies and pleaded guilty to three.

"It was a bad thing to do," Vairin's lawyer, Yolanda Lehner, said in court last week. "My client should not have been involved." But she maintained the youths broke in believing the residence was empty, and that Vairin watched in horror as the elderly man was attacked.

The victim sat behind me in court, radiating quiet indignation. He told the DOC investigator he wanted the youths to "get what's coming to them," but also that the trauma of this crime paled compared to what he'd experienced in World War II.

SINCE THIS BREAK-IN, VAIRIN HAS HAD MINOR SCRAPES WITH THE LAW – notably an altercation with his sister in 2003, for which he received two years of probation. But he's held jobs and met the conditions of his probation. The DOC investigator called him "a dutiful and loving father" and said he is "working hard at becoming a mature pro-social adult after experiencing a horrendously hostile, alienated and rebellious youth."

The prosecutor, Assistant District Attorney Doug McLean, was in no mood for mercy. He asked for a 10-year sentence, twice what the DOC recommended. He told the court that "a weekly newspaper" had previously put "a lot of pressure" on the DA's office, without which "we would not have given Mr. Meesouk the incredible consideration he got in these cases." His bosses, he implied, had wrongly caved to outside pressure.

Lehner, in turn, spoke of her client's deep remorse and steps he's taken to turn his life around. And she urged the court to consider the immigration consequences. A jail term of under a year – even 364 days – would give Vairin at least a fighting chance to avoid deportation. She argued for this: "I'm not saying Vairin Meesouk should not be punished. But I'm asking the court not to punish too much. And too much is being deported."

Vairin read a statement, expressing remorse and claiming to have changed. "I have a stronger foundation," he said, breaking down. "I'm a father now, and I am currently employed fulltime.... In the future, I will not commit any further offenses."

Judge Daniel Moeser acknowledged some positive steps the defendant had taken, but also the seriousness of his crime. He then sentenced him to three years in prison, followed by five on extended supervision. He agreed this could trigger deportation but said, "that's a consequence of committing a crime like this."

Deputies slapped on the cuffs and led Vairin away. The involvement of immigration authorities is now virtually assured. He'll likely spend the rest of his life behind bars or in permanent exile.

"I'm sorry," Lehner told Vairin's family afterwards. "I'm so sorry I couldn't stop it."

Perhaps no one could have. Except maybe Vairin – back when he was 17, before his chances ran out.

JANUARY 12, 2007

Vairin Meesouk was released from the state prison system in December 2009 into the custody of U.S. Immigration and Customs Enforcement. On March 1, 2010, a judge ordered his deportation to Laos.

Shedding Light on Records

Walter H. Besley may well have been Wisconsin's first open-government crusader.

Back in 1853, five years after Wisconsin became a state, Besley, the clerk of circuit court in Jefferson County, billed the county board of supervisors $22 for two expenses: wood to furnish his office and a large box of candles to light and warm it.

The board rejected the expenditure. Besley sued and won. The board was ordered to pay these expenses, plus interest and "the costs of suit."

In 1856, the Wisconsin Supreme Court heard the case on appeal. It affirmed the circuit court's ruling, citing a state law mandating that the clerk and other county officials "keep his office open during business hours, Sundays excepted, and all books and papers required to be kept in this office shall be open for the examination of any person."

The court said the Legislature's intent was clear, "to accommodate the wants of the citizens" who had business to transact. "To require these officers to keep their offices open during business hours," it wrote, "and yet provide no means of warming or lighting them, would be simply absurd."

While the law did not require the clerk "to keep a tavern" – which presumably would also accommodate the wants of some citizens – "it is clearly the object and intention of the statute that these county offices shall be kept open, and in a suitable condition…." Thus the expenses presented by Besley were "a proper and legal county charge" that the board was wrong to reject.

This case, *The County of Jefferson vs. Besley,* was uncovered recently by Bob Dreps, a lawyer at the Madison office of Godfrey & Kahn, who was researching the authenticity of an entry on Wikipedia, the online encyclopedia.

The entry, "Freedom of Information in the United States," states that the nation's first open records law was passed in Wisconsin shortly after it became a state.

This was news to me and other members of the Wisconsin Freedom of Information Council. We knew the state's current public records law was passed in 1981, replacing an earlier version that was on the books since 1917. But Wisconsin's pioneering role in this area was apparently lost to history – until this Wikipedia entry.

IN SEARCH OF MORE INFORMATION, I VISITED THE STATE LAW LIBRARY. There I located a bound volume of the Revised Statutes of 1849 in the State Law Library, a book so old that some its pages had come loose. There, under Chapter 10, Section 137, was the statute cited by the Supreme Court.

It required every sheriff, circuit court clerk, county board clerk, register of deeds and county treasurer in the state to "open for the examination of any person" all of their books and papers. Any officer who neglected to comply "shall forfeit for each day he shall so neglect, the sum of five dollars."

Five dollars was a lot of money in those days – more than 200 current dollars, according to one inflation calculator. A public official who refused to let the public see records faced serious consequences. (The law is still on the books, under 59.20(3), and the fine is still $5 a day!)

But this statute would not have meant much for the citizens of Jefferson County had Walter Besley not gone to the mat to defend their right for a place to review records and candles to provide light and heat.

The citizens of Wisconsin owe a debt of gratitude to Besley – and modern-day counterparts including Brian Buswell, who sued a school district for using a deliberately vague meeting notice so the public wouldn't know what the school board planned to decide. Earlier this year, the Wisconsin Supreme Court deemed this improper, and instructed public bodies to make fuller disclosure.

Credit goes also to the citizens group that won an important case against the city of Milton, which reached a secret deal to subsidize an ethanol plant. "Now," the mayor of Milton recently stated, "we're taking care to make sure everything is done properly." Hooray for that.

Throughout Wisconsin are people committed, in word and deed, to the public's right to know. Now and then, we should light a candle in their honor.

DECEMBER 2007

This column was written for the Wisconsin Freedom of Information Council and published in papers and on websites across the state.

Gableman, Unfit for Any Office

My old friend Charlie Sykes has a good line about the difference between liberals and conservatives. "Conservatives," he says, "think liberals are wrong. Liberals," he adds, "think conservatives are evil."

It's a point well taken. The left does tend to demonize the right. That this is a vice-versa proposition makes it no less unsavory.

One thing I've learned over the years is that conservatives can be intelligent, perceptive, even caring and compassionate (in addition to being wrong). There is much to admire in their hardscrabble, self-reliant view of the world.

Not so with Burnett County Judge Michael Gableman, the undistinguished conservative challenging Justice Louis Butler in the April 1 election for state Supreme Court. Gableman is beyond wrong. More than any other person I've encountered in 25 years of covering politics, he deserves to be seen as ... if not evil, then certainly its mixed-up cousin, vile.

I'm not saying this lightly. Recently, I wrote a column in defense of Supreme Court Justice Annette Ziegler, a target of the left's overheated attacks. I think people slavish in their allegiance to corporate and state power have every right to seek seats on the state Supreme Court.

That Gableman fits this mold has been obvious from the start. He has repeatedly signaled, sometimes overtly, his dissatisfaction with court rulings that minutely expanded the rights of criminal suspects and the ability of injured parties to sue. His message to groups like Wisconsin Manufacturers & Commerce, which is spending vast sums on his behalf: Put me on the court, and I'll have your back.

That's fine. That's how our system works. Where Gableman crosses the line is in his willingness to lie to get elected. Not little white lies. Not statements on which reasonable people can disagree. Not things said in error, due to confusion or forgetfulness. Lies. Outright, brazen, calculated and bald-faced lies.

Everyone knew this was going to be an ugly campaign, but no one anticipated how low Mike Gableman would be willing to go. He is a man without honor, or shame.

Gableman casts his rival as a "judicial activist" who's soft on crime and heedless of the rule of law. That in itself is untrue. Butler and Justice Patrick Crooks are the court's centrists, joining with the majority nearly all the time.

Butler, whose brother is a Miami police officer who took a bullet to the head in the line of duty, has voted to uphold criminal convictions in 97 percent of the cases that have come before the court. (One measure of how much Gableman has degraded the race is that Butler brags about this.)

An ad run by one of the shadowy conservative groups seeking to install Gableman claims he's "sided with criminals nearly 60 percent of the time."

The group is lying, and so is its candidate. Gableman signed a pledge promising to "publicly repudiat[e] dishonest negative ads made by independent groups against our opponent." He has not done so.

Gableman is also minting his own falsehoods. He defines New Federalism as "the rights of defendants unbound by anything but the personal political views of the majority of the court." In fact, it is simply the notion, backed by the U.S. Supreme Court, that state courts should look to their own constitutions in deciding cases.

Judges and especially justices have a duty to educate the public on matters of law – not set out to deceive them for purely political and self-serving reasons.

GABLEMAN'S MOST EGREGIOUS TRANSGRESSION AGAINST TRUTH AND decency is his ad picturing Butler alongside a black rapist. The ad says Butler found a "loophole" in the law, after which the man raped again. An ominous voice-over asks, "Can Wisconsin families feel safe with Louis Butler on the Supreme Court?"

In fact, the man served his full sentence on the first offense. Butler, then with the state Public Defender's Office, had won the man the right to a new trial, but the Supreme Court reinstated his conviction.

The ad has left most observers shocked – not by Butler's behavior, but Gableman's lack of scruples.

"I am troubled that a candidate for our highest court would belittle our constitutional right to counsel," wrote Dodge County District Attorney Steven G. Bauer, explaining his decision to withdraw his endorsement of Gableman. "I am equally troubled by Gableman's cavalier disregard for accuracy in his representations to the public through this ad. The integrity of the criminal justice system should not be allowed to be tarnished by one man's ambitious desire for higher office."

The Wisconsin Judicial Campaign Integrity Committee, an independent watchdog created by the State Bar, has asked Gableman to pull this "contemptible" and "deliberately misleading" ad and issue an apology. Gableman, whose signed pledge also obliges him to refrain from "personal negative attacks," has not done so.

Sykes, a respectable conservative, was moved to "throw a flag on our own team" in a recent blog post. "The case in the ad is not one Butler handled as a judge or justice." And even as a defense lawyer, Butler played no role in the rapist's eventual release. "So the claim that Butler was somehow responsible for the subsequent rape is completely unfounded."

Wisconsin Citizen Action has filed a complaint against Gableman with the state Judicial Commission. It says he's broken the code that requires judges to act in a way that builds public confidence in the integrity of the judiciary.

Clearly, Gableman has defiled that code, and the Judicial Commission should discipline him. The man is not just unfit to be a Supreme Court justice; he is unfit to be a judge, or hold any public office.

MARCH 28, 2008

On April 1, 2008, Mike Gableman narrowly defeated Louis Butler; it was the first time in 40 years that a sitting Wisconsin Supreme Court justice was ousted from office. The Wisconsin Judicial Commission subsequently filed an ethics charge against Gableman, for his ad accusing Butler of having found a "loophole" that led to the release of a sex offender. But a review panel recommended dismissing the charge, buying Gableman's argument that the deliberately misleading ad couldn't be punished because its component parts were true. In other words, noted one of the panel's judges, he found a loophole! On June 30, 2010, the Wisconsin Supreme Court deadlocked, 3–3, on whether the charges against Gableman should proceed, which kept this from happening. Half of his colleagues felt he had made knowingly false statements; the other half that the ad was merely "distasteful." Gableman proclaimed victory.

For the Love of Newspapers

I don't recall seeing either of my parents ever reading a book. I'm pretty sure they didn't even own any, except for a Bible, which, bless their hearts, they also didn't read. But every morning my father would buy a *Milwaukee Sentinel* (he always left for work at 5 a.m., before the paper would have been delivered) and every afternoon the *Milwaukee Journal* arrived at our door. They read those papers front to back. I grew up reading them, too.

At 13, I got my first paper route, one of several. Through college and afterward, I worked for the *Milwaukee Journal*'s circulation department, delivering papers to carriers and vendors, collecting money, keeping the books. In 1982 I co-founded a Milwaukee newspaper called *The Crazy Shepherd*, now the weekly *Shepherd Express*. Four years later I landed my first and only fulltime job, here at *Isthmus*.

Newspapers are a huge part of my life, part of who I am. I've always considered them essential. The idea of not reading a daily newspaper strikes me as a dereliction of one's duty to be an informed citizen.

A few months ago, on the final season of HBO's "The Wire," a character recalls being a kid watching his dad peruse the paper each morning. That's why he became a journalist: He wanted to be part of something that important.

The fictional newsroom in the show is, like most real newsrooms these days, in crisis. The industry is reeling from drops in circulation, revenue, investor confidence and public regard.

Papers from *The New York Times* to *Isthmus* are cutting staff. The *Wall Street Journal* was sold to Rupert Murdoch. *The Capital Times* and now the *Daily Telegram* of Superior have ceased daily print publication. The price of stock in Lee Enterprises, half-owner of the *Cap Times* and *Wisconsin State Journal*, has fallen from nearly $50 a share in 2004 to barely more than $3 a share today.

As Mia Farrow says in *Rosemary's Baby*, when she wakes up and realizes she's being raped by the Devil: "This is not a dream. This is really happening!"

That many newspaper companies remain highly profitable seems not to matter. They are seen as anachronistic, a throwback to an earlier age, unsustainable.

But what most galls me is the public's increasingly supercilious attitude. It's become fashionable to bash the print media as unreliable, at a time when newspapers are a beacon of credibility compared to the blowhards on cable TV and the bloviators of the blogosphere.

THE OTHER DAY I GAVE A TALK TO A LOCAL ROTARY CHAPTER. I MADE some point about excessive government secrecy, and one of the gentlemen in attendance opined that it was perfectly understandable, given the media's predilection to get things wrong.

I was of course gracious and politic in my response, but I think this fellow is full of it. Of course the media make mistakes, and I would never defend everything my colleagues do, especially at the national level.

But the truth is that newspapers get an amazing number of things right. Numbers, dates, names, context, nuance – we check and double-check. We don't go all viral spreading ridiculous lies, like that Barack Obama is a Muslim. We publish corrections when we're wrong. How many doctors or lawyers or politicians do that?

I once had an editorial intern break into tears over an error so inconsequential I can no longer recall it. He hated getting something wrong, as does every reporter I know. (Again, I flash to "The Wire," where a reporter makes an early-morning call to the copy desk to make sure he hadn't misstated a statistic. Waking up in cold sweats is part of this job.)

As I told the Rotarians, there's a simple way to educate yourself about what it takes to be a reporter: Go to any event in your community that you know will be covered in the local paper. It can be a debate, a day of court testimony, a press conference, an appearance by a visiting newsmaker, even a baseball game. Pay close attention and take copious notes. Then go home and write up a story about what you've just seen. The next day, compare what you've written to the story that appears in print. I guarantee you won't look down your nose at newspaper reporters ever again.

And covering events is just a small part of what newspapers do. The job gets a lot tougher. Enterprise stories, analytical stories, stories that require special expertise. Long hours. Low pay. And for what? So people can cluck about how irrelevant newspapers have become?

If it sounds like I'm angry, I guess I am. I'm angry that newspapers are falling into disrepute. I'm angry that people don't respect the quality control that goes into news reporting; they seem to think any idiot with Internet access is worth listening to. I'm angry that some young people feel they don't need newspapers – or, apparently, anything else in the way of information about their community.

I submit that those of us who care about newspapers and the quality information they provide ought to help ensure their continued existence. That may mean subscribing instead of reading them free at work or online. It may mean placing ads in papers instead of some online service. It certainly should mean recognizing that ads are what make papers possible, and that newspaper advertisers deserve support.

It's not enough to hope that newspapers stick around. We need to fight for them.

JULY 18, 2008

Too Green for Madison?

With $4-a-gallon gasoline and likely global environmental catastrophe, the mayor's desire to incorporate ideas of the sort he saw during a recent visit to Madison's sister city of Freiburg, Germany, is abundantly sensible and more than a little exciting. But you'd never guess that from the local reaction.

"So Mayor Dave wants to build a 'car-light' neighborhood," exclaimed *Isthmus* columnist Rick Berg. "How ridiculous!" He snickered that Europe, unlike the U.S., has very dense population centers, and that the mayor merely needed to "check it out on a map" to see that this idea would not work here.

The next time Cieslewicz visits Germany, Berg urged, he should "leave the wacky ideas over there."

Wacky ideas? Building a neighborhood that maximizes passive solar in how it's platted, links up with hoped-for commuter rail and de-emphasizes auto reliance? *That's* wacky, but acting as though oil is an infinitely renewable resource is not?

Further, contrary to Berg's assumptions, Freiburg and Madison are actually quite similar. (Hmmm, maybe that's why they're sister cities!) Both are university towns with just over 200,000 residents. But one has hugely popular car-light neighborhoods, and the other does not.

Freiburgians somehow manage to survive. Trams provide clean, reliable transportation. "Pedestrians are everywhere," relates Cieslewicz. "I didn't see a single vacant storefront." Cars can still be used; "it's just that the entire neighborhood isn't designed around them."

The sad truth is that cities all over the world are embracing innovative approaches that conservatives here would shoot down in a nanosecond.

Streetcars downtown? The mayor's gone mad! Stop him before he wastes our tax dollars again. Commuter rail? How ridiculous! People here *like* high gas prices, traffic jams and trouble finding parking. They'd *never* trade these for fast and efficient mass transit!

BERG'S RANT APPEARED IN THE SAME ISSUE AS A LETTER TO THE EDITOR from Clareen Erickson of Waunakee, who opined that Madison's mayor "wants to force 'car-light' neighborhoods down our throats."

First of all, why should a person in Waunakee flip out over a green neighborhood in Madison? Doesn't Waunakee have everything urban life has to offer, including some restaurants and a bowling alley, so people there never need venture outside its borders?

And how exactly is creating a neighborhood that's less dependent on fossil fuel an act of brute force? Don't like it, don't move there.

Presumably, some people care more about the planet than Exxon-Mobil's profits ($11.7 billion in the second quarter of 2008 alone). They'd like streets where children could play without dodging cars. They'd get a charge out of selling energy back to the power company on a sunny day.

But if any such people are in Madison, they're being awfully quiet.

Cieslewicz suggests it's irresponsible for cities to keep designing neighborhoods as though high gas prices and global warming (for which American consumption is disproportionately to blame) did not exist. He likens it to automakers who remained committed to gas-guzzling SUVs despite clear signs that the market was changing.

So when Madison is planning a new neighborhood that will occupy 2,800 acres and house 20,000 to 30,000 people, he asks, "does it make sense to base that plan on the old paradigm of cheap gas or the new paradigm of expensive energy? What would be better for our economy and our environment in the long run?"

The conservatives who have dominated reaction to the mayor's plan emphatically embrace the old paradigm. Local radio squawker Vicki McKenna told me the mayor is "asking the rest of us to support a choice by a very small number of people that will cost the rest of us millions of dollars."

She also believes the mayor's green neighborhood scheme is meant to grease the skids for commuter rail. What's wrong with that? "I don't want to live like that," says McKenna, as though this idea were akin to drinking raw eggs for breakfast. "No one's going to take a train to work."

Indeed, she says even the phrase "car-light" conveys "a hostility to personal mobility. Why? You can't force people to make the choices you prefer them to make. Most people prefer a car."

Maybe McKenna is right. Maybe people in Madison only care about what's most convenient for them. They want to drive everywhere. They aren't interested in reducing auto or energy use. You can put them on a commuter train when you pry their car keys from their cold, dead fingers.

Maybe that's why, when someone like Cieslewicz proposes a visionary neighborhood that could be a national model, drawing visitors and acclaim from far and wide, most people here keep their mouths shut and eyes averted as conservatives rip him to shreds. Maybe he's getting the reaction he deserves, for trying to force unwelcome ideas down people's throats.

AUGUST 29, 2008

In mid-2009, Rick Berg joined a Madison delegation to Freiburg and came back enthusiastic about its car-light design features. The mayor's green neighborhood plan was approved by the Madison Common Council and is now in the planning stages.

Justice is Everybody's Business

In April 2008 I wrote an article about an astonishing legal filing in the Ralph Armstrong case. It alleged that a Dane County prosecutor, by then retired, not only failed to investigate a tip that pointed to a wrongful conviction but set out to destroy evidence that might have proven this.

The article did not take sides. It merely reported what the filing alleged: In the mid-1990s, Dane County prosecutor John Norsetter was contacted by a woman from Texas who said Steve Armstrong had admitted to the 1980 rape and murder of which his brother Ralph was convicted.

Accompanying the filing were detailed affidavits from two women who described this confession, and their efforts to call attention to it. One of them purportedly spoke to Norsetter, Ralph Armstrong's original prosecutor.

Norsetter failed to pass on this information and in 2006 ordered testing that destroyed what remained of a DNA sample, in violation of an existing court order. Steve Armstrong died in 2005, the same year that the state Supreme Court overturned Ralph Armstrong's conviction on other grounds. He was awaiting retrial when the revelations about his brother came to light.

My article promoted an outraged reaction – but not the sort you might expect.

"Sure we've had our share of mistaken convictions and overzealous prosecution in Dane County, but this is one [case] where people need to tread carefully," wrote one poster on *TheDailyPage.com* Forum. "What I see is Leuders [real accuracy buff here] being used by Armstrong's defense attorneys in a PR campaign to make Armstrong look like a victim of a corrupt DA.... Shame on you Leuders and shame on *Isthmus*." Other respondents voiced similar criticisms.

In late July, Reserve Judge Robert Kinney, having heard the allegations against Norsetter, as well as a vigorous defense of his actions by the state, agreed that "a series of conscious decisions" had tainted the conviction beyond redemption. He dismissed the charges, a decision the DA's office has decided not to appeal.

Ralph Armstrong, who has always maintained his innocence (even though it's meant a longer sentence), is on his way to being released from his Wisconsin prison, due to prosecutorial actions *Isthmus* was skewered for even mentioning.

I tell this story because it points to a larger issue, one that ought to concern the entire community. Ordinary citizens and even political leaders rarely challenge the criminal justice system, no matter how often we're reminded of its fallibility. Even folks who flock to public meetings on other local issues sit on their hands when it comes to prosecutors and police. It's a real problem.

Already, we give these people vast powers – to arrest, to prosecute, to overlook transgression, to deprive of liberty – and immunize them from most lawsuits when they screw up. And then, on top of that, we spare them the bother of having to explain themselves. Indeed, the most common public reaction to allegations of injustice is to reflexively defend the system, as though it were too fragile to withstand scrutiny.

IN ANNOUNCING THAT IT WAS NOT APPEALING JUDGE KINNEY'S DECISION, the Dane County District Attorney's Office issued a statement, which read in part:

"[The] record demonstrates that prosecuting attorneys and their colleagues in the Madison Police Department pursued this case in good faith at every stage of the process, and that any errors that occurred during the course of the investigation and prosecution were the product of innocent mistake or oversight."

That settles that. Thanks.

Except, as Columbo might say, for one little thing: Norsetter heard from a woman who said Steve Armstrong had credibly confessed, providing explicit details. He later ordered a DNA test that could not distinguish between brothers but used up the sample.

What makes the system so certain this was an innocent mistake?

Even if it were, that doesn't eliminate the need for answers and accountability. Where are the editorials from Neil Heinen and the dailies? Why hasn't noted local blogger Dave Cieslewicz weighed in?

Because the justice system always gets a pass. We snooze, we lose.

A decade ago I wrote several articles about a 15-year-old girl who was charged with a crime for slightly changing her account of a sexual assault. The person she accused was convicted of a crime. So was the girl's father, for calling her a slut and beating her up after the DA's office led the way in turning against her.

Dane County Judge Maryann Sumi dismissed the charge against the girl and chided the DA's office for bringing it. Then it was up to the community to respond. So far as I know, only one person did. Madison resident Moria Cue circulated a petition expressing outrage. She ultimately forced a high-level meeting with the DA's office, and I believe made it less likely that future rape victims will be treated this way.

We need police and prosecutors, and no community has more honorable people at the helm than Madison Police Chief Noble Wray and Dane County DA Brian Blanchard. But we also need citizens like Moria Cue, looking over their shoulders, asking for explanations.

SEPTEMBER 4, 2009

Part Two

INVESTIGATIONS

Sign in Florence, the county seat. Photo by Bill Lueders

What Happened in Florence County?

Between June and August 1986, the state Department of Health and Social Services investigated the Department of Social Services in Florence County. The investigation, in two parts, involved a total of 17 DHSS staffers from throughout the state. It was, by one official reckoning, "the most extensive and comprehensive review ever undertaken by the Department of Health and Social Services."

The allegations that prompted the probe were serious. Social service workers in Florence County were said to have coerced welfare recipients into abortions and sterilizations; used threats of criminal prosecution and false charges of child abuse to force conduct desired by the agency; wrongfully denied and restricted benefits; and used social service funds for personal gain.

No such charges were ever confirmed. The final DHSS report, released in late February of this year, lists 30 mainly procedural problems uncovered in the review, including a finding that the agency director was not working full time in this capacity and could perhaps have part of his salary disallowed. But the report complimented the county for having low error rates and concluded that the agency and its employees "were subjected to an extremely stressful and detailed review because of allegations which proved to be unfounded."

Reaction to the report, at least in some quarters, was jubilant. The Florence County Department of Social Services, in a press release printed in the local weekly paper, the *Florence Mining News*, said it had been "completely and totally exonerated" by the investigation. Later, the county board chairman and social service board used the same medium to publicly upbraid members of the community who had made charges against the agency to begin with.

In other quarters, however, the report raised more questions than it put to rest. Did the state look in the right places? Did it respond appropriately to what it found? Is the DHSS, the state's largest agency, capable of being an effective monitor of county social service departments?

In an era of increasing experimentation with workfare and other programs for welfare recipients, these are questions of great importance. The answers, at least those suggested by the Florence County experience, are not reassuring.

"It appears to be a whitewash," one state staffer says of the final report. "What we found were real, real significant problems. Anything you might have heard as far as treatment of people of any type of situation that sounds highly unusual or perverse or unthinkable in the 20th century is probably true."

FLORENCE COUNTY, LOCATED IN THE EXTREME NORTHEAST CORNER OF THE state near Iron Mountain, Mich., is beautiful though impoverished. The land is mainly forest land, with a few farms and scattered remnants of the area's erstwhile mining days. Although twice the size of Milwaukee County, it contains only about half as many people (4,172 in 1980) as the average Madison aldermanic district.

The county seat, Florence, is unincorporated. Most county offices are located in a 98-year-old courthouse building in the center of town. A sign on the door to the sheriff's office on the main floor reads, "If you don't like police, next time you need help CALL A HIPPIE." In the basement is the Department of Social Services.

Florence County's director of social services since 1958 – and the most controversial man in town – is Duane A. Folz. Most area residents call him George, although some use another moniker: the Godfather. The title is a traditional one in Florence County; before Folz it was used in reference to the late chairman of the county board.

In addition to being social services director, Folz heads up the 5142 Board – an entity providing services to the disabled and chemically dependent – for which he receives a combined salary of $40,407. Folz is also coordinator of the county's Economic Development Commission, for which he supposedly receives no additional compensation, and is a partner in a local land-development company.

A lot of suspicion and not a little fear attend the mention of Folz's name in Florence County. One shopkeeper, looking anxiously about to see who might overhear, calls him "a ruthless liar." Other residents are convinced Folz is benefiting illicitly from his numerous involvements.

Folz, for his part, refused repeated requests for an interview. "I'm paranoid," he admitted at one point. "I'd be crazy not to be."

To an extent, Folz is justified in claiming the paranoiac's defense: People really are out to get him. One notable Folz foe is Frederick (Rick) Prohaska, a charismatic 34-year-old who blames Florence County for a host of personal harassments. Prohaska has approached officials and attended meetings while wired with a hidden tape recorder, written letters to agencies throughout the state, and organized critics of the Social Services Department.

Another galvanizing force is Charles Grabski, formerly Folz's friend and a county social service worker. Grabski was fired by Folz in 1978 on grounds that were later ruled inappropriate by the U.S. Department of Health, Education and Welfare. Passionate and embittered, he has been fighting the county ever since.

"There's a real serious problem up here in relation to ... the U.S. Constitution," says Grabski, the former head of the county's Democratic Party. "There's no way in hell that I can see that's a viable document here. It's just not. They don't go by the rules or the laws and they seem to get away with it. Why I don't know.... We tell people about it and the next thing we know those people we tell are covering it up."

THE STATE'S INVESTIGATION INTO FLORENCE COUNTY SOCIAL SERVICES was prompted by a number of complaints received in early 1986 – including those from Prohaska, the county taxpayers association (which complained about Folz using Social Service dollars for economic development activities, including trips to Houston and Las Vegas) and Fred Hatch, an attorney from St. Germaine in nearby Vilas County who has represented a number of clients in legal proceedings against the department. Folz also requested an investigation.

It began with a preliminary review in June, in which, according to an early draft of the state report, "technical or substantive errors" were found in all 30 of the AFDC [Aid to Families with Dependent Children] cases randomly sampled for review. On the basis of this finding, DHSS ordered a complete review of active income maintenance (primarily AFDC and food stamps) and general relief cases. This was accomplished by rotating teams of DHSS workers from Madison and regional offices throughout the state.

The most common recollection of those who participated is that Florence County's files were an absolute mess – poorly organized and lacking adequate documentation. Indeed, some recall making joking reference to what they called the Gasp Factor: how long it took for a new person arriving on the scene to look into a Florence County social service file before he or she audibly gasped. ("It didn't take long," says one.)

Several staffers report being followed on some occasions. Although many clients interviewed had no complaints, some told of harassment and threats. At one point DHSS investigators Mary Ann Cook and Jim Dalland rented a hotel room in Iron Mountain to meet with clients were who afraid to discuss their experiences within county limits.

A total of 210 cases were reviewed, 112 of which involved an interview with the client. Some staffers did not find anything out of the ordinary, according to reports to supervisors obtained by *Isthmus* under the state's Open Records Law. Others were troubled by what they found.

Clients seemed uninformed of their right to a hearing, said one. "There is an overapplication of procedures that at best are 'a little much' and at worst are client harassment," said another. "There appears to be a great deal of punitiveness on the part of the agency," said a third. "I'm glad I'm not poor and on aid in Florence County."

AMONG THE MORE INTERESTING ASPECTS OF THE STATE INVESTIGATION is what it did not investigate. For instance, it did not look into charges that welfare recipients were coerced into abortions or sterilizations.

This was the subject of a civil suit heard in federal court in September 1986. The suit, brought by attorney Hatch, charged that a young woman named Margarette Coffin was pressured into having an abortion by Florence County social worker Rich Kallman. Kallman denies there was any coercion ("abortion is a very personal matter; it was up to her to decide," he tells *Isthmus*), and after nearly a week of testimony it took the jury less than 90 minutes to agree.

Left unexamined by the state were a number of similar allegations. Former social worker Grabski, for instance, recounts being ordered by Folz to inform one client that the county would pay for her medical expense to have a baby only if she agreed to a subsequent tubal ligation. The woman, says Grabski, refused, seeking medical assistance elsewhere.

Also not investigated were charges that child abuse and neglect complaints are used as a means of harassment. The omission is especially interesting in light of Kallman's remark that one reason the department owns a paper shredder is to destroy sensitive material dealing with child abuse and neglect cases. According to Mary Dibble, a specialist with the DHSS's Bureau of Children, Youth and Families, county agencies are required to retain documentation on all child protection investigations.

The final DHSS report does address charges that participants in the county's Occupational and Skills Training (OST) program were coerced. Participation in this program was supposed to be completely voluntary. But county welfare recipients received letters stating that unless they reported to their assigned county work crew, they would be prosecuted for nonsupport of their children.

One such letter, addressed to James Marefke from social worker Robbin Ghere, warns: "I will be referring your case to the district attorney on Feb. 7, 1985, unless you notify me ... that you have become employed or that you are willing to participate in the Opportunity and Skills Training Program." (With legally constituted workfare programs, the only permissible sanction is reduction or denial of benefits.)

During this period, as many as 40 individuals worked on various OST work crews in Florence County. Participants say they were all required to work 32 hours a week, regardless of the amount of benefits received. Marefke, for instance, received $201 a month plus $45 to $89 in food stamps, meaning he was compensated at a rate of less than $2.25 an hour.

OST participants performed a number of tasks, some under contracts with the U.S. Forest Service and other agencies. Marefke says he drove a bus for senior citizens, despite the fact that his driver's license had been revoked. Participant Danny Hartman says his tasks included moving toxic chemicals and digging up live electric cable with a metal shovel in the rain. "They didn't give a shit," says Hartman. "Free labor, what the hell."

Mike Boettcher, who began as an OST participant in October 1983 and later became a paid foreman for one of the largest workfare crews, began each day picking up crew members who needed rides. When he reported difficulties getting some men to come along, he says he was told by OST coordinator Dennis Peterson, "If necessary, get the sheriff and force them to go to work at gunpoint."

On another occasion, when a tour group that included county board members and State Sen. Lloyd Kincaid (D-Crandon) visited his work site, Boettcher says he was told by Folz, "Whatever you do, be sure the men don't tell these people that we're forcing them to work." Program participant Mark DeGrave, who was within earshot, confirms the remark.

"They forced them to work, then sold their services, and no one knows where the money went," says attorney Hatch, who would like to represent program participants in a lawsuit against the county. But OST coordinator Peterson denies that any wrongdoing took place. "Have you read the review that the state had done?" he asks. "The state cleared up all of that. Our office was cleared."

THE FIRST DRAFT OF THE STATE'S "REVIEW OF THE FLORENCE COUNTY Department of Social Services" is dated Sept. 2, 1986. The final report is dated Feb. 2, 1987. At least two other versions were produced in-between.

Although similar in organization, the early and final drafts differ dramatically in size, content and tone. In the final draft, the state lists 30 findings together with its recommendations and the agency response. In every case, the agency response is: "Agency agrees."

Among the findings included in the early drafts but omitted from the final review: "The director actually spends less than half his working time on appropriate agency activities"; "The disorder of the case records is extreme"; and "In one instance the director admitted to harassment of a client by delaying benefits."

The early drafts also state that clients expressed fears of retribution from social service staff; that incomplete documentation in some cases "makes accurate review impossible"; and that "case records contain a wide variety of information about clients including sheriff's reports, allegations from citizens, etc., which do not appear to have a direct bearing on the determination of eligibility and benefits."

In addition, an entire section on general relief – state-mandated emergency assistance to the poor – was pulled from the final report. Among the findings regarding that program in early drafts was that 21 of the 27 cases reviewed, or 78 percent, "contained decisions in conflict with state statute or had incomplete or no documentation." The section also listed four county general relief policies that apparently violated state law, including that "all able-bodied adults living with their parents are ineligible for general relief" and "couples living together without benefit of marriage will not be eligible."

The decision to drop general relief from the report was made by Jim Meyer, who was appointed administrator of the Division of Community Services by Gov. Tommy Thompson. In a written response to *Isthmus*, Meyer explains: "The state did not contribute to county general relief for the period of time in question, the department did not have general relief guidelines or standards for the period of time in question, and the department had no oversight regulations or policy."

Assistant administrator Gerald Born, who coordinated the investigation, concurs. The state's control over county relief was "strictly advisory," says Born, a former Madison alderman. "We thought this advice would be helpful to them, and since they didn't think it was we decided not to fight about it."

WHY DID THE STATE TAKE SO LONG TO RELEASE ITS REPORT, AND WHY WAS it substantially changed?

Attorney Hatch thinks he knows. "Word was out that there was enough out there that if it were to all hit the fan, it would be very embarrassing to [then-governor] Tony Earl," he says. "It was hard enough for Tony Earl to defend his welfare program. For the Earl administration to have taken a department of welfare to task was just a suicide thing."

Former DHSS secretary Linda Reivitz scoffs at the suggestion. "Anybody who makes that judgment just isn't aware of how small a piece Florence County is," she says. Both Reivitz and Born say that showing the report to the county to give it a chance to correct errors and present its side of the story was part of the state's intention from the start. Meyer believes the report was initially drafted as it was – "hard-nosed, more allegation than fact" – to leverage a settlement. And Born suggests this strategy was a success: "We were most interested in getting them to proceed in a certain fashion, and I think we did that."

According to a DHSS monitoring report dated April 29, Florence County has implemented, or made progress toward implementing, all 30 of the recommendations spelled out in the report. But has it? One of the recommendations is that "OST staff should meet with state staff early in 1987 to thoroughly review all forms of communication with clients.... A problem-resolution system should be developed. Toward this end the state will make available Mr. Tad Mengesha who coordinates the food stamp workfare program for the department."

The monitoring report states that the "agency has had contact with Tad Mengesha," who spent a day in Florence County. But any notion of developing a problem-resolution system is news to Mengesha, who thought his only task was to make sure the program complied with federal requirements; it did. "I guess somebody suggested without my even knowing that I would be reviewing the program," he says.

Similarly, another recommendation calls on the agency to "discontinue use of the director's rubber stamp in the place of his required review and signature" in protective service cases. Says the monitoring report, "Agency has discontinued the use of the director's rubber stamp signature." But *Isthmus* has obtained a copy of a letter in a protective service case dated April 9, 1987, in which the director's rubber stamp signature was clearly used.

"They've never apologized and they haven't stopped," asserts agency critic Prohaska, explaining why he will continue to fight. "Their only concern is, 'How can we keep it up with them watching us?'"

The other side is also unhappy. According to social worker Kallman, "the entire department has been unfairly accused of a number of things."

CONSIDERING THE NUMBER OF THINGS THE DEPARTMENT HAS BEEN ACCUSED of, Kallman's claim is no doubt true. And yet it seems clear that something terrible has gone on here, a conditioning of fear that has not yet been purged.

"The truth hasn't come out at all," says a local resident, who in the next breath adds, "Never while I'm living here, never while I have children here, will I ever tell what I know."

As Hatch sees it, the crux of the problem is the state's traditional unwillingness to involve itself in county affairs. Rural counties, he argues, can pretty much do as they please, especially when it comes to matters that do not provoke a lot of popular concern – such as the way people on public assistance are treated.

A state DHSS official familiar with the Florence County investigation agrees. "I think what's really going on is something nobody wants to deal with, and that is ... the state/county relationship and the tradition of local control," he says. "There is really no will on the part of the department to come down hard on the counties. In any situation where you have 'Who do you believe?' the bureaucrats are always going to come down on the side of each other."

Within the next three years, food stamp workfare will be mandatory in each of Wisconsin's 72 counties. The Thompson administration is pioneering other workfare programs in counties throughout the state. The agency in charge of making sure these programs are administered properly is the state DHSS.

What are the lessons of Florence County? DHSS quality control reviewer Barbara Zellmer, in a letter to Born in response to the first draft report ("nothing in this report should be deleted," she advised), offered these reflections: "It would be too simplistic to assess Florence County staff or regional and central office staff all the blame. It is too complex for that. The blame is shared. I hope there will be no cop-outs.

"We found out about the mess, examined the mess, and have made suggestions to clean the mess up. Whether it will be cleaned up remains to be seen. But those are not the only issues. We have to look at how it got started to insure that nothing like this ever happens again.... If we don't start looking for root causes, and some preventive measures, God knows what's down the road."

JUNE 5, 1987

Duane "George" Folz resigned as Florence County's director of human services in December 1988 but continued to head its Economic Development Commission until 2004.

A Reasonable Doubt

I t reads like a mystery, but with a distressing lack of resolution only a work of nonfiction could contain. It has the elements of a suspense novel, but no heroes or heroines. Perhaps it is simply a tragedy.

Isthmus has learned that D. Kaye Gapen, dean of the UW–Madison's General Library System, was the principal suspect in an investigation last year by UW and state investigators into the hitherto unreported theft of $2,905 in cash from the proceeds of a library-sponsored book sale. (Checks totaling $15,626 were also taken, but were later returned via campus mail.)

A web of circumstance linked Gapen to the crime. The state, however, ultimately opted against prosecuting the case on grounds that the evidence was not sufficient to establish guilt beyond a reasonable doubt. According to a Justice Department memorandum dated Dec. 7, 1989, one year to the day after an envelope containing the money disappeared:

"Dean Gapen had access to the money and would have had sufficient knowledge to know that it was available for the taking. In addition, her actions ... were consistent with her attempting to cover up the theft. We would also be able to show that Gapen lacks skills as a money manager and was in tight financial straits at the time of the theft." (Gapen's skills as a money manager have recently been called into question for another reason: the 15-library system's projected $800,000 deficit for the current fiscal year.)

The Justice Department memo also notes "certain inconsistencies" in statements made by library staffer Deborah Reilly, who supervised the book sale, that might have frustrated efforts to prosecute Gapen. Assistant Attorney General Steven Tinker wrote that although he did not believe Reilly took the money, "we would not be able to disprove [this] beyond a reasonable doubt...."

Gapen, 45, became a prime suspect in the case following a routine check of bank records. UW investigators found that on Dec. 9, 1988, two days after the envelope was to have been delivered to the UW Foundation, Gapen deposited $1,940 in cash into her checking account – in denominations that "closely matched, as nearly as could be determined," those in the stolen envelope. This money was then used to make a $2,038 mortgage payment.

Prior to this deposit, Gapen did not have enough money in her account to pay her mortgage. Indeed, Gapen, who admitted to investigators that her financial condition was "precarious," had fallen behind in her payments. Bank personnel had contacted her about this situation on Nov. 15, and she promised full payment by Dec. 1. But no check was issued until Dec. 10, the day after the deposit.

"It was entirely a coincidence and that's all it was," says Gapen, who will receive a salary of $92,475 for the current academic year. "I'm innocent, and it was a coming together of circumstances that nobody can control."

As for her fortuitous cash deposit, Gapen told investigators ... but wait, we're getting ahead of the story.

IN JANUARY 1988, UW ALUMNUS RICHARD STOCKWELL OF NEILLSVILLE, Wisconsin, donated 8,700 books from his collection to the UW Foundation, the university's fundraising arm. The books were appraised by the Memorial

Library, which picked out the volumes it wanted to keep and sponsored an auction to sell the rest.

That auction was held Dec. 1 through Dec. 4 of 1988 and was overseen by Reilly, the library system's external relations coordinator. Reilly brought proceeds from the sale home each night and on Monday, Dec. 5, counted the money with her secretary, Catherine Shapiro. The agreed-upon total: $18,531, including $2,905 in cash.

On Dec. 7, Reilly and Shapiro prepared the proceeds for the UW Foundation. The money and checks were placed in an envelope, which the foundation was informed would be delivered by courier.

Here's where the inconsistencies creep in. Reilly told the campus Department of Police and Security that she set the envelope on a counter in the duplicating room when she was interrupted by a phone call, and could not remember putting it in the out-basket for courier pickup. Later, when interviewed by Special Agent Elizabeth Feagles of the Justice Department's Division of Criminal Investigation, Reilly definitely remembered having put it in the basket.

In addition, when the theft was first reported to the campus police, Reilly placed the amount of missing cash at $905, not $2,905. Confronted later with this discrepancy, Reilly said Shapiro had simply forgotten to put a 2 in front of the 9 – an explanation the secretary disputed and Assistant Attorney General Tinker concluded "did not hold water."

Reilly insists these inconsistencies are insubstantial. It was, she says, "a very natural thing to [initially] doubt that I had placed the envelope in the basket." To this day, "I can't swear I put the envelope in the basket, although to the best of my knowledge I did."

As for the $2,000 discrepancy, Reilly says the book sale was "a minor project" compared to other endeavors at the time. "When it comes right down to it," she says, "there is no reason why anyone should have remembered the breakdown between the cash and checks. Only the total was important."

At any rate, it didn't become known that the money was missing until Dec. 9, two days after the delivery was supposed to have taken place, when Reilly received a phone call from the UW Foundation. Reilly, whom Shapiro described to investigators as being very alarmed, began to search the office. She told Gapen about the disappearance, and was purportedly advised against contacting the police. According to Feagles' report, "Reilly [says she] felt that Gapen was more annoyed than concerned because she seemed to feel that the envelope would show up."

On Dec. 19, Reilly told Gapen that she intended to ask the issuers of the stolen checks to write new ones; it was then that Gapen decided to call the police. The next day, after the campus cops interviewed Reilly, Gapen and Shapiro, a university envelope directed to Reilly arrived in the campus mail. In it were the missing checks; the $2,905 in cash was gone.

FROM THE START, UW INVESTIGATORS WERE CONVINCED THAT THE THIEF was a library employee — in part because such a person had easier access to the envelope and also because an outsider probably would not have bothered to return the stolen checks.

Early in 1989, Gapen, Reilly, Shapiro and the courier who was supposed to have delivered the money were all asked to sign bank-disclosure forms and submit to polygraph tests. All signed the forms, and Reilly, Shapiro and the courier agreed to take tests.

But Gapen drew the line on the polygraph — not only for herself but for her employees. A memo from Gapen to Reilly dated Feb. 26 states: "Do not take a ploygrahp [sic] test under my orders.... This has all been both demeaning and pointless." (Gapen later denied ordering Reilly not to take the test. Rather her point, as Feagles phrased it in a report, was that "Reilly was not to assume that Gapen had required her to take a polygraph examination.")

If Gapen's opposition to the polygraph — which she says is unreliable and inadmissible in court — aroused suspicions, the inspection of her bank records drove them home. In addition to the $1,940 deposit, UW investigators found that Gapen, contrary to what she had reported, maintained two auxiliary checking accounts in other states and had a history of bouncing checks.

Among these, ironically, was a $100 check Gapen had written to the book sale. The check was returned by the UW Foundation and professedly called Gapen's to attention by secretary Shapiro "on more than one occasion." Last June, six months after the sale, the UW investigator reported that Gapen's invalid check "remains in the secretary's desk and is a source of embarrassment, at least to the secretary."

UW Chancellor Donna Shalala and attorneys were briefed on the investigation. In late June, campus police and security chief Ralph Hanson and acting vice chancellor for legal affairs John Tallman both wrote the state Justice Department, asking for help with, as Tallman put it, "an unusually sensitive matter." That led to Special Agent Feagles being tapped, with most of her work being done from mid-July to the end of August last year.

Feagles interviewed about a dozen people, some more than once, and obtained numerous records, many of which concern Gapen's finances. Feagles found ample evidence to support Gapen's earlier assertion, proffered "several times" to UW investigators, that she was not "a good money manager."

Between July 1988 and February 1989, Gapen overdrew on her Madison checking account 11 times, each time incurring a $10 penalty. Between January 1988 and August 1989, she was hit five times with $59.96 late-payment penalties on her home mortgage. Feagles said Gapen admitted having "very large debts to approximately 10 different credit card companies." On her American Express Platinum Card alone, Gapen's minimum monthly payment at the time of the theft was $540; she missed her payment for December 1988.

Late last year, the UW's library system – with a current annual budget of $14.2 million and 300 fulltime employees – was found to be running $800,000 in the red. Gapen cited unexpected equipment purchases and unavoidable increases in staff and salaries. But the Library Assembly, a group representing campus librarians, was not consoled. "The suddenness and extent of this budget crisis have serious implications for the quality of our working lives," the group wrote Gapen. "How could the deficit reach such proportions without anyone noticing?"

On Aug. 28, 1989, Feagles and another special agent interviewed Gapen at the UW. They asked how she happened to deposit $1,940 in cash on Dec. 9, after missing earlier deadlines for paying her mortgage. Gapen said she had been awaiting "a $5,000 to $8,000 tax return" and other checks; when these did not arrive in time, she tapped into a cash reserve she had been saving for Christmas.

According to Feagles' report, Gapen "went on to explain that she attempts to save $100 to $200 a month by stashing her daily change in a canvas bag which she keeps in a bookcase at home." The agents noted that Gapen's deposit consisted of 20-, 50- and 100-dollar bills, which hardly squares with ordinary definitions of "change." States Feagles in her report, "Gapen conceded that occasionally she took some of the money to the bank, had it consolidated into large bills, then took it back home and put it in the bag."

In his memorandum of Dec. 7, Assistant Attorney General Tinker concluded that his department "would not be able to disprove Dean Gapen's explanation beyond a reasonable doubt." Hence, he concluded that, in the absence of new information, the case should be set aside.

HERE'S WHERE THE STORY GETS REALLY STRANGE. IN A LETTER TO TINKER dated March 26 of this year, Gapen's attorney, Bruce Rosen of Madison, said his client was "not content with your decision not to prosecute her for the alleged theft.... It is imperative to have her name, reputation and good standing in the community cleared of any false innuendo."

Thereupon Rosen made a "formal" albeit admittedly "unusual" request to have Gapen submit to, of all things, a polygraph examination. If Gapen passed the test, Rosen wanted Tinker to "issue a statement exonerating her for responsibility for this incident."

Tinker, in his reply of March 29, flatly declined, asserting "I have serious questions about the reliability of these exams and of your client's involvement in this theft." He also expressed surprise at the request, noting Gapen's earlier refusal to take a polygraph "and her suggestion, if not an order, to her staff not to take one."

Gapen says her initial qualms about taking the polygraph were overridden by the desire to clear her name: "There are only so many ways to say you are innocent." Still, she has no plans to submit, as Tinker suggested, to a polygraph sans the conditions stipulated by Rosen.

Rosen did not return phone calls. Melany Newby, UW vice chancellor of legal affairs, refused to comment and blocked efforts to obtain comment from Chancellor Shalala. Gapen says she has not been sanctioned by the university or suffered any negative consequences as a result of the probe – "and properly so."

According to Rosen's letter to Tinker, "the rumors and innuendo that appear to be circulating within the community motivate us to make this request of you." What rumors and innuendo is this referring to? That statement, says Gapen, "was referring to the possible outcome of what would happen if somebody like you were to write an article."

APRIL 17, 1990

Kaye Gapen, embroiled in further controversy over an alleged conflict of interest (an internal probe cleared her of wrongdoing), resigned from the UW–Madison in September 1990. She went on to become library director at Case Western Reserve University and to start her own consulting company – Northern Lights – specializing in digital information management. In December 2007, she was named vice president of academic affairs and provost at Trinity College in Washington, D.C., a position she left in June 2010.

Adam Korbitz, 1991. Photo by Brent Nicastro

Obsession

This February, 10 days after attending his daughter's wedding in Madison, Melvin Veloon of Rubicon, Wis., received a letter that began: "I do not want to shock you, but your daughter Heidi is in the greatest of danger. You must help her."

Veloon, who has a heart condition, summoned his wife, Elnora. The letter said the Veloons' new son-in-law, a UW–Madison graduate student from India named Girish (pronounced Ga-reesh) Bhat, was "in the U.S. illegally" and had married Heidi in order to "fraudulently obtain residency status."

By participating in this arrangement, the letter warned, "Heidi is committing a very serious crime and could go to prison." Furthermore, she was at risk because "Mr. Bhat is a violent and dangerous man." Thus the marriage should be "annulled immediately."

The letter was signed, "A concerned friend." Elnora Veloon reached a different conclusion: "It looks like the work of a jealous girlfriend."

Also enclosed was an ominous array of information, including a list of Bhat's "known associates" (names, addresses, driver's licenses and Social Security numbers), the newlyweds' marriage certificate, and even Bhat's supposedly confidential visa and passport numbers.

Police later learned this letter was composed – and data sheets compiled – by Adam C. Korbitz, 27, a former military officer, federal agent and licensed private investigator who has taken up the cause of Michelle Ninneman, a Madison woman who once dated Bhat.

Ninneman, a 24-year-old UW student, charges that Bhat has been harassing her for nearly two years. Bhat, 31, says these accusations are baseless. Korbitz, a first-year UW law student, believes Ninneman.

The letter to the Veloons was part of a week-long spree of harassment admitted to by Korbitz, an earnest, trusting fellow who calls Bhat "the most frighteningly evil man I have ever encountered." Korbitz also stalked Bhat, made threatening calls, sent cryptic letters and emerged as a suspect in mail tampering and other crimes. But the Dane County District Attorney's Office has refused to press charges, in part because it is already prosecuting Bhat based on allegations made by Ninneman.

Korbitz, currently the subject of a UW anti-harassment probe, is continuing his war on Bhat, primarily through well-written and seemingly well-documented letters loaded with hyperbole, innuendo and unproven accusations. (There is, for instance, no credible evidence that Bhat is in the country illegally.) His goal: to destroy Girish Bhat's life. That is, to break up his marriage, cost him his career, get him thrown out of school, in jail, and/or out of the country.

"He's acting as a judge and jury," complains Bhat of Korbitz, whom he has never met. "What if he's wrong? He's never even thought of that."

GIRISH VENKATARAMAN BHAT WAS BORN IN BELGAUM, INDIA, AND received a degree from Christian Medical College in 1982. He worked for a year as an apprentice surgeon and for 18 months as a senior research fellow. In July 1985 he came to Madison to pursue a Ph.D. in cancer research, and is today one of four graduate students under the tutelage of Howard Temin, winner of the 1975 Nobel Prize in medicine.

Brilliant, good-humored and handsome, Bhat wears his emotional immaturity on his sleeve. He says he never even dated until June 1986, when he was 27. That first relationship lasted a year and a half. Bhat and Ninneman began dating in April 1989.

Bhat says the couple dated until September, broke up, got back together in February 1990 and broke up for good last May. But Ninneman claims – and Korbitz believes – that her romantic involvement with Bhat lasted less than two months. After that, she says she became unnerved by his possessiveness and broke things off, but he followed her everywhere and pestered her with calls and letters.

Early in the relationship, Ninneman was in a restaurant with her friend Victoria Thomas, voicing her suspicions that Bhat followed her. Just then, Thomas says, Bhat walked in and admonished Ninneman because he hadn't known where she was. Thomas witnessed similar episodes later on.

It's clear from Bhat's letters to Ninneman, sometimes more than one a day, that he was obsessed with her. One written on June 10, 1989, begins: "I know I'm imposing on you. I know I'm driving you crazy. I know I'm putting pressure on you. I know I may be destroying what little affection you have left for me."

By this time, Ninneman says she wanted nothing more to do with Bhat ("I told him more than 100 times to leave me alone"), but agreed to meet him on a few occasions only in order to get him to stop. During an interview, Ninneman, her voice quaking, her eyes red from crying, says Bhat frightened her and "wore me down to a point where I had no self-esteem."

Even after Bhat allegedly violated her when she let him into her apartment, Ninneman says she was too "brain-warped by him" to call police. Korbitz, comforting Ninnemann by rubbing her neck, chimes in that Bhat is "the master of the mind-fuck."

IN THE EARLY MORNING HOURS OF APRIL 25, 1990, NINNEMAN SAYS SHE was walking home from a party – "not drunk at all" – when Bhat drove by and offered to take her home. When Bhat drove to his Ingersoll Street residence instead, Ninneman says she bolted into the house to call police, but Bhat slammed her against a wall and "hit me so hard my feet picked up." Then, as Bhat allegedly pinned her to the ground, Ninneman says she scratched him in self-defense.

Bhat's version is different. He says Ninneman, "totally drunk," had called him for a ride, then kept opening the car door as he tried to take her home. So he drove instead to his house, whereupon she allegedly broke his glasses, scratched his face from behind and, inside the house, began striking him. Bhat says he slapped Ninneman once to make her stop. Police, summoned by neighbors, arrested Bhat for battery.

In a statement written the following day, Bhat's then roommate, Leo Ocola, who was home at the time, affirmed that Ninneman had called Bhat for a ride and that the couple argued loudly when they arrived at the house: "I heard Girish telling Michelle to stop hitting him." There was a thud, and Ocola found Ninneman on the floor. Bhat's face was badly scratched: his glasses lay broken in the car.

According to Bhat, Ninneman hit him often; his letters contain many references to her allegedly violent behavior. But while faulting Ninneman's conduct, Bhat says he loved her "unconditionally."

Tony Minardi, Bhat's roommate from August 1989 to August 1990 – long after Ninneman claims to have stopped dating Bhat – recalls one incident in Bhat's room. "I heard the hitting going on and him saying, 'Michelle, stop hitting me,' and her saying 'I can't stop hitting you.'"

Sue Evans, Bhat's roommate from September to December 1989 – when even Bhat says the pair had split up – remembers warning Bhat about his behavior, which included checking up on Ninneman and leaving soup by her door. The next day, Nov. 30, Ninneman filed a police complaint.

But also during this period, Evans says Ninneman stayed over on at least one occasion and left "sappy" messages on the answering machine: "He would try to break it off and she would start it up again." As Evans sees the situation, "Here's two really emotionally retarded people. They didn't know how to handle themselves."

After the April 25 incident, Ninneman wrote a letter asking that the charges against Bhat be dropped. She admitted to being drunk, calling Bhat for a ride, and initiating the fight. The charges were dismissed last August on the prosecutor's motion. Today, she says Bhat "basically forced me" into making that statement.

But Ninneman made the same admissions to Bhat's friend Sonia Kandathil. Moreover, it seems clear from that conversation, which Kandathil secretly recorded, that Ninneman hoped to keep dating Bhat. "I want to work on it," she said of their relationship, which she described as "really sick."

ON MAY 17, 1990, NINNEMAN PETITIONED FOR A RESTRAINING ORDER against Bhat, claiming he continued to harass her – including by ringing her doorbell and pounding on her bedroom window in the middle of the night.

Judge Moria Krueger granted the petition in a hearing on May 25, ordering Bhat not to contact Ninneman or come within 50 feet of her. Since that time, Bhat says he has not sought or desired contact with Ninneman. But Ninneman says Bhat is still in pursuit. All through last summer, she says, he followed her about, though generally at a distance of more than 50 feet. She also reports getting dead-air phone calls in the middle of the night.

On Oct. 29, 1990, Ninneman reported five separate violations of the restraining order. On that day, she was sitting at a table with friends at Steep & Brew on State Street when Bhat came in and sat at a table near her. Later that night, she charged, Bhat made three phone calls to her home. Ninneman also reported that four days earlier Bhat had followed her at the Memorial Union.

Bhat admits visiting Steep & Brew that night but says he never even saw Ninneman. He denies following her or making any of the calls: "Why would I want to violate the restraining order and bring trouble on myself?"

But why would Ninneman make such allegations if they weren't true? Bhat speculates Ninneman is jealous of his relationship with Veloon. He notes it was exactly one week after his Feb. 5 wedding that "all hell broke loose."

On Feb. 12, Bhat found two of his car tires punctured. That same day, someone posing as Bhat canceled his phone service and had his mail forwarded to a cemetery. Two days later, there was a message on Bhat's answering machine: "Mr. Bhat ... Be careful what you do." The next day someone left unsettling messages for Heidi at her old apartment. One said, "I followed Girish home last night. Tell him he isn't a very smart man."

At 10:59 that evening of Feb. 15, Bhat fielded a call at home from "a concerned friend" who told him to show up at the Plaza bar on Henry Street, Bhat's usual haunt, at 11:30. Bhat and his friend Minardi arrived, but no one approached them. Later they found a note on Bhat's car: "Mr. Bhat: You were 23 minutes late. We know what you've done. We are watching you."

At 1:42 a.m., Bhat got a message that was later traced to a pay phone: "You looked surprised ... when you and Tony saw our note. Oh, and by the way, where is Heidi?"

On Feb. 19, Bhat and Veloon arrived at the UW police station for a prearranged conference just as Ninneman was leaving with a white male companion. That night, Bhat and Minardi entered the Plaza and saw Ninneman and the same man – Korbitz – who immediately called 911 to report that Bhat was violating the restraining order. Minardi took his picture; Bhat left the bar.

The officer dispatched to the scene found Ninneman, restraining order in hand, with Adam Korbitz, but said that because Bhat had walked out no violation occurred. Both Ninneman and Korbitz are angered by this. Says Korbitz, "There's no question in my mind [Bhat] was looking for Michelle that night."

Later that evening Bhat received a call traced to the Plaza in which a disguised male voice howls: "Fuck you. We are at the Plaza. Fuck you. We are drinking beer, bastard. You can't be here. Fuck you. Fuck you. Bye-bye...."

The next day, Bhat received a threatening letter at work ("I am the mystery man who has been haunting you"). The letter was signed Richard Kimball, from TV's "The Fugitive." The same name was signed to a personal ad in the *Daily Cardinal* congratulating Bhat and Veloon on their marriage.

WHILE ALL ON THIS WAS GOING ON, BHAT WAS THE SUBJECT OF TWO requested restraining orders. On Feb. 19, his first girlfriend, Joanne Hatley (not her real name), sought a restraining order against him in Dane County court. On Feb. 27 the order was granted – based largely on allegations regarding Bhat's lovesick conduct in 1988.

Bhat's lawyer unsuccessfully argued that Hatley was acting at Korbitz's instigation. Hatley refused to be interviewed for this article but conveyed through Korbitz that she did not want her name used. Korbitz, meanwhile, has been using her name freely in letters to university and law-enforcement officials, even providing lurid representations of her sexual relationship with Bhat.

On Feb. 20, Korbitz also sought a restraining order against Bhat, citing Bhat's arrival at the police station and his appearance at the Plaza. Touting his credentials as a former federal agent, Korbitz called Bhat "a cunning, violent and dangerous man" who posed "a very real threat to my safety." (Korbitz admits that Bhat has never threatened him, nor has he ever seen Bhat harass Ninneman.) The petition was denied when Korbitz failed to appear in court.

Bhat and the Veloons – Melvin, Heidi and sister Holly – met with Madison police officer Bernardo Bernal on Feb. 22, to complain about Korbitz. The next day Korbitz called police to "straighten out the situation."

Korbitz, interviewed by Bernal and Detective Lou Gebler, confessed to most of the items on Bhat's characteristically meticulous list of "incidents of harassment" – except for the most serious ones: puncturing Bhat's tires, stopping his phone service, transferring his mail and making the "Fuck you" call. He even gave Bernal copies of letters he had sent the Immigration and

Naturalization Service (INS) and mentioned the "neighborhood watch" posters bearing Bhat's picture that he put up near Ninneman's home.

According to Bernal's report, Korbitz wanted to "intimidate and harass" Bhat because he believed Ninneman's allegations against him. Bernal then called Ninneman to set up an appointment. This purportedly drew a call to Bernal from Margot Ninneman, Michelle's stepmother, advising him to "lay off" the case. Margot Ninneman is a Madison police officer. Michelle's father, Terry Ninneman, is the village of Shorewood's chief of police.

Apparently undaunted, Bernal and Gebler recommended that Korbitz be charged with harassment and unlawful use of the telephone. But Assistant District Attorney Fred Erhardt declined, professedly because the offenses involved only civil forfeitures and because "we've got an impending prosecution against the victim." Bhat is facing five misdemeanor counts of violating Ninneman's restraining order against him. Erhardt instead recommended that Bhat get a restraining order against Korbitz.

What does Detective Gebler think of this decision? "Look, I've got to work with the DA," he says. "I don't want to go into that."

ADAM CHASE KORBITZ, THE SON OF A PHYSICIAN (HIS FATHER) AND A

hospital head nurse, was born in Monona, attended Monona Grove High, and received a B.A. in anthropology from the UW–Madison in 1985. He served as an officer in the U.S. Navy, where he says he "investigated offenses involving naval personnel" aboard the U.S.S. Peleliu, and as a special agent with the Defense Investigative Service in Madison, part of the U.S. Department of Defense.

In 1989, Korbitz left the military to work as a private detective in Madison. Although his license is still valid, he shut down his practice last fall to become a full-time law student.

Korbitz and Ninneman met in late November last year and became friends, largely because of his interest in her tale of harassment. Says Ninneman, "He's the first person I spoke to [who] made me feel somebody cares and wants to help."

Soon Korbitz began gathering information on Bhat from public records – and elsewhere. Recently, he obtained records from Bhat's medical college in India by posing as a prospective employer. "Did I lie to obtain it?" he asks of this record-culling method, for which Bhat was billed. "Damn right."

Korbitz says he got Bhat's visa and passbook number by walking into the UW foreign students office and asking to see Bhat's file because "this guy is harassing a friend of mine and I think he's in the country illegally." UW officials say all office workers are carefully trained to treat such records as private. Campus police Detective Gary Moore investigated, but concluded there was no way to prove that Korbitz had done anything wrong.

But what really turned Korbitz into a vigilante was his perusal of Bhat's letters to Ninneman: "I felt like I stood on the edge of the abyss and stared into the mouth of hell." Most of the letters amply illustrate the obsessive nature of Bhat's affection, but it was an atypical dispatch, dated June 15, 1989, that most aroused Korbitz. In it, Bhat claims to be a Satanist who admires Hitler, thinks all women are "sluts and whores," enjoys incest, is high on marijuana "24 hours of the day," tortures his laboratory animals and as a surgeon in India used to murder his patients.

The only thing is, the letter is transparently facetious. Bhat says he wrote it because Ninneman was always accusing him of terrible things, and thus he thought a tongue-in-cheek confession might pave the way to her heart. Korbitz, however, solemnly asserts: "I have no reason to doubt the statements Bhat makes about himself.'"

In recent weeks, Korbitz has sent Bhat's letter to Dr. Temin, McArdle Lab senior scientist Isle Riegel, the dean of students office, the new head of the UW campus police, the Dane County District Attorney's Office, the FBI, the INS, INTERPOL, Bhat's attorney, Sens. Robert Kasten and Herb Kohl, and Rep. Scott Klug. When Riegel replied that Temin "feels that this matter is not his business," Korbitz went through the roof.

"Dr. Temin does not feel it is his business that his graduate student, his researcher, his university employee has threatened to rape, torture, mutilate and murder another university student?" he exclaimed in his letter to Klug. "I am astounded."

So is Dr. Riegel — at Korbitz's crusade against Bhat, whom she has known for six years. "I think Girish clearly used some bad judgment in his dealings with women when he first came into this country," she says. "But I don't think Girish would want to hurt a soul."

Heidi Veloon agrees. "Who does he think he is?" she demands of Korbitz, calling Bhat "the least violent man I've known in my life."

Meanwhile, Korbitz is working on other fronts. In a March 9 letter to Detective Dawn Johnson of the Dane County Sheriff's Department, he discusses Bhat's sexual "predispositions," quotes from his love poems to Ninneman and speculates that he worships Satan — all in an attempt to implicate Bhat in the recent murder of a woman at Goose Lake. Korbitz has also written the FBI to suggest Bhat as a suspect in a March 1989 bombing in San Diego.

ALTHOUGH BHAT AND KORBITZ WOULD NO DOUBT BE REPULSED AT THE very idea that they have anything in common, it's true they both believe firmly in their own blamelessness.

Korbitz crows that the District Attorney's Office has "cleared me of any criminal conduct" regarding what he now calls "a few harmless pranks" – his week-long spree of harassment against Bhat. And he's furious that the UW dean of students office is now investigating him for possibly violating the UW's controversial anti-harassment rule, the penalties for which range from a reprimand to expulsion.

The real issue, he insists, is Bhat's violence toward women – and the fact that the system has allowed him to go unpunished for too long.

Bhat, meanwhile, blames his troubles all on Ninneman, and even suggests she timed her allegations to frustrate the expected June completion of his Ph.D. (In recent weeks, Ninneman has twice showed up at the Plaza when Bhat was present. On April 4, *Isthmus* contributing writer W.P. Norton watched her stare at and walk past Bhat, then leave after a few minutes. Last Saturday night Ninneman stayed longer, and Bhat left the bar.)

"There's absolutely nothing to say I've harassed this woman except her word – nothing," Bhat exclaims, noting that Korbitz has not been punished at all. "If I had done or confessed to a portion of the things he's done or confessed to, I would find my ass in jail."

That may yet come to pass. Bhat has refused to plea bargain away the charges that he violated his restraining order against Ninneman. A trial date has been set for June 27. If convicted of all five counts, Bhat faces a maximum $5,000 fine and 450 days behind bars.

APRIL 19, 1991

In December 1991, Girish Bhat pled no contest to a single reduced charge of noncriminal disorderly conduct, and paid a small fine. He did not receive a Ph.D. from the UW, in part due to the turmoil of this case; he and Heidi remain in Madison, where she is a social worker. Michelle Ninneman, with a new married name, still lives in the Madison area. Adam Korbitz got his law degree from the UW–Madison in 1993 and is now government relations coordinator for the State Bar of Wisconsin. He describes himself on his blog profile as a "sometime raconteur and occasional astronomer," with a particular interest in "the search for extraterrestrial intelligence."

Inside Turtle Lake casino, 1994. Photo by Bill Lueders

Indian Takers

In 1987, when Lewis Taylor was first elected to the St. Croix Tribal Council, he had a clear goal: "to bring this tribe out of poverty." Back then, the St. Croix owned almost nothing except a few patches of land; today, in 1994, their casino gaming operations net upwards of $30 million a year. But in the tribal community near Hertel, Wisconsin, where Taylor lives, evidence of this newfound wealth is hard to find.

The tribal office is so sparsely furnished that it's hard to imagine the St. Croix have a dime. A pile of garbage decorates the main road, attended by a large dog that chases passing cars. Taylor, chain-smoking, shows off a field of old government-donated vehicles used for contract construction jobs and touts a pitiful plan for economic development: a convenience store to "take advantage of" the tribe's partial exemption from the federal cigarette tax.

"We're proud to no longer be dependent on handouts for survival," says Taylor, chairman of the five-member council. Instead, the St. Croix – like dozens of other tribes that today run 220 Indian gaming operations in more than 20 states – are dependent on gambling, an activity that by its very nature promises more than it delivers. And, like many tribal players, the St. Croix are coming up short.

No one disputes that the Chippewa band has derived substantial benefit from casino operations; about half of its scattered 1,400 members (those with enough St. Croix blood) now receive $1,000 monthly distributions. But the biggest jackpot winners have been the St. Croix's partners, Roy C. Palmer and Ronald G. Brown, two white businessmen from Palatine, Illinois.

Palmer and Brown, as sole owners of the Indian-sounding Buffalo Brothers Management, Inc., have pocketed tens of millions of dollars from the St. Croix's two casinos in western Wisconsin, where they employ no staff and incur few expenses. In 1992, the pair raked in $13.8 million in profits, more than twice the $6.5 million that went to the tribe. Last year, they siphoned off at least another $13 million, and this spring they negotiated a buyout of their management contract for a reported $36 million.

This is money for which Palmer and Brown need not do anything – not even go away. They continue to be involved with the St. Croix's casinos – operations known for their shoddy treatment of workers, Indian and non-Indian alike.

Worse, this unlucky alliance between the St. Croix (officially the Lake Superior Band of the St. Croix Chippewa) and the Buffalo Brothers, Palmer and Brown, has spurred corruption at the tribal, county, state and federal levels. Officials have been bribed, tribal elections have been influenced, critics have been threatened, harassed and even shot at. All the while, regulators in Wisconsin and Washington, D.C., have, with one notable exception, stood by and winked. And the one regulator who spoke up was promptly fired.

"The Buffalo Brothers are a perfect example of what's going on in the country," says Clyde Bellecourt, the Minneapolis-based cofounder and national director of the American Indian Movement. "They're supposed to be working for the tribe, but that's not what's happening."

BELLECOURT, WHO HAS PARTICIPATED IN PROTESTS AGAINST THE BUFFALO
Brothers (including, in late April, a brief occupation of the much larger
casino at Turtle Lake), sees the St. Croix and other tribes as victims not just
of exploitation but of circumstance: "Our people weren't prepared for this.
One day we have tribal governments led by people with a sixth-grade education. The next day we wake up and boom – we've got a multi-million-
dollar business in our backyard."

Most Native Americans, including St. Croix tribal members who have
led the charge against the Buffalo Brothers, take a positive view of Indian
gaming. This new frontier, opened by the court decisions and the 1988 Indian
Gaming Regulatory Act, has given tribes an unprecedented opportunity to
stake a claim to economic independence.

Some have made the most of this opportunity. Wisconsin's Oneida
tribe has used the proceeds from its self-managed Green Bay casino to set
up a scholarship fund for tribal members. Connecticut's Mashantucket
Pequot – whose Foxwoods casino, also managed by the tribe, now nets more
than $1 million a day – are building a $130 million museum to preserve
their heritage. The St. Croix's casinos have made a deep dent in local
unemployment and welfare rates and helped band members to become self-
sufficient, some for the first time in their lives.

But overall, Indian gaming – last year a $3 billion industry – has been
a mixed blessing. Indians who receive gaming proceeds lose federal assistance
and see their subsidized rent shoot up. Bellecourt says he's heard stories
that make him want to cry, of young Indians blowing "thousands of dollars" on limo rides. And while alcohol abuse is still the number-one problem
facing Native Americans, they now also have access to cocaine and designer
drugs.

"It's killing us. It's killing our people," says Bellecourt. "They never
had money in their lives and they don't know what to do."

It is precisely this lack of money that made the tribes vulnerable in the
first place. In the mid-1980s, when Indian gaming evolved beyond bingo
halls into video poker and other electronic games, few had the funds to
purchase this equipment. Borrowing from banks was out of the question,
since the legality of these early operations was in doubt. But some folks were
still willing to help the poor Indians out.

Glenn Hall, a Wisconsin Lac Courte Oreilles band member, recalls
that 90–10 profit splits were once common throughout Wisconsin and
Minnesota. The Indians got a 10 percent share for making space for the
machines; the owners got 90 percent for providing them. "These guys

pretended to be the tribes' friends," says Hall, "but in fact they were stealing from them."

It was in this capacity — as leasers of gaming machines — that Roy Palmer and Ron Brown in 1988 began their lucrative involvement with the St. Croix. Brown, a former high-school track coach, got into the business through a video rental chain he ran with his brother. Palmer, a lawyer who in 1974 was a key figure in a major Illinois scandal (described by that state's Better Business Association as "a scheme ... to control the regulation of the Illinois savings-and-loan industry"), gave up private practice to go into Indian gambling.

"We got into the game early and took some risks," Palmer told the *St. Paul Pioneer Press*. "It worked out very well."

NOT SURPRISINGLY, PALMER AND BROWN STAYED ON BOARD AS THE gravy train headed for its next stop: full-scale casinos. In January 1991 the pair, then operating as the sole proprietors of an outfit called Interstate Gaming Services, Inc., signed a five-year contract to lease gaming machines to the St. Croix. In August 1991, Palmer and Brown's other company, Buffalo Brothers, Inc., entered a seven-year pact giving it the exclusive right to develop, manage and operate the band's casino at Turtle Lake. In September, it entered a similar agreement for the smaller casino at Danbury.

The management contract granting Buffalo Brothers 30 percent of the net revenues from Danbury and 40 percent (the highest allowed) from Turtle Lake was approved by Earl Barlow, then area director in Minneapolis for the Bureau of Indian Affairs. These high percentages and long terms — as opposed to two-year pacts for 2 percent to 5 percent cuts said to be the norm in Las Vegas — are typical of the contracts approved by Barlow and other BIA officials. Barlow was suspended last fall and later forced to retire after it emerged that he and an assistant accepted free meals and gambled at casinos he regulated, winning more than $20,000 in jackpots while billing the government $31,000 for travel costs.

Besides their huge slice of the overall profits, Palmer and Brown were collecting 30 percent of the leased gaming machines' gross profits through a concurrent contract with Interstate, which was not reported to the BIA. And any capital secured by Palmer and Brown for casino construction was paid back as a loan by the band.

Paul DeMain, managing editor of *News from Indian Country*, a twice-monthly newspaper published in northern Wisconsin, says such arrangements have "caused some tribes to generate debt while having million-dollar cash flows." The bulk of the profits are going to the white businesspeople with whom they enter gaming-related contracts. DeMain cites the Minnesota's Mille Lacs tribe, which owns two casinos managed by Grand Casinos, Inc. One of the firm's founders last year gave each of his two children stock valued at $30 million; the Mille Lacs' take for 1993, meanwhile, was $24 million.

The Buffalo Brothers have also fared well. In 1992, Brown reported total adjusted gross income of $11.9 million, up from $53,267 two years before. Palmer's 1992 income was $12.3 million, virtually all from Indian gaming. Last year, the two men listed total assets of more than $70 million.

In 1993, the Office of the Inspector General for the U.S. Department of the Interior found excessive fees totaling $62 million in 18 of the 26 tribal management contracts it reviewed. Its November 1993 report noted that in almost every case where a contractor secured financing for an operation, the tribe was paying it back, with interest, in addition to the management fee. The office also reviewed 13 leasing agreements and found that the tribes paid $40.3 million for gaming equipment they could have bought for $3.2 million. Additional losses were attributed to theft and embezzlement.

"It's clear that the Indian gaming industry is a tempting target for criminal activity and exploitation," says U.S. Rep. Robert Torricelli, the New Jersey Democrat who is author of a bill to tighten regulation of Indian gaming. The response from BIA Secretary Ada Deer, whose agency had approved many of the contracts under review, was to "agree with the report that some tribes may have entered into unconscionable contracts and leases" but "disagree that the Bureau of Indian Affairs could have done more to prevent this situation."

Deer and National Indian Gaming Commission Chairman Anthony Hope took issue with most of the report's recommendations, stopping them dead in their tracks. Hope, the congenial son of comedian Bob Hope, thinks most of the problems are being corrected through tighter regulation and the machinations of the market (some tribes are now smoothly running their own operations). Hope admits there are "plenty of cases where things are going on that shouldn't be," but says the government's response is limited by its commitment to tribal self-determination: "The basic notion is that the only way they're going to learn to stand on their feet is to fall down once in a while."

THE BUFFALO BROTHERS, LIKE OTHER OUTSIDERS WHO SECURED
management contracts, initially knew little about casino management. Their hastily assembled management team included such casino veterans as Barbara

Tidd as chief financial officer. After the rush to prepare the Turtle Lake casino for its May 1992 opening, Tidd reviewed the financial arrangements and was appalled to discover how much of the profit was going to Palmer and Brown.

In June 1992, a meeting of the St. Croix tribal chairman and casino brass, including Palmer, was held at Tidd's behest. As she recalls, it didn't last long: "Roy started screaming, 'You fucking bitch.'" Fired shortly thereafter, Tidd gave tribal council member Mary Washington documents regarding casino finances that provided the basis for a federal lawsuit filed "on behalf of the St. Croix tribe" by Washington, fellow council member Kenny Mosay, and his father, Chief Archie Mosay, the band's spiritual leader. Named as defendants were Buffalo Brothers, Interstate, Palmer and Brown.

The suit, which argued that the Interstate lease pushed the Buffalo Brothers' take well beyond the 40 percent maximum allowed for management companies, was shot down at the district and appellate levels. But the publicity generated by its December 1992 filing prompted the St. Croix and Interstate to terminate this contract. Still, acquiring ownership of the machines cost the band at least another $2 million – on top of the more than $9 million in lease fees it paid in 1992. This for machines the tribe could have bought, on credit, for $4 million.

In justifying their sweetheart lease, Palmer and Brown told the tribe that each gaming machine would earn about $40 a day. But, in securing a loan for these machines, the pair prepared a prospectus confidently (and correctly) predicting earnings of between $150 and $225 a day.

On May 26, 1993, Michael Liethen, then director of the Wisconsin Gaming Commission's Office of Indian Gaming, recommended in a draft report that Buffalo Brothers, Inc. be sent packing for having "abused the trust placed in it ... to unjustly enrich its owners at the expense of the tribe." That same day, Liethen was suspended by Commission Chair John Tries. When Liethen later released the report in response to a federal court subpoena from the plaintiffs in the lawsuit against Palmer and Brown, he was fired.

Tries, formerly Gov. Tommy Thompson's personal chauffeur, insists the commission had good cause for its actions. But Liethen calls the commission's stated reasons "a pretext for improper political considerations or a cover-up of other improper activities within the commission." He believes the action taken against him – which came just after a meeting between Tries and Buffalo Brothers attorney Ray Taffora, formerly the governor's chief legal counsel – "was an effort to interdict my recommendation regarding the Buffalo Brothers."

Gaming officials deny this, but in fact have since mothballed Liethen's report and tolerated the Buffalo Brothers' continued looting of the St. Croix. Explains Wisconsin Gaming Commission spokesman Bill Clausius, "It's paternalistic to suggest we should be stepping in and blocking bad business deals."

LIKE OTHER TRIBES, THE ST. CROIX CONSIDER THEIR BUSINESS enterprises exempt from basic labor laws. That means casino employees do not receive workers' compensation or unemployment compensation, and they are not covered by laws governing minimum wage, discrimination and sexual harassment.

Jerry Sondreal, managing editor of the weekly *Amery Free Press*, says he's spoken to "100 to 150 people who have what I consider to be legitimate complaints" regarding the casino's labor practices. "It's a total reign of terror."

Last December, the Wisconsin Legislature's Special Committee on Gambling Oversight heard testimony from 19 former St. Croix casino workers. It was one horror story after another. Laurie Kirwan, a cocktail waitress, said her supervisor would routinely run his fingers through her hair and once tried to bite her breasts (she quit; he didn't have to). Karen Nerison, a waitress, was fired after she became pregnant (her supervisor said she was going to the bathroom too often; normally, casino waitresses get just one five-minute break per eight- or nine-hour shift). Gretchen Cottingham, the head of housecleaning at the adjacent hotel, testified in tears that she was never given a reason for her termination: "I called the hotel and they said, 'You no longer work here.'"

At one point during the hearing, the committee chair, Rep. Marlin Schneider, angrily asked tribal attorney Howard Bichler whether the U.S. Constitution was suspended on Indian lands. Replied Bichler, "In some respects it is." Tries agrees, saying federal law governing compacts between states and tribes "would not allow us" to include language regarding workers' rights. This even though there *is* compact language requiring compliance with state building codes.

In an interview in March, casino marketing director Joseph Hunt derided the former workers' complaints: "This is a good operation. We do not condone sexual harassment. We do not condone mismanagement. To even insinuate that the Buffalo Brothers are not sensitive to these issues is really an insult." In April, Hunt himself was fired, part of a spate of high-level cannings that also include the casino's chief financial officer and its director of security, Louis Merrill, who subsequently helped Bellecourt and about 60 others take over the casino early on the morning of April 24.

The dissidents closed off the casino for several hours and occupied the casino boardroom until later that day, when they met with Chairman Taylor and other tribal council members to air their grievances, mostly regarding the Buffalo Brothers. Afterwards, Bellecourt, Merrill and newspaperman Sondreal, who covered the occupation, were served restraining orders barring them from the casino and its environs, (The orders were later lifted.)

On April 29, state Rep. Harvey Stower, who has been on the warpath against the Buffalo Brothers for months, hand-delivered a letter signed by Chief Archie Mosay to the office of U.S. Attorney General Janet Reno. The letter alleges that "our current tribal council is being bribed and bought by the Buffalo Brothers" and urges the Justice Department to investigate.

The Justice Department forwarded the letter to the Bureau of Indian Affairs and the U.S. Attorney for the Western District of Wisconsin, which won't confirm whether an investigation is underway. Sources say federal investigators are unlikely to get involved, especially now that the Buffalo Brothers are professedly on their way out.

Why has the St. Croix's leadership continued to affiliate with the Buffalo Brothers despite overwhelming evidence that the tribe is being ripped off? "There's no doubt in my mind," says Bellecourt, "that they have been bought off." This would hardly be unprecedented.

Glenn Corrie, the owner of a management company that ran gaming operations for the Wisconsin Winnebago, received an 18-month prison term after he confessed to paying hundreds of thousands of dollars in bribes to members of the tribe's business committee. Corrie's company was kicked out by a federal judge in January 1992 – but not before controversy over the arrangement drove the Winnebago to the brink of civil war, culminating in an arson attempt and shootout at one of the tribe's casinos.

Palmer and Brown's relationship with the St. Croix has been just as fractious. After Washington and Mosay filed suit against the Buffalo Brothers in December 1992, their $30,000 annual salaries – up from about $8,000 in the days before gaming – were terminated. ("It's fair," asserts Taylor. "If they're not satisfied, cut them out. I learned that from the white man.")

Last summer, Mosay and Washington were ousted from the council in elections held one day after tribal members received an unauthorized $1,000 per-capita payment drawn from casino profits – along with a letter scurrilously attacking Mosay, who lost by two votes. A building owned by the Buffalo Brothers was used for an election-eve rally, catered by the casino. A casino van was dispatched to Minneapolis to transport select tribal members – those who supported pro-Buffalo Brothers candidates – to the polls. The BIA was asked to nullify this election result; it refused.

CRITICS OF THE CASINO HAVE ALLEGEDLY BEEN FOLLOWED, THREATENED

and had their phones tapped. Bob Reynolds, a former casino head of security, last August had five bullets fired into his truck from another vehicle.

Other threats have been directed against the tribe as a whole. Last December, the council claimed in a letter to tribal members that protests against the Buffalo Brothers had caused a decline in casino profits, which might force it to "decrease or eliminate ... per-capita payments, [the tribe's] loan program, daily work programs, housing projects, benefits for elders and children, education programs, and tribal pow-wows."

Bellecourt sees such discord as an ominous portent for the St. Croix and other tribes. "I believe that gaming is a major conspiracy against Indian people," he says. "I think it's a form of termination." Once tribal corruption reaches critical mass, he fears, "the federal government will step in and put us in receivership."

National Indian Gaming Commission chair Hope offers a divergent, though equally dismal, prognosis. Gambling, he observes, is an inherently wasteful endeavor: "It's not a product, provides no product, does nothing. It's a net drain on any economy." In 10 or 20 years, he predicts, the current gambling boom will reach a saturation point and communities will no longer stand for it. "Gambling died out in the 1840s and 1890s," he says. "It's going to die out again."

At the moment, however, gambling is in ascendance and Indian tribes – whose gambling share, says Hope, is 5 percent to 8 percent of the national total – are along for the ride. And while management companies are on the way out, the determination of white outsiders to cash in on Indian gaming appears as strong as ever.

Michael Liethen, now general counsel for the Wisconsin Winnebago, notes that Golden Nickel Corporation, one of the management companies the tribe turned to after being burned by Corrie, has bought up all the land around the Winnebagos' flagship casino near Wisconsin Dells. "We're absolutely landlocked," he says. "It's obvious they're exploiting us rather than working with us."

As of late June, more than a month after Taylor notified the state that the buyout was complete, Palmer and Brown were still at the casino, taking care of business. They could keep drawing money from the operation for some time to come. The terms of the buyout have still not been disclosed to state gaming officials or band members, some of whom are now trying to force a tribal referendum on the deal. The tribal council has responded by sending a "red alert" to band members, urging them to resist "this small faction and their dissident supporters who want to destroy the economic base of the tribe." State authorities and the FBI continue to investigate.

No matter what happens, the imprint of the Buffalo Brothers on the St. Croix will be long and deep. Perhaps the best emblem of this can be found inside the Turtle Lake casino, in the etched glass panels that adorn the Buffalo Brothers Saloon. There, among the exquisite renderings of Indian scenes – wolves, soaring eagles, Indians on horseback – is the graven image of Roy Palmer and Ron Brown. The two men are dressed in frontier garb, rifles in hand.

AUGUST 1994, THE PROGRESSIVE

This article was retooled from a series that ran in Isthmus *in April 1994; it appeared in* The Progressive *under the headline, "Buffaloed: Casino Cowboys Take Indians for a Ride." The Buffalo Brothers eventually did walk away from the St. Croix tribe, with Palmer going on to other Indian gaming ventures. He later told* Time *magazine, of his involvement with the St. Croix: "We did not do one thing wrong." In 1999, a federal jury ruled in favor of Michael Liethen's claims that he was wrongfully terminated; the state subsequently agreed to a $290,000 settlement.*

Tommy Thompson, 1994. Photo by Bob Rashid

My Free Lunch with Tommy

Elaine Pulver is standing, as I am, outside a dining room at the Concourse Hotel, waiting for Tommy Thompson. A nice, mom-like woman of perhaps 50, Pulver happened to learn that the governor is meeting his senior staff there for lunch.

She tells me she's from Elroy, Thompson's hometown, and has known him for many years. The last time they met, Pulver told Thompson of her difficulties finding a job as a high school administrator; he urged her to keep trying. Now, after four years of trying, she's landed an assistant principal job in Oconto, north of Green Bay. And so she's waiting for Tommy Thompson, to say thanks.

"I feel like a groupie," Pulver tells me, as she writes the governor a note.

The reason I'm waiting for Tommy Thompson is different. After nearly a month of trying to set up an interview with the governor, the clock is running out. That morning Mark Liedl, the governor's oily campaign flak, told me Thompson wanted to do an interview – but that he, Liedl, advised against it. Why? "I don't think he's going to get a fair shake."

Apprised that access to Thompson might be based on such calculations, I've decided to signal my intention to stalk the governor, if necessary, to get my 45 minutes. Maybe even bring in Michael Moore.

John Matthews, the guv's acting chief of staff, meets me in the hall at the Concourse and straight away is on the horn. A few minutes later press secretary Kevin Keane whisks me away, as I bid adieu to Pulver, who gives me her note to give to Thompson. ("I'll get it to him if I have to *mail it*," I promise.) We go to Thompson's office in the Capitol, and learn he's already at the Concourse. We go back to the dining room, the door opens, and I am standing before some two dozen top Thompson administration officials as Tommy Thompson shakes my hand and invites me to join him for lunch.

So I tell the story of the woman in the hall and present Thompson with her note thanking him for his encouragement. He studies the signature as I head for the buffet.

"One of my old girlfriends," he cracks, and the room explodes with laughter. "One of the few that said thanks," someone shouts out.

As he eats, the governor holds court, calling on his team members to give the lowdown from their departments. All the news is good – especially the news from Carol Skornicka, secretary of the Department of Industry, Labor and Human Relations, that state manufacturing jobs are at their highest levels since 1979 and Madison's 2.1 percent unemployment rate is the lowest in the nation.

"You hear that," Thompson harangues me, good-naturedly recalling his regular trashings in *Isthmus*. I am reduced to citing a rare exception: Charlie Sykes' pro-Thompson analysis during the 1990 campaign. "That's why you're not letting him do it again!" jokes Thompson. Everyone laughs. He is enjoying this.

When the luncheon ends, I am left in a daze of positive Republican energy, with Thompson and a half-dozen of his associates. This is an experience I will remember later, as I contemplate a popularity that has brought Thompson praise from George H.W. Bush, much of the national press, and rocker Ted Nugent (who calls the guv "a politician with a major set of gonads"). I will remember it as I watch Thompson issue blustery proclamations during the gubernatorial debates and jot the observation "He's a demagogue" in my notes. It is an experience his handlers would have been foolish to deprive me of – especially as the thought, unwelcome as a nightmare, insinuates itself into my brain: *"I like this guy."*

I trust I will snap out of it. The interview begins.

IN 1986, WHEN THOMPSON CLINCHED THE GOVERNORSHIP, I DUBBED HIM

"a preposterous hick from Elroy who drives like an idiot and then lies his way out of traffic tickets" – a reference to Thompson's driving difficulties in the days before he had an $84,000-a-year chauffeur. His victorious campaign against Democrat Tony Earl, I noted, had been based "almost exclusively on misstatements of the record and shameless appeals to bigotry and ignorance."

This year, Thompson is said to be a shoo-in, but still he's hitting below the belt. The week before our interview, Thompson broke his vow against negative ads with an attack on his Democratic opponent, state Sen. Chuck Chvala, for voting to raise the salaries of prisoners.

It turns out that this outrage, an appropriation buried in the bowels of the 1983-85 state budget bill, hiked salaries a mere 5 percent (prison wages range from $.20 to $2 an hour) – a cost to the state of $112,600 over two years. Chvala says he didn't even know about the pay hike. And Thompson, then Assembly Minority Leader, was not bothered enough to include it among the budget items he sought to expunge.

Now, 11 years after the fact, Thompson wants to turn this thin reed into the smoking gun that proves his Democratic rival is soft on crime. He's even using his vastly superior campaign war chest – Thompson, already the longest-tenured governor in Wisconsin history, may redistribute more than $7 million to win an unprecedented third term – to pay telemarketers to scare the bejesus out of professed Chvala supporters by warning them he voted to increase prisoners' pay. (Chvala himself got one such call. "Oh, you've got the same name here," exclaimed the caller, doubtless another success story in Thompson's endless stream of good employment news.)

The ad, which *The Capital Times* denounced as "dirty politics," shows Thompson at his worst: unscrupulous and coldly opportunistic. It recalls his recent decision, unprompted by any penological imperative, to remove weightlifting equipment from state prisons. Its whole point, as in Thompson's seemingly tireless crusade against welfare, is to focus popular resentment against the less fortunate – in this case, prisoners.

That's ironic, because Thompson owes a debt of gratitude to prisoners, whose burgeoning numbers provide him with a ready answer to criticisms that, during his tenure, the size and expense of state government has substantially increased. "What do you want me to do?" he asks. "Build prisons and not staff them?"

Indeed, devoting an ever greater share of the state's resources to locking people up is central to Thompson's vision for Wisconsin's future.

"And this year," Thompson declared during his first debate with Chvala, "there's going to be an additional $50 million to operate the prisons. And it goes along nicely with the economic growth in the state of Wisconsin. You know, Wisconsin's economy is on fire.... Why? Because of Tommy Thompson."

When I ask Thompson – who as chair of the state Building Commission approved $1 million in recreation facilities, including a weight room, for a prison now being built – about the pay-for-prisoners ad, he responds with righteous indignation. "Mr. Chvala has ever since he's announced ... spoken untruths about my record," says Thompson. "He's spreading all these idle things, attacking me on running for president, attacking me on my money raising, making false accusations, talking about special-interest money when 44 percent of his money comes from PACs and only 4 percent of mine [does]. He has misconstrued all along my record."

Geez. This guy isn't Goliath. He's Genghis Khan. And he's just getting warmed up.

In contrast, Thompson says, his campaign has stuck to facts. "All we ever do is point out public records, that are documented, that are not false, not subject to opinion.... All I did was point out: 'But Chuck, for 12 years this is how you vote, this is your record.' And here's where Tommy Thompson has consistently stood, and I'm proud of my record of accomplishment and success. In fact. I don't know of any other governor in the country that's had a record of success like mine. And I'm proud of it."

THOMPSON'S TENDENCY TO REFER TO HIMSELF IN THE THIRD PERSON
suggests a curious detachment, as though Tommy Thompson were a product and the 52-year-old politician merely its pitchman. He may or may not believe in what he's selling but, by golly, there's no doubt that Tommy Thompson believes in himself. He wants others – from folks like Elaine Pulver to folks like me – to believe in him, too.

"Actually, Bill, it's no big problem," he says when I ask him how he intends, without raising the sales or income tax, to come up with the $1 billion needed to fulfill his and the Legislature's Hail Mary commitment to deliver property-tax relief. "You just diagram it out."

He proceeds to do just that: $500 million in additional revenue from new economic growth in 1995; this amount plus another $500 million the following year; $115 million in Medicaid savings, $15 million in surplus. "So that's 1.65 billion over two years. One-point-six-five billion, and I haven't even worked up a sweat yet."

Wow. Maybe coming up with a billion dollars a year really *won't* be difficult – not for Tommy Thompson.

Chvala, asked the same question, is more honest, but his answer is less appealing. He admits some tax hikes will be needed, just as Thompson has imposed many new taxes and fees: "We have to tell the public there is no free lunch." (Then how did that turkey sandwich get on my plate?)

The issues fly by and the governor swats them:

• Thompson says his efforts to reduce property taxes have been frustrated by liberals like Chvala, but now that the Senate is under GOP control some real progress is being made: "The biggest property-tax reduction bill ever signed into law was signed by me, within this past session, and Mr. Chvala didn't vote against it."

• Thompson has led the fight to get local spending under control, largely by standing up to the teachers union. "You know, it would be much easier to not fight and have the teachers union on my side," he says, pounding the table with his fist. "It would be much easier. But it's wrong [pound]. You've got to have cost controls. You've got to change [pound] the way we set up contracts [pound], and then you can do something [pound] about property taxes."

• It's "absolutely not true" that the Thompson administration engages in cronyism, and no big deal that some of Thompson's political appointees have stepped down in disgrace: "I've made over 5,000 appointments since I've been governor, and a handful haven't worked out.... It's much less than one-half of 1 percent. So 99.5 percent of my appointees have been excellent."

• Those almost nonstop fundraisers Thompson attends (provided that organizers promise a total take of at least $25,000) and memberships in the Governor's Club (open to anyone who gives Thompson at least $500 a year) do not in any way mean that access to the governor is for sale. "Absolutely not. Absolutely not. I've been successful at raising money. And I have never – I want you to know this – I have never called anybody for money."

BUT THOMPSON'S SLICKEST SPIEL IS ON WHAT IS EUPHEMISTICALLY

called welfare reform. He says Chvala has been "the anchor on the boat" on this issue, until recently. "Now he wants to be the propeller."

Not only is this a great line, it may well be Thompson's strongest selling point: If his agenda is so faulty, why are Chvala and the Democrats trying to one-up it?

On welfare, the Democrats last year pushed through a plan to abolish AFDC in Wisconsin by 1999 (offering, typically, no clue as to what should replace it). And Chvala is chiding Thompson for not also agreeing to wipe out general assistance.

"Now they're trying to get out in front of me on welfare reform," Thompson tells me. "They've fought me so long, now they want to get out because I've made it a popular issue."

In truth, getting tough with people on welfare has long been popular enough to enjoy broad bipartisan support: Gov. Earl started the wheels in motion before Thompson gave the issue his own energetic spin. The difference between the two parties' approaches, to the extent there is one, is that the Democrats have taken to welfare bashing because they lack ideas of their own. Thompson, meanwhile, thinks it's the right thing to do.

"I do not believe welfare does anything but hurt the people on welfare," he thunders. "And I am giving people hope, giving them an opportunity to get off welfare."

Of course, there's no evidence he's doing any such thing. The few studies that have been done – despite the Thompson administration's efforts to suppress them – suggest that Wisconsin's welfare initiatives have been abject failures. The 22 percent reduction in AFDC rolls the governor crows about likely owes more to the economy than to welfare tinkering, although the latter undeniably deserves credit for spurring a 328 percent increase in the state AFDC program's administrative costs.

Finally, Thompson's rhetoric aside, grateful former welfare recipients are hardly among his core supporters. In this and other areas, Thompson has sold Wisconsin a bill of goods. But what a truly great salesman he is!

Listen to him sell his agenda for the state's economy. It's the topic he goes off on when I ask what courage there is to his agenda, shaped as it is by his desire to be popular and maximize his hold on government.

"What did I come in on?" he asks, characteristically using a rhetorical question to punctuate his speech. "I came in on economic development. Created that. Completely changed the business climate in this state. When it wasn't popular. I took on the Democrats, I took on *Isthmus* and everybody in making economic development the powerhouse."

IN THOMPSON'S VIEW, STANDING UP FOR BUSINESS TAKES A LOT OF GUTS, of the sort Chvala lacks. "He tears down, I build," Thompson told the *Wisconsin State Journal*. "If he ever did get elected, the state would fall apart because his negative attitude would drive businesses out and [he] would increase taxes and spending."

Chvala sees such tactics – including the pay-for-prisoners ad – as evidence of Thompson's moral bankruptcy. "Tommy Thompson is a man who gathers political capital to himself and never spends it for any useful purpose," the challenger says. "He appears to be almost a total political animal. I can't name a single area where he's stood in front of an audience and said, 'I know you disagree but the state needs to go in this direction.' He has also pandered to what I would perceive as being the lowest common denominator.

"That's foreign to my view of what you should be doing in public life. To me, to do what Tommy Thompson does, why be there? Just stick your finger up in the wind and go in that direction. You're supposed to be providing leadership and a vision of what needs to be done."

It's a good rap and a solid critique of Tommy Thompson the politician – regardless of whether Chuck Chvala has the chops to do a better job. But in the clash of ideas and images, how can it compete?

Our interview is nearly over. I ask Tommy Thompson if he has anything else to say. "No," he answers. "I just don't know why you're so angry. I can't imagine it."

And with that, the feel-good governor goes back to work, having gathered a bit more political capital to himself. His performance may not change any minds, but it certainly helps clarify why Elaine Pulver – and a lot of other folks – will have no trouble deciding whom to vote for Nov. 8.

OCTOBER 14, 1994

Tommy Thompson easily won reelection in 1994 and again in 1998; in 2001 he became U.S. secretary of Health and Human Services under George W. Bush. In 2002, Sen. Chvala was charged with 20 felonies for misconduct in office; he pled guilty to two counts and was sentenced to nine months in jail.

Victory celebration at *The Progressive*, 1979. Photo by Brent Nicastro

The H-Bomb Case Revisited

I n 1979, a federal judge in Milwaukee blocked *The Progressive*, a Madison-based magazine, from publishing an article regarding H-bomb design. The case has inspired two books, a play and dozens of articles. Yet what this extraordinary event really merits is a major motion picture, perhaps directed by Oliver Stone – or, better yet, Woody Allen. Here's how I envision the opening scene:

There's a sharp clicking of shoes as a messenger walks down hallways and through guarded doors before handing an envelope marked "Top Secret" to an important-looking man, who nods, then continues the envelope's journey into the Oval Office. President Jimmy Carter cracks open the seal, and reads a one-page memo from U.S. Attorney General Griffin Bell, notifying him of the government's determination to block publication.

Rows of perfectly square white teeth disappear into a frown as Carter scrawls his response on the memo's top: "Good move, proceed. J"

Instantly, the scene shifts to a small, messy office in Madison, where an ill-dressed middle-aged man is rifling frantically through mountains of clutter on his desk. Erwin Knoll, editor of *The Progressive*, at last locates a crumpled manuscript entitled "The H-Bomb Secret: How We Got It, Why We're Telling It." He grabs his coat and dashes out the door, accompanied by Sam Day, the magazine's managing editor, as they head to meet a delegation of high-ranking officials from the U.S. Departments of Energy and Justice. "I love it!" exclaims Knoll on the way.

Give or take a few details. this is what happened on March 2, 1979, in Washington, D.C., and Madison, Wisconsin. It's the ultimate study in contrasts, as the full might and authority of the U.S. government was about to come crashing down on a tiny political magazine.

The meeting between *The Progressive*'s editors and attorneys and the government delegation ended without resolution. The officials said the article, written by an ambitious freelancer named Howard Morland, contained "restricted data" that, if published, would threaten national security. Knoll responded that he was "incredulous that a writer with Morland's limited background ... could so readily penetrate what you are describing as perhaps the most important secret possessed by the United States."

In short order, *The Progressive* formally rejected the government's offer to rewrite Morland's article, removing the "restricted data." On March 9, 1979, Federal Judge Robert W. Warren of Milwaukee granted a temporary restraining order blocking publication. It was the first time in U.S. history that the government had censored a publication on national security grounds.

For the next six months and 19 days, *The Progressive* and its editors were prohibited, under the 1954 Atomic Energy Act, from "publishing or otherwise communicating, transmitting or disclosing" the restricted information in the H-bomb article. It was a historic confrontation between the rights of the press and the power of the state, and, in the end, *The Progressive* prevailed – but only to a point.

IN EARLY 1978, SAM DAY LEFT HIS JOB AS EDITOR OF *THE BULLETIN OF the Atomic Scientists* and came to *The Progressive* with a mandate to make nuclear issues a main focus of the magazine. In April, he traveled to Indiana for a formal debate against Charles Gilbert of the Department of Energy, which runs the nation's nuclear weapons program. Afterward, over a beer, Day expressed his desire to tour the nation's nuclear factories, and Gilbert, to his surprise, agreed.

While preparing for his travels, Day learned about a New Hampshire activist named Howard Morland who had put together an interesting slide show on nuclear weapons. The two met and decided that Morland would accept the DOE's offer to tour the plants, in search of the Teller-Ulam Idea, a closely guarded "secret" of H-bomb design. Morland, a former Air Force pilot, found it egregious that such a secret still existed, providing a pretext for shutting off public access to information about nuclear weapons.

Knoll, formerly a reporter and editor for *The Washington Post*, had seen often enough how government officials used claims of secrecy to evade accountability and cover up abuses. He took an especially dim view of nuclear secrecy – predicated on the dubious notion that, were it not for seditious breaches, "they" might not figure out how to build "our" bombs. Five nations had independently mastered this achievement, with no help from the Rosenbergs. The Big Lie that nuclear proliferation hinged on access to some sort of secret was, Knoll believed, responsible for nearly all of political repression – the spy scares, the witch hunts, the loyalty purges – that had confounded progressive change in Cold War America. Knoll leapt at this chance to boldly challenge the nuclear-secrecy mystique.

Morland spent the remainder of 1978 touring plants, researching publicly available literature, and meeting with scientists knowledgeable about nuclear weapons. He found that the more he knew, the easier it was to obtain information. (At one point, Morland asked the scientists at one plant whether a particular piece of equipment "is used to press lithium-6 deuteride powder into a shaped, ceramic-like material for later machining." After a long, shocked pause, one of the scientists answered "Yes.") He respected the expertise of weapon makers; they, in turn, responded to his sincere desire to know.

In January 1979, Morland wrote the first draft of an article on the H-bomb secret, complete with diagrams showing key principles of H-bomb design. The article, as rewritten by Day, spilled the secret of the Teller-Ulam Idea in its very first graph: "The secret is in the coupling mechanism that enables an ordinary fission bomb – the kind that destroyed Hiroshima – to trigger the far-deadlier energy of hydrogen fusion. The physical pressure and heat generated by x- and gamma radiation, moving outward from the trigger at the speed of light, bounces against the weapon's inner wall and is reflected with enormous force into the sides of the carrot-shaped 'pencil' which contains the fusion fuel."

A copy of Morland's article sent to an MIT scientist for review was passed on to the DOE, which pushed the panic button. After a series of emergency meetings, Bell sent his memo to Carter, and the government sent its delegation to Madison.

THERE WAS, UNTIL 1979, ONLY ONE OCCASION IN U.S. HISTORY WHEN
the federal government sought to stop something from being published. It happened on the other end of this same decade, in 1971, when the Nixon administration moved to suppress the Pentagon Papers. But the U.S. Supreme
Court promptly voted 6–3 to reject this censorship attempt, with Chief Justice
Warren Burger declaring that "prior restraints on speech and publication
are the most serious and least tolerable infringement on First Amendment
rights."

In *The United States of America v. The Progressive, Inc., Erwin Knoll,
Samuel Day, Jr., and Howard Morland*, the Carter administration tried again.
This time it succeeded, thanks to Judge Warren – a conservative Republican
appointed by Richard M. Nixon in August 1974, one day before he resigned
in disgrace.

The March 9 hearing lasted 90 minutes. The government claimed that
publication of Morland's article would result in "grave, direct, immediate
and irreparable harm to the national security of the United States" – adjec-
tives selected to meet the precise criteria for prior restraint set by the Supreme
Court in the Pentagon Papers case. Warren sided with Uncle Sam, proclaiming: "I'd like ... to think a long, hard time before I gave the hydrogen bomb
to Idi Amin." He also falsely called the article "the recipe for a do-it-your-
self hydrogen bomb."

Meanwhile, government officials led by Defense Secretary Harold
Brown contacted *The New York Times*, *The Washington Post* and *The Los
Angeles Times* to discourage them from rallying to *The Progressive*'s defense.
The New York Times withheld judgment, while the other two papers came
out strongly against *The Progressive*. *The Washington Post*, Knoll's alma
mater, was especially hostile: "As a press-versus-government First Amendment
contest, this, as far as we can tell, is John Mitchell's dream case – the one
the Nixon administration was never lucky enough to get: a real First
Amendment loser."

Perhaps the harshest blow was delivered by legendary journalist I.F. Stone,
Knoll's mentor and longtime friend. Knoll and Ron Carbon, *The Progressive*'s
publisher, had lunch with Stone and others in Washington, D.C., where they
were making contacts regarding the H-bomb case. Stone, to Knoll's horror,
denigrated the magazine's desire to print Morland's article. "He thought it was
stupid," recalls Morton Minz, a *Washington Post* reporter who was present. "He
was quite affirmative and astringent about it."

Critical letters flowed into *The Progressive*. "I hope the government
wins its case, as the First Amendment was never meant to cover irrespon-

sibility of this kind," wrote one reader. Another called Morland's article "a craven effort to gain publicity and subscribers. If I had a subscription, I'd cancel it." (Knoll wrote back, "It's always a good idea to subscribe, so you won't be caught in that predicament.")

Knoll took the lead in defending the magazine's image. "The government's assertions are demonstrably absurd," he wrote in a column for *The Washington Post*. "The contention that an enterprise with *The Progressive*'s pathetically limited resources can penetrate the 'secrecy' of the nuclear establishment is, on its face, preposterous."

FROM THE START, THE CASE AGAINST THE PROGRESSIVE TOOK ON Kafkaesque tones. The government blocked the magazine from showing Morland's article to any scientist who lacked security clearance. Court filings were purged of references to articles that had appeared in magazines and encyclopedias. Knoll and other defendants were not allowed to see many of the affidavits submitted on their behalf. They were subject to court decisions they could not read, based on proceedings they were not allowed to attend.

Despite these constraints, unprecedented in the history of American jurisprudence, the magazine managed to turn the tide, winning support from scientists who knew that the so-called secrets in Morland's article were obvious from publicly available literature and the media, which grew wary of the government's increasingly bold exertions in the name of national security.

On Sunday, March 25, *The New York Times*' lead editorial came down squarely on *The Progressive*'s side, calling the government's charges "lame in both logic and law. The shouts of alarm are more dangerous than the danger they describe. The government is doing its best to intimidate the Milwaukee judge and to incite the public against the magazine."

Meanwhile, independent researchers were proving the fallacy of the government's position. *Milwaukee Sentinel* reporter Joe Manning spent a week researching nuclear weapons, using only materials available in public libraries. Manning concluded that Teller and Ulam "may have come up with some sort of arrangement that would compress the fuel through the use of soft x-rays from the atomic bomb blast reflected off the bomb casing wall." Bingo.

Then, on May 8, a 23-year-old Harvard student named Dimitri Rotow found, on the shelves of the Los Alamos Scientific Library, a report declassified four years earlier that disclosed vitally sensitive information about hydrogen bombs. The DOE immediately closed the library to launch a document-by-document search of the shelves. Sen. John Glenn, the chair of a subcommittee overseeing national security, demanded a high-level probe.

The government's own attorneys – including Frank Tuerkheimer, then the U.S. attorney for Western Wisconsin – at this point urged that the prosecution be dropped. (Tuerkheimer says he was "really shocked" when he got his first look at Morland's article: "I saw things in the boxes marked off as 'censored' that I had known in high school, when I was interested in nuclear physics.") But Bell refused, declaring, "There is sometimes honor in taking a weak position."

In late May, Sen. Glenn sent the DOE a copy of a letter he had received a month earlier from four scientists complaining about the government's own inconsistency and negligence in letting "restricted data" into the public domain. The DOE responded by classifying the letter, which by this time had been sent to a half-dozen newspapers. Despite threats of criminal prosecution, the letter was published in *The Daily Californian*, a Berkeley student paper.

More disobedience followed. Chuck Hansen, a California-based nuclear-weapons buff, objected to the government's "purely political" case against *The Progressive* in an Aug. 27 letter to Sen. Charles Percy of Illinois. The letter speculated as to the nature of the Teller-Ulam idea and the concepts underlying H-bomb design.

The DOE classified Hansen's letter. Government agents showed up at Percy's office and Hansen's home, demanding surrender of all copies. It also sent warnings to known recipients – including the *Wall Street Journal*, the *Chicago Tribune* and the *Daily Californian* – claiming the letter contained "restricted data." On Saturday, Sept. 15, the government went into a federal district court and obtained a judicial restraint against *The Daily Californian* on national security grounds.

NEWS OF THIS LATEST SPASM OF CENSORSHIP ROCKED THE MADISON

Press Connection, a paper produced by striking employees of Madison's two daily newspapers. That morning's edition reported that the paper had obtained a copy of Hansen's letter. All day long, the staff half-expected the office door to be kicked in by federal marshals in search of the forbidden document. When the government censored *The Daily Californian*, a decision was made to publish the letter in a special Sunday edition of the *Press Connection*, along with an editorial explaining why. The staff worked into the night to get the issue on the streets, thwarting any attempt to prevent publication on the paper's usual schedule.

The next day, Monday, Sept. 17, the Justice Department held a press conference to declare that it was dropping its case against *The Progressive* because "the publication of an article containing restricted data ... by a newspaper in Madison" had rendered the issue moot. The *Press Connection* was deluged with media attention, much of it negative and sensational. "It was a zoo," recalls former editor Ron McCrea. "The national television networks came in. We were inundated. It was an incredible media onslaught. We received many really hateful calls and death threats."

The Progressive claimed victory. "We are obviously delighted that this attempt to deprive Americans of information to which they are fully entitled has been beaten back," said Knoll, before popping open a bottle of champagne for photographs that appeared around the world. "We hope the government will think a long, hard time before it mounts this kind of censorship again."

Privately, Knoll and the other defendants were bitterly disappointed. Just four days before, on Sept. 13, the Seventh Circuit Court of Appeals in Chicago heard oral arguments on *The Progressive* case. The panel of three appellate court judges took a decidedly skeptical view of the government's claims. It looked likely that they would come down strongly against Warren's decision, vindicating *The Progressive* and giving future courts yet another clear precedent for rejecting prior restraint.

But the government's decision to drop the case confounded all that, leaving key issues unresolved. Even Judge Warren, whom I interviewed in April 1995 (he died last August at age 72), felt the government acted to "cut their losses." In fact, he said, "I was a little disgusted with the government. If they started this thing, they should have had faith in their cause. And apparently, they didn't."

IN EARLY OCTOBER 1979, THE PROGRESSIVE PUBLISHED MORLAND'S article, without any changes. Morland, who now lives in Arlington, Virginia, credits *The Progressive* case with helping change "the cultural attitude" toward secrecy claims. Today, he says, "the cult of military secrecy is a thing to be ridiculed. And I'd like to think part of that has to do with what we were doing in the 1970s and 1980s to create a new national consensus."

Most experts agree that the evidence presented to Judge Warren did not justify the imposition of prior restraint and that the Supreme Court, had things gone that far, would have ruled to this effect. But this didn't happen, and instead the case stands as an example of how the government, aided by a federal judge, successfully used the Atomic Energy Act to block publication. "Judge Warren saw the State's asserted interest as preeminent and simply refused to enforce the plain language of the First Amendment and First Amendment case law," groaned one legal scholar.

Brady Williamson, one of *The Progressive*'s attorneys, looks on the bright side: "Nobody went to jail, and the article got published. This case will be remembered as the time a federal judge appointed by Richard Nixon accepted at face value a series of government affidavits that on their face were incredible, and were proved so."

When I interviewed him four years ago, Judge Warren admitted that the government misrepresented the threat posed by Morland's piece, but he nonetheless defended his decision to block publication: "I was raised in a time when country was important. And the protection of country and its security had a very high priority among our panoply of values. Now, these days, if the U.S. and its government decide they have to engage in some action around the world, I'm appalled by the way everybody feels free to question it, beyond what I think is reasonable. ... I think I'm of a generation that felt that, if it was necessary to protect the integrity of the United States, you didn't challenge it. On the other hand, nowadays it seems that you grab a placard and away you go. Or sit down and pour blood on books or something."

Warren also claimed censorship was appropriate "because a country like China, or a country like Russia, could save literally years" of research by disclosures in the piece. When I pointed out to Warren that, by 1979, both these countries had had H-bombs for decades, he made an even more astounding display of his ignorance: "I don't remember. Atomic bombs maybe, but this is thermonuclear, and of course there's a vast difference."

Erwin Knoll spoke and wrote often about the H-bomb story. One of the last things he wrote – it came out shortly after his death in November 1994 – was for the *William & Mary Bill of Rights Journal*. Knoll expressed his "sincere regret" over one thing: his decision to obey Warren's injunction. "If such circumstances were to arise again," he promised, "I would publish and be damned."

MARCH 5, 1999

This article is drawn in part from my 1996 book, An Enemy of the State: The Life of Erwin Knoll.

Gerard Berge at the prison, 2000. Photo by Kevin J. Miyazaki, *Milwaukee Magazine*

Sizing Up Supermax

A historical marker proclaims Boscobel's distinction as the birthplace of Gideons International, the group that puts Bibles in hotels. A 10-foot wooden turkey pegs it as the "Wild Turkey Capital of Wisconsin." But no signs direct visitors to the community's newest asset, the Wisconsin Supermax Correctional Institution.

The prison, off Highway 133 on the city's northern edge, is surrounded by pine trees and orange signs that say "No trespassing, State of Wisconsin – Owner." The $47.5 million facility is ringed with concentric fences, each topped with razor wire.

I pull into the parking lot and take a few photographs. Within seconds, a patrol vehicle drives slowly past. My picture-taking, I later learn, has caused a security alert, including notification of Warden Gerard Berge.

A guard demands a photo ID, then barks into a phone receiver, "It's him." Past a locked door, another guard takes my picture and scans my hand into the prison's high-tech identification system. I remove my keys and pens but still set off the metal detector. I continue removing items: ring, watch, belt, boots. "Hopefully, there no metal in your pants," the guard jokes.

This is the same process family members must go through before they can "visit" with inmates via the closed-circuit video terminals inside this lobby building. There are 13 terminals, none in use. A guard tells me the half-full, 509-bed prison averages six visits a *week*.

Two guards escort me to the warden's office. Along the way we pass through six more locked doors and gates, all controlled by guards in the tower above. One of these fences is designed to deliver a lethal dose of electricity. I don't ask which one, or test my luck.

Warden Berge greets me warmly. His office is in the same building as the inmates, but is separated, I'm told, by three more layers of security. On a bookshelf behind Berge is a novelty statuette. "That's my Yes Man," he says pleasantly, explaining that it comes in handy at staff meetings. The smiling figure says things like, "I couldn't agree with you more completely." It's a prison administrator's dream.

It soon emerges, however, that Berge's ideal model is actually a Yes I Can Man. He acknowledges that supermaxes elsewhere have failed, but says Wisconsin is determined to succeed. He insists his prison is nothing like the "high-tech torture chamber" that critics have made it out to be.

But the evidence Berge offers falls short of demonstrating a true break from what has come before, and already, there is ample evidence that Wisconsin's Supermax represents the realization of its critics' worst fears.

"The obvious question is, 'Who's going there and why?'" asks former state Department of Corrections (DOC) chief Walter Dickey, now a UW–Madison law professor. "I worry about sending people there as punishment. I worry about sending people there who are a pain in the ass – verbally or lawsuit-wise. I worry about the mentally ill most of all."

In fact, all these things are happening. Supermax, intended for "the worst of the worst" among Wisconsin's inmates, is quickly filling up, mainly with inmates who are, on the evil meter, underachievers. As of early August, the prison had 277 inmates, at least some of whom can be categorized as troublesome but not violent. The prison is being used as a disciplinary tool and to serve as a warning to other inmates. One in 10 inmates is mentally ill, and they are especially vulnerable to the extreme isolation that Supermax entails. And the prison is, in the main, a repository for racial minorities.

Supermaxes have become the hottest trend in corrections – there are now at least 57 of them run by three dozen states and the federal government – despite overwhelming evidence that they do more harm than good. Courts have repeatedly verified allegations of systemic abuse. Human rights groups say these prisons constitute cruel and unusual punishment and meet the definition of torture under international law. Psychologists who study solitary confinement agree they cause severe and lasting psychological damage.

"I'm concerned about putting people in an environment where everybody admits you're likely to become insane," says state Sen. Gwendolynne Moore (D-Milwaukee), calling Supermax confinement "a strategy designed to make people mentally ill."

As for the multitudes who couldn't care less about how people in prison are treated, there's this: Many if not most of those serving time in Supermax will someday be back on the street, letting their bottled up rage and resentment spill forth like blood from a slashed artery.

"We're creating much more vicious, dangerous individuals who we're all going to encounter again in our lives," says Moore. "It's not that I'm feeling for the prisoners so much as I fear for Wisconsin citizens as a result of this strategy."

WARDEN BERGE, FOR HIS PART, DISMISSES SUGGESTIONS THAT SUPERMAX is too harsh to handle. "We have very intentionally designed this place, physically and programmatically," to counter the dangers of isolation. In particular, he claims, there is a great deal of interaction between inmates and staff.

For instance, says Berge, meal trays are dropped off and picked up three times daily, which he counts as "six interactions." And medical personal stop by once a day. But all these contacts occur through locked doors, and staff are discouraged from having substantive conversations with inmates.

Supermax contains two basic cell types. The first, where all inmates start off, measures 7-by-12 feet and consists of solid concrete and steel, except for a thin vertical slit of glass in the door. All conversation takes place via intercom. About half the cells have cameras, so that inmates can be monitored.

The other type of cell measures 8-by-12 feet and has shutters on the doors that, when open, provide an 11-by-27-inch window to the world. A smaller percentage of these cells have cameras, and most have TVs, through which all programming, from education to chapel services, is delivered.

Each cell contains a concrete-slab bed on which a mattress can be placed, a combination sink/toilet/mirror, and an upright stand with a caged shower spout. The toilet flushes at regular intervals; the shower turns on for seven minutes twice a week at prearranged times. No watches or clocks are permitted.

A light remains on 24 hours a day. Supermax inmates never see the sun or sky, although some natural light filters through a horizontal strip of glazing at the top of each cell.

Inmates are confined to their cells for 24 hours a day four days a week. On the other three days, they have an opportunity for one hour and 20 minutes of out-of-cell time in which they are led, alone, to either the law library or exercise areas that are only slightly larger than their cell and contain no equipment. Many decline.

Whenever an inmate is moved within the prison, he is handcuffed and shackled and has at least a two-guard escort. Strip searches are conducted whenever an inmate is placed into observation or transferred from one unit to another.

Except in the rare event that an attorney arrives with papers to sign, Supermax inmates at the most restrictive levels never have face-to-face contact with each other or any outsider. All visits take place via the video terminals, and all conversations are monitored by guards. Media access to inmates, even via video terminals, is strictly forbidden. On this point, says Berge, "the department is pretty insistent."

The one saving grace, from inmates' point of view, is that they can communicate with their immediate neighbors through ventilation ducts. Berge says this avenue of human contact was completely unintended. Indeed, prison engineers tried to correct this problem, without success.

FROM THE START, WISCONSIN'S SUPERMAX WAS THE PRODUCT OF politics. The first public mention was Gov. Tommy Thompson's 1996 State of the State speech: "And once this plain, stark and austere facility is built, that's where Wisconsin's most vicious criminals will go. The Supermax will be a criminal's worst nightmare."

Up until that time, says Dickey, "I never heard anybody from corrections suggesting it was something we should have." Indeed, he says then-DOC Secretary Michael Sullivan "told me he argued vociferously for allocating the money in different ways" – especially on supervised community placements.

In some respects, Supermax is the perfect emblem for a prison system hijacked by politicians. They're the ones who have rushed to hike sentences, abolish parole and turn buzzwords like "three strikes and you're out" and "truth-in-sentencing" into policy, often against the advice of people who work closely with offenders.

As a result, Wisconsin's adult prison population now stands at 20,682, up from 5,736 when Thompson took office in January 1987. The state leads the nation in exporting prisoners, with 5,700 doing time at contract facilities in other states. And still, the state's 30 adult prisons, with a total capacity of just under 11,000 beds, are severely overcrowded.

State Sen. Moore suggests this boom has little to do with crime rates, which in Wisconsin have fallen for eight consecutive years. In legislative discussions on prisons, she says, "We don't even talk about dangerous criminals. We don't even talk about victims. We talk about the number of jobs that are created. We talk about receipts."

Supermax is by far the state's costliest prison, due to the extremely high level of security and the fact that, unlike other prisons, inmates do not prepare meals, do laundry or mop floors. Currently, the inmate-to-staff ratio is about one-to-one. Next year, when Supermax is in full swing, its projected $12.7 million operating budget and 400-450 inmate population (assuming some beds are left open for emergencies, as Berge would like) will add up to a per-inmate cost of about $30,000 a year. This is more than twice the per-inmate cost at maximum-security Waupun.

Dickey believes the prison system has a need for "close custody" of some offenders, those "who are so damaged that they act very aggressively toward others." Back when he headed the DOC, from 1983 to 1987, "we probably had a dozen guys that fit that description." A more contemporary indicator of need, he says, is the number of inmates in administrative confinement, kept separate from others for reasons of safety or security.

Last fall, when Supermax opened, the Wisconsin DOC had 50 inmates in administrative confinement, and 41 others being considered for such placement. But the population of Supermax is now nearing the 300 mark and, at current growth rates, the prison will be full by the end of this year.

Supermax is home to offenders like Christopher Scarver, who bludgeoned Jeffrey Dahmer and another inmate to death in 1994. But it also houses folks like Howard Beech, a 27-year-old whose original conviction was for attempted robbery in 1991. Since then, he has had two run-ins with guards, which brought additional four-year terms. Michelle Beech, Howard's wife, says he has had trouble in prison because he is mentally ill, diagnosed as bipolar.

Beech's current sentence is for a February 1998 incident in which he threw a temper tantrum, broke a table, and threatened a guard with the leg.

But the guard was never hit and, in a pre-sentencing report "did not want to recommend" additional prison time.

What's more, says Michelle, Howard has maintained a good conduct record since he returned to custody in August 1999. In fact, he got a satisfactory review at Portage on March 1, less than two weeks before being transferred to Supermax.

"He should be being integrated back," says Michelle, noting that her husband's mandatory release date is December 2001, before he can complete the regimen required to get out of Supermax. "He shouldn't be further from society."

DOC RULES SAY SUPERMAX IS MEANT FOR INMATES "KNOWN TO BE assaultive, violent or sexually aggressive." But that's just the start. Also eligible are those who have destroyed property, present "safety and security risks" due to gang activity, are considered "major escape or flight risks," or "otherwise threaten the orderly operation" of the prisons they're in.

Dickey says these guidelines lack the "clarity and specificity" needed to protect against overuse. He's not surprised: "When I was involved in rule-making, there was always pressure to draft rules as vaguely as possible. Then you can do anything you want."

Jerry DeMaio, a UW–Madison law student and editor of the *Wisconsin Law Review*, has written a thesis on Supermax entitled "If You Build It, They Will Come." It argues that Wisconsin's severe prison overcrowding, "coupled with admission and release standards that are vague and overbroad," add up to the likelihood that overclassification will occur.

Clearly, there is glaring racial disparity. Of the first 215 inmates sent to Supermax, only 62 (29 percent) were white. The majority – 128, or 60 percent – were African American, with Hispanics making up most of the rest. Spins DOC spokesperson Bill Clausius [formerly with the state Gaming Commission], "It's not like, 'Oh, you're black, you can't come in here!'"

A similar policy of inclusiveness applies to the mentally ill. Ted Garlewski, the DOC's chief psychologist, says that while some such inmates are screened out, being mentally ill does not preclude Supermax placement "if we think it's something they could handle." According to Berge, 25 of Supermax's first 242 inmates were receiving psychotropic medication, which Garlewski says is the best indicator of mental illness.

And there are signs that Supermax is being used to punish political activity. Exhibit A in this category is Shaka Shakur, a self-described "revolutionary nationalist and socialist" who ended up finishing out his

Wisconsin term at Supermax before being extradited to Indiana in March. Shakur got in hot water at another Wisconsin prison for possessing writings that included such statements as, "We must employ all means necessary to protect and support black people within prison walls."

Shakur, 34, also suspects he was singled out because, in Indiana, he participated in a hunger strike and lawsuit that forced one supermax to convert most of its cells to less restrictive uses. Still, this and another Indiana supermax remain so severe they were lambasted by the international group Human Rights Watch. But Shakur, who served years in Indiana's supermaxes, thinks Wisconsin's Supermax "takes the cake in terms of its sensory and perceptional deprivation and social isolation."

SUPERMAXES NATIONALLY HAVE BEEN CALLED "BREEDING GROUNDS FOR mental illness" and "virtual incubators of psychoses." Stuart Grassian, a Harvard Medical School professor who has spent more than two decades studying the psychological efforts of solitary confinement on prisoners, reports that common symptoms include hallucinations, panic attacks, obsessive thoughts, paranoia and problems with impulse control. "The harm caused by such confinement," he writes, "may result in prolonged or permanent psychiatric disability [and] may seriously reduce the inmate's capacity to reintegrate into the broader community upon release from prison."

A recurring phenomenon at supermaxes is self-mutilation, which experts say is done by inmates to "ensure themselves that they exist" and to prompt a reaction, even if it's a brutal one. Horror stories abound. At Arizona's supermax Special Management Unit II, one inmate castrated himself with an eating utensil and another tried to gouge out his own eyeball with a pencil. At the new supermax in Tamms, Ill., an inmate carved into his own flesh and ate scraps of the bloody tissue, then ripped out the sutures and rubbed feces into the reopened wounds.

At Wisconsin's Supermax, says Berge, "At least to date, our clinical staff have not seen the type of mental health deterioration that allegedly is going to be a given." But the most serious effects may take time to manifest. And letters from inmates confirm the pain that extreme isolation can bring.

Adam Procell, a former honor student who was convicted of murder in Milwaukee in 1996 at age 15, was among the first Supermax inmates to arrive. In letters to me, he has described an atmosphere of mind-numbing emptiness to which he has responded with defiance. He got in trouble for covering the camera in his room when he used the toilet, and has at times refused orders to leave his cell, prompting his forced removal. "So what if I get hurt?" he wrote, explaining that his 130-pound frame is no match for a cell-extraction team. "Bones heal, and physical pain heals fast. The mental pain of being treated like you aren't anything doesn't. I have too much pride to get walked over."

Howard Beech, in a letter to state Sen. Judy Robson, says the prison's conditions – the light that's on constantly, the dearth of outside-the-cell time, the lack of human contact, the absence of privacy – produce "thoughts of suicide, intense feelings of rage." He worries about what Supermax is doing to his fellow inmates: "This place is cruel and will make these people want to be the same."

THE GOAL OF SUPERMAX IS TO MODIFY BEHAVIOR THROUGH A SYSTEM of graduated privileges. Before becoming eligible for programmatic release, inmates must advance through five levels. Each level entails slightly greater privileges – for instance, the ability to make two six-minute calls per month instead of one. Any major conduct report will lead to a demotion in levels, and even repeated minor ones can result in an inmate not advancing.

Based on the required lengths of stay at each level, Berge anticipates that the typical inmate will spend around 30 months – two and a half years – at Supermax. This assumes that the inmate, after perhaps a setback or two, eventually does everything that's expected of him.

In fact, there's nothing to prevent Supermax from keeping inmates who never get with the program – due to obstinacy or mental illness or a lack of interest in the meager additional privileges they receive – for years or even decades. And despite the emphasis on controlling behavior, the prison has seen, in Berge's words, "lots of disruptive conduct." An open-records request confirms that hundreds of major conduct reports have been issued for things like threats, disobeying orders, disrespect and damaging property.

In January, an inmate was beaten by other inmates when a computer malfunction caused 26 cell doors to suddenly spring open. Three assaults of staff by inmates have been referred for prosecution, including an incident last December in which a fully shackled inmate headbutted a guard. Several inmates have destroyed the TVs in their rooms; these will not be replaced until they make restitution, no matter how long they're in Supermax. In late May, as many as nine inmates participated in a week-long hunger strike; DOC officials claim they have no idea why.

And there have been incidents of self-mutilation. In one case, Berge says, an inmate cut his arms "very superficially" with a pilfered razor blade. He was placed in clinical observation, in restraints, because the blade couldn't be found. On a previous occasion, the same inmate swallowed part of a razor blade and was placed in restraints until he excreted it. Berge says this inmate "is attempting to manipulate his way out of here, and this is the method he's attempting to use."

Berge takes a similar hard line regarding complaints about inmates being woken up by guards every hour all night long. "We've got some inmates who try to sleep in a way other than the way they're required to sleep," he says, explaining that covering one's face with a blanket in the always-lighted cell is against the rules. "It goes with the program. If that's what you want to do, you probably won't have a peaceful night of sleep."

THE MOST TROUBLING SUPERMAX INCIDENT DID NOT HAPPEN AT Supermax. In April, an inmate at the Racine Correctional Institution hanged himself to prevent his planned transfer to Wisconsin's harshest prison. "I told you I wasn't going to go there," wrote the inmate, David Hatch, convicted of killing two people, including a police officer, in 1985.

Milwaukee Circuit Reserve Judge Fred Kessler, who presided over Hatch's trial in Beloit and considers him "a real bad guy," was shaken by news of the hanging. "I was reminded of Devil's Island," he says of Supermax. "It starts to cross over into cruel and unusual punishment, and it reflects badly on society."

Such moral qualms also emanate from within the DOC. "This is really the cruelest thing that has ever been created," says one senior corrections official who spoke on condition of anonymity. "If it were done in a war, the people who would subject their enemies to treatment like this would be tried as war criminals."

The official says "many enlightened people in the department are very disappointed these resources are being diverted to this end" but is pessimistic anything will change because corrections is now the purview of politicians who believe, "The harsher the better."

But the problem is not just with politicians, it's with the people they seek to pander to. Letters to the editor from Supermax critics are met with responses from folks who want prisons to be places where inmates suffer. Supermax, advised one letter writer to the *Milwaukee Journal Sentinel*, "should be a standard means of confinement across the board."

Supermax's opening last fall was preceded by a six-day open house during which vendors sold sodas, sausages and T-shirts. Tens of thousands of people, including some 3,000 schoolchildren bused in from around the state, toured the facility. According to press accounts, some visitors were angered to see TVs in cells, thinking this was too great a luxury.

Against this backdrop, Sen. Moore advances a notion revolutionary enough to get her solitary: "I think inmates have rights. I think they're human beings. I believe you can rehabilitate people."

What's needed, says Moore, is "a major education of the public" to counteract existing notions about crime and punishment. People have come to accept that spending money on prisons "is going to make them safer," when in fact the opposite may be true, if the prisons being built are "driving prisoners crazy, creating more violent ones."

AUGUST 18, 2000

This article is a shorter version of one that appeared in Milwaukee Magazine. *Madison attorney Ed Garvey credits these articles with prompting him to get involved in several years of litigation on behalf of Supermax inmates, winning federal court rulings that changed the prison's rules regarding confinement, recreation and the imprisonment of the mentally ill. Berge remained warden until 2004.*

Brian Burke outside court, 2002. Photo by Steve Apps,
© *Wisconsin State Journal*, reprinted with permission

The Undoing
of Brian Burke

O n the morning of July 1, 2002, Brian Burke emerged from a Madison courtroom into bright lights and a phalanx of reporters shouting questions. It was like one of those television courtroom dramas where the media appear as an insensate mob, thrusting microphones and clicking cameras, creating a humiliating gauntlet through which the hapless defendant must pass.

"No comment," pleaded Burke, as he shuffled his way through a thick knot of inquisitors. But his attorney, Robert Friebert of Milwaukee, fielded questions on the spot and even after he and Burke left the building and strode briskly down the street, TV crews in tow. Friebert was indignant and unequivocal.

"Sen. Burke did not engage in any improprieties," he insisted, calling the 18 felony counts just issued against his client "gross overkill." There was no "pay-to-play," in which legislative favors are traded for campaign donations. Friebert said the Dane County prosecutor who brought the charges had a serious conflict. And he reiterated the breathtakingly audacious argument he had just made in court: that Burke could not be arrested or subjected to criminal proceedings while the Legislature was in session.

As one of the reporters in this unseemly throng, I took notes but kept my focus on Burke. He's commonly described as "boyish," the kind of guy who inspires joking references to Dorian Gray. On this day, however, Burke looked every bit his age, 44, and seemed inexpressibly weary and sad. The camera lights shone on the thin film of tears that welled up in his eyes.

How on earth had it come to this? Burke was among Wisconsin's most powerful and respected Democrats, considered a near shoo-in for the job of state attorney general. And then suddenly he's facing a maximum though unlikely sentence of 100 years in prison for "misconduct in public office" and other alleged crimes. His quest for the state's top law enforcement job had to be abandoned and his political career can now be described in a word: over.

Burke, who represented Milwaukee in the state Senate for 14 years and co-chaired the Legislature's mighty Joint Finance Committee (he did not seek reelection in 2002), was the first and perhaps most surprising target of criminal charges stemming from a John Doe probe that began in the summer of 2001. For several months, he stood alone as the poster boy of the so-called caucus scandal. He was eventually joined by other legislative leaders, including fellow Democrat Chuck Chvala, the now-former Senate majority leader (20 felonies, including three counts of extortion) and three Republicans: former Assembly Speaker Scott Jensen (three felonies, one misdemeanor), Assembly Majority Leader Steve Foti (one felony) and former Assistant Majority Leader Bonnie Ladwig (one misdemeanor). Also caught up in the dragnet have been aides to Burke, Chvala and Foti.

In many respects, Burke still stands apart. The charges against him have little to do with the now-defunct state caucuses, partisan branches of the Legislature that committed wholesale violations of rules against campaign work by state employees. In fact, much of the conduct for which Burke is facing criminal charges occurred *after* a series of articles in the *Wisconsin State Journal* focused attention on the caucuses and prompted prosecutors in Madison and Milwaukee to launch the John Doe probe.

Moreover, Burke's alleged conduct is at once more petty and less comprehensible than that of his fellows. He's charged with eight felonies for claiming $88 per diem payments to which he was not entitled. And while

Chvala, Jensen, Foti and others allegedly broke laws in their zeal to augment the power of their parties, Burke stands accused of crimes prompted strictly by personal self-interest and to cover up past wrongdoing.

There is another respect in which Burke differs from his fellow lawmaker-defendants. While all of them have declared their innocence and vowed a vigorous defense, Burke has gone further, declaring his outrage.

"Let me say this as clearly as possible: I haven't done anything wrong," Burke told a hushed Senate chamber in early July. "I haven't broken the law." He bitterly accused Dane County District Attorney Brian Blanchard, who brought the charges, of seeking "to destroy my family to further his own interests." Burke even claimed that Blanchard, whom he branded a lawbreaker and liar, had targeted him "because of my well-earned reputation for honestly serving the people of Wisconsin." He concluded by expressing his belief that "good will ultimately triumph over evil."

This much can be said for sure about Brian Burke, based on his years of public service and his months as an accused felon: He is not a common criminal. There is a reasonable basis for him to take umbrage at the charges lodged against him. They may indeed amount to overkill and in other ways be unfair. But it also says something about Burke's character – and that of the scandal-wracked Legislature as a whole – that he resolutely refuses to acknowledge how his own choices have been the agent of his undoing.

BURKE INITIALLY AGREED, IMMEDIATELY AND WITH ENTHUSIASM, TO BE interviewed for this article. While my letter urged him to take some time to think it over, he called me within minutes of its receipt. He suggested we do at least two interviews, one in Milwaukee and one in Madison.

But our interviews never took place. Instead his Senate staff appraised me that Burke's attorneys advised against it. "Brian loves to speak to the press," said aide Andrea Rowe. "Now he's in a strange position where he can't speak."

Actually, he can and has – not just in his statements from the Senate floor but also, just before charges were filed, in an interview with the *Milwaukee Journal Sentinel.* He also released a statement offering wild speculation about prosecutor Blanchard, who admitted receiving minor help from the Senate Democratic Caucus during his 2000 campaign, saying he clearly "used the power of his office to overcharge me, thereby allowing him to claim that his own admitted misconduct was not very serious." (Ultimately the State Elections Board ruled that Blanchard had committed only a minor infraction and imposed no penalty.)

In withdrawing from the attorney general race, before any charges were filed, Burke said the inclusion of his name on a list of lawmakers under investigation would be a "distraction." But he claimed his main reason was health-related, having to do with a herniated disc in his neck. In what he should have seen as a bad omen, no one believed him.

Burke lives in Milwaukee on 51st Street near North Avenue in a four-bedroom, one-bathroom brick house with an assessed value of $132,500. As he made it a point to tell his Senate colleagues, it does not have central air or cable TV. His family's "new car" is a 1991 Cutlass. Burke's job as a state senator paid $44,233 a year (plus per diems – $17,512 in 2001). Whatever it was that propelled him into politics, it was not to get rich.

The youngest of seven children in an Irish Catholic family, Burke has credited his parents – his father was an administrator at Milwaukee's Veterans Administration Hospital, his mother a nurse – and the rhetoric of John F. Kennedy for inclining him toward public service. A graduate of Washington High School and Marquette University, he got his law degree from Georgetown in 1981. He worked as an assistant prosecutor for the Milwaukee County District Attorney's Office before being elected to the Milwaukee Common Council in 1984. In the fall of 1988, he ran for the state Senate seat vacated by John Norquist, squeaking through a six-person Democratic primary with 33 percent of the vote. It was the last serious electoral contest he faced.

Michael Murphy had little interest in politics when he agreed to work on Burke's council campaign. He was a friend of Burke's wife, Patty – both had been geology majors at the University of Wisconsin–Milwaukee – and was impressed by Burke's community ties. Murphy became Burke's sole staff member and ultimately his successor as alderperson, a position he still holds. Burke was one of just two Common Council members to vote against awarding the city's cable contract to Time-Warner, because, says Murphy, "he felt the process wasn't fair." And as a state senator whose district included much of his old aldermanic area, he remained in contact over issues of concern.

Ald. Murphy calls Burke a "consummate family man" and "great dad" to his three daughters. He also describes Burke as "very private" and "emotional." It's the same note sounded by another old friend, Milwaukee lawyer and recurring candidate Matt Flynn. After heaping praise on Burke ("I just like him and I think everybody I know likes him"), Flynn tells how Burke reacted to a perceived betrayal.

Early in the race for attorney general, Flynn decided to endorse Burke's rival, former U.S. Attorney Peg Lautenschlager, whom he has known for many years and who managed one of his past campaigns. When Burke found out about this, says Flynn, "He was like a wounded puppy. He was very cute about it." At more than one event, Flynn says Burke would "corner me with wounded eyes," asking, in so many words, "Matt, how could you?"

Flynn sees this as part of what makes Burke a rare and wondrous specimen. "A lot of politicians, their responses are fake," he says. "They'll tell you what you want to hear." But not Burke: "He's one of the few people in politics I've ever had an honest conversation with."

As a senator, Burke became a darling of environmentalists for his efforts to protect air and water, preserve green space, promote recycling, oppose mining and reduce pollution. He was a main force behind legislation that spurred the cleanup and redevelopment of abandoned industrial sites, as well as a bill to require local governments to devise comprehensive land use plans. Burke consistently made Wisconsin's Environmental Decade's Clean 16 list based on his legislative voting record. He's also won awards for his work on behalf of sexual assault victims, Vietnam vets, Hispanics, Jews, law enforcement and the military.

Spencer Black, who recently stepped down as Assembly minority leader, praises Burke's record. "I served with him for many years. He was a top-notch legislator – very hard-working, very intelligent, very conscientious. He always seemed very principled to me."

Burke's self-image is wrapped up in notions of us vs. them, good vs. evil. His biographical materials boast that as an assistant district attorney in Milwaukee, he "stood up to gang leaders and deadbeat dads alike." He's "a champion of consumer rights" and is intent on "cracking down on white-collar crime and corruption."

On criminal justice issues, Burke touts himself as the author of "hard-hitting" initiatives to add police, combat gun violence and improve the treatment of crime victims. But he also highlights his advocacy of community policing, drug treatment and addressing the "root causes of crime" – poverty, abuse, failing neighborhoods. "Everybody talks tough," he's said, "but we've also got to be smart."

Marla Stephens, director of the appellate division for the State Public Defender's Office in Milwaukee, says that despite Burke's background as a prosecutor, he always grasped the importance of adequately funding other players, including her office. And as one of Burke's constituents, she appreciates his efforts to clean up Menomonee Valley and fund the Hank Aaron State Trail. When he was criminally charged, Stephens wrote him to say, "I'll always remember and respect you for the good work you did."

Jay Heck, a former legislative aide and caucus worker, recalls that when Burke took office in early 1989, "It seemed clear to everybody that he was going to have a fairly bright future." He was soon appointed to a host of key committees, including Joint Finance. Yet Heck "always got the sense that Burke felt he was entitled to more than he was getting. He felt under-appreciated."

IT'S REALLY NOT FAIR TO BLAME THE CAUCUS SCANDAL ON THE SMALL group of people who have been criminally charged. None of them were operating in a vacuum; after all, 19 people were granted immunity in the John Doe probe. What happened was the ethical breakdown of an entire system, including those who failed to exercise appropriate oversight.

One legislative aide explains it using a sports analogy: "Two teams are playing basketball. There's a hard foul and everyone looks at the ref. He doesn't call it. Next time down the court – boom! – another hard foul, this time by the other team. No call. From now on, that's the way the game is played. We used to have good rules and a good ref. We don't anymore."

That the state's legislative caucuses evolved over time into full-fledged political machines was an open secret. A 1996 *Isthmus* article on former caucus staffer Mo Hansen blew the whistle on this activity, loudly and clearly. But no one paid any attention, least of all the agencies charged with enforcing the laws in this area.

"The Ethics Board and Elections Board are completely lame; they haven't done their job," says former Burke aide Barry Ashenfelter. "They knew this stuff was going on."

The abuse was so rampant and so well-known that Madison's *Capital Times* was able to steal some of the *State Journal*'s thunder by running an editorial entitled "Clean Up Caucuses" three weeks before the latter began its investigative series (which many in the Capitol and local press knew was in the works). Both legislative parties, the editorial noted, "have for years been fueling their political operations with taxpayer dollars."

In addition to asleep-at-the-switch regulators, DAs in Dane County were noticeably reluctant to involve themselves in investigations of alleged Capitol misconduct. But Brian Blanchard, a former federal prosecutor with no prior political experience, pledged as a candidate to take such matters seriously, and to many peoples' great surprise, actually did, launching a John Doe probe within weeks of the *State Journal*'s series.

Given the "anything goes" culture that had been allowed to fester in the Capitol, it's not surprising that the targets of this probe, Burke included, feel victimized by a sudden rush to take the rules seriously. Perhaps when he insists, "I haven't done anything wrong," what he means is "I haven't done anything unusual." And in this, he may be right.

Barry Ashenfelter was fresh out of law school when he joined Burke's staff in early 1992, filling in for an aide on maternity leave. He ended up staying 10 years, ultimately becoming Burke's chief of staff. "I like Brian Burke and think he's a good guy," attests Ashenfelter, who now works for the Humane Society of Wisconsin. "I really think he did more to improve the public good in the last 15 years than most groups of 100 people do in their entire lifetimes."

Ashenfelter, who was especially drawn to environmental issues, found that Burke, after a short while, was willing to give him "free rein to negotiate legislation" in this area. Even more impressive was Burke's independence because he didn't need to raise campaign funds. "Until he ran for attorney general, he didn't care what lobbyists thought," says Ashenfelter. "His seat was safe." (Burke faced only token opposition in 1990 and 1994 and none at all in 1998.)

As Joint Finance co-chair, Burke battled road builders and their allies who, says Ashenfelter, "protect the transportation fund like it was the Holy Grail." Burke and two Republicans, Scott Jensen and John Gard, "were the only ones fighting for more aid to municipalities, more bus service and repair of existing highways." (This area, explains Ashenfelter, is "not a partisan thing. Most Dems do whatever the road builders want, too.")

But Ashenfelter goes on to make some disturbing admissions about the gradual erosion and eventual disintegration of the boundary between legislative and political work that occurred in Burke's office and, no doubt, throughout the Legislature as a whole. "When I first started, I was really careful to take vacation time" or work only evenings and weekends on behalf of legislative candidates, doing things like stuffing envelopes and going door to door.

Over time, however, Ashenfelter stopped being so scrupulous. "The line just blurred," he says. "It just didn't seem to matter. It just seemed like nobody cared." He cites the lack of reaction to *Isthmus'* article on Mo Hansen: "What was anyone to think?"

Ashenfelter, who according to the criminal complaint used state equipment to process campaign checks and participated in campaign-related meetings on state property, rationalized his conduct on grounds that he was putting in 50- to 60-hour weeks, so taxpayers were still getting their money's worth. Besides, he says, "70 percent" of what legislative aides do – from putting out newsletters to arranging public appearances – is "about getting their legislator elected." He calls it "campaigning in disguise."

Now Ashenfelter, who was neither granted immunity nor criminally charged, calls the political work done on state time "a horrible mistake," admitting, "Everyone knew we were doing wrong." And while he feels bad for both Burke and Chvala, he thinks the people who make and have the power to change laws ought to live by them. "We all should be held accountable."

THE CRIMINAL COMPLAINT AGAINST BRIAN BURKE ALLEGES THAT, DESPITE a clearly articulated rule against using state offices, staff and supplies "for any campaign activity," he had his state Senate aides process contributions, prepare campaign finance reports and write letters to donors. He allegedly got irked over one staffer who declined to do campaign work, saying others were "busting their asses."

Burke aides Tanya Bjork and Raghu Devaguptapu, both now charged with relatively minor offenses, apparently cooperated fully with investigators. Both are former Assembly Democratic Caucus staffers who say Burke hired them explicitly to do campaign work, including fundraising. Burke allegedly told Bjork he wanted to raise big money during the small "window" of opportunity, perhaps six months, created by the state budget process.

Devaguptapu, meanwhile, compiled "call sheets" of potential donors and set up meetings with lobbyists. The complaint identifies five meetings in March and April 2001 in which lobbyists were hit up for contributions to Burke's attorney general campaign. While it was usually Devaguptapu who did the asking, the complaint says Burke "definitely knew" money was being sought.

During a meeting with lobbyists from the Wisconsin Realtors Association in a state Capitol conference room, Devaguptapu allegedly asked for $25,000. "You're crazy," replied the lobbyist, "we've never given that kind of money."

The Realtors, in a statement, confirm that such a comment was made and that the Greater Milwaukee Association of Realtors subsequently gave $5,000 to Burke's campaign. The statement calls the meeting "atypical" in that it took place where prohibited, on state property, and says the amount sought was "disproportionately large and for … an election [attorney general] in which the Realtors historically had not been involved."

In other cases, Burke allegedly made direct requests, at one meeting going around a room of lobbyists, asking, "What are you going to do to help me become attorney general?"

Burke, according to Bjork, would often overstate the degree to which he was in accord with lobbyists, saying things like, "Yes, I'm with you" even if his traditional positions differed from those of the interest group. But Burke, unlike Chvala, is not accused of making explicit promises or threats. The Realtors, in their statement, say "there was no attempt by Sen. Burke or his staff to connect the contribution to a specific legislative action" and that no one felt "threatened or coerced to make a contribution."

Hence the protestations by Burke and his attorneys that there was no "pay to play." But the complaint does allege that Burke came awfully close. At a meeting with lobbyists for the Wisconsin Dental Association, he allegedly sought a $10,000 contribution after being asked to introduce an amendment regarding dental care in rural areas. The group gave him $8,000 and Burke offered the amendment, which did not pass.

The 34-page complaint is sprinkled with intimations that Burke knew what he was doing was illegal. He allegedly instructed his campaign treasurer to record reimbursements to Bjork and Devaguptapu for expenses like gas and stamps in a way that made it look as though they were being paid consulting fees for campaign work. He brushed off warnings about using his state cell phone for campaign-related calls and his office for campaign-related business. And when Bjork urged him to start paying half of one Senate aide's salary using campaign funds, he pointedly refused, saying this sudden shift would look too suspicious – that is, it would raise questions as to whether this staffer had previously been doing campaign work on state time.

In October 2001, Burke received the first of two subpoenas from the John Doe probe, this one seeking records regarding Devaguptapu's activities. The following month, Burke allegedly directed Bjork to delete references to meetings with lobbyists from his Capitol office computer. He also told her to change references to "call time" spent contacting potential donors to "constituent time" and to delete campaign-related materials from the computers of two former staffers.

Burke received a second, much broader subpoena in early March 2002. According to the complaint, when Burke saw that a calendar printout generated in response to the subpoena still contained campaign-related entries, he got mad and ordered Bjork to make additional deletions. Investigators later recovered 13 deleted entries from Burke's seized office computer that did not appear on the printouts he produced under this subpoena.

Before leaving Burke's staff in the fall of 2001, Devaguptapu, who now works for the national Democratic Legislative Campaign in Washington,

D.C., produced two memos for his successor. One listed upcoming fundraising events for the Burke campaign, the other was an assessment of various lobbyists. The complaint says Burke made handwritten additions to this second memo and discussed it with his new aide, referring to lobbyists who did not contribute as "deadbeats." He allegedly decided to recreate a clean copy in case it was subpoenaed and "expressed anger" when he suspected, correctly, that the aide had turned over the marked-up list.

There's more: Upon learning that Devaguptapu relinquished records regarding lobbyist contacts, Burke allegedly told Bjork, "Why couldn't he burn those in the fireplace or flush them down the toilet?" And when Bjork was pulling together documents in response to the second subpoena, Burke is said to have instructed her not to include campaign materials, so she tossed more than a dozen campaign-related messages in the recycling bin. At least this action was environmentally correct.

WELL BEFORE IT BECAME A TARGET OF THE JOHN DOE PROBE, BURKE'S BID for state attorney general was raising eyebrows. In September 2001, the nonpartisan watchdog group Wisconsin Democracy Campaign produced a report called "Hey Bidder, Bidder ..." about the alleged auctioning of state government favors to special interests. Burke was one of four main "auctioneers," along with Chvala, Jensen and then-Gov. Scott McCallum. The group said Burke "used his position to vigorously seek large special-interest contributions to fuel his run for attorney general, [raising] substantially more – $222,513 – than any other member of the entire Legislature during the half of 2001 when the budget was being considered."

The report also charged that while Burke had sponsored a campaign finance reform bill, he "subsequently did nothing to move the measure through the legislative process." Grumbles Mike McCabe, the group's executive director, "He didn't even bother to testify on behalf of his own bill at hearings throughout the state."

More red flags went up in early 2002 when McCabe's group, in reviewing Burke's campaign finance reports, found no evidence of any paid staff for a campaign that by then had raised more than $440,000. No paid manager. No paid consultants. No office. No outside help of any kind except from a firm engaged in direct mail and telemarketing.

"It was pretty obvious to us that there had to have been some state employees involved in running his campaign," says McCabe, who also noticed the hiring of former caucus workers Bjork and Devaguptapu. "It looked to me and to a lot of people that his staff was being turned into a campaign organization." He's astounded that even after the *Milwaukee Journal Sentinel* ran an article on these concerns, Burke didn't even have the good sense to "put a campaign manager on the payroll for appearance's sake."

For all candidates, says McCabe, the enormous cost of getting elected creates pressure to cross lines and cut corners. But Burke's behavior strikes him as even more extreme: "What he did was so reckless and so foolish, it's a reflection of how strong his ambition was."

Many observers speculate that Burke was the first lawmaker charged because he was a Democrat and prosecutor Blanchard did not want it to look as though he was only going after Republicans. Blanchard agrees he "prioritized" the Burke investigation over others but says it's because of "the nature of the job" Burke was seeking. "He was running for the highest law enforcement position in the state and we were getting new information at a time when the campaign for attorney general was under way."

All total, Burke raised just over $500,000 for his aborted bid for attorney general, including this year's receipts. That sounds excessive, especially given that, as of January 2002, Burke had $403,663 on hand compared to Peg Lautenschlager's $13,613. But by the election last November, when Lautenschlager eked out a narrow victory, she had apparently raised and spent about $465,000. Granted, much of this money would have flowed to Burke, as it did to her, in the campaign's final months. But his zeal to get a huge head start no longer appears all that misguided.

Former aide Ashenfelter says Burke was just following advice: "That's what his friends in Milwaukee told him to do — save all of your money for [ads on] TV." He says these friends included Burke's attorney Friebert. Ironically, some of these contributions are now going to Friebert and others at his firm. Several weeks before the charges were filed, Burke sent a form letter to contributors, seeking authorization to use their donations for his legal defense ("It would mean a lot to me and my family"). Within a few weeks, he was able to transfer $100,215 from one pot to the other; more funds may have been shifted since. And Burke has as of yet made no progress on his public promise to repay the nearly $9,500 in legal fees passed on to taxpayers.

DESPITE ALL OF THIS, THE CHARGES AGAINST BURKE INSPIRE RAGE IN some quarters.

"I think this whole prosecution is an abuse of prosecutorial discretion," fumes Burke's friend Matt Flynn. He chalks it up to a DA who "wants to make a name for himself and is also politically ambitious." There is no evidence, he says, that votes were bought. "A great many people in both parties" solicit contributions, and the laws against doing so on state property are not consistently enforced, making the charges against Burke selective and unfair.

Some observers think prosecutor Blanchard, perhaps miffed by Burke's alleged efforts to conceal evidence, engaged in piling on. Burke couldn't agree more, asserting in one statement, "While I vigorously deny having done anything wrong, even if I had, 18 felony counts represents a wildly overblown charging decision."

Of particular concern are the eight separate felony charges, each carrying a maximum $10,000 fine and five years in prison, for allegedly submitting false $88 per diem claims involving a total of 10 days. "If he did it, it's wrong," says a Capitol insider who considers these charges among the most bothersome, since they involved personal gain. "But I don't think $880 in falsified expense reports should be punishable by 40 years."

Burke's lawyers have argued in court filings that if the rules regarding per diems were violated – which they don't concede – the responsibility for enforcement belongs to the Legislature and not the DA's office. Longtime Senate Chief Clerk Don Schneider is unaware of any other instance in which criminal charges were filed over per diem claims. On the other hand, he also can't think of any occasion when these were internally enforced: "In the 26 years I've been clerk, this is the first time any question has been raised."

Similarly, Burke's defenders contend that no one has ever been criminally charged for seeking contributions on state property. Even if Burke did this, they say, the charges amount to nitpicking. Had he asked lobbyists for money at a coffee shop near the Capitol, it would have been perfectly legal – and, in fact, commonplace.

"Reality is that the entire campaign finance system is based on implicit quid pro quos," says the Capitol insider. "It happens all the time. The only thing they got Brian Burke on is he didn't walk across the street to do it."

Brian Brophy, Blanchard's predecessor as Dane County DA, agrees that the charges amount to overkill. Unless Blanchard's goal is to send Burke to prison "for many, many years," says Brophy, now a criminal defense attorney, the charges are inappropriate. "I think that when we talk about filling our jails with nonviolent criminals, certainly Mr. Burke would qualify. Even if the charges levied against him are true, this is someone who has done an enormous amount for the state."

Lester Pines, the Madison attorney representing Tanya Bjork, has a different perspective. "The Legislature and the courts have over the last three decades made it easier than ever for prosecutors to bring charges" for all manner of offenses, he says. Now that some lawmakers are on the receiving end, it occurs to them that this is unfair. "To that, I say, 'Duh!'"

Recently, Pines had a client "charged with 16 counts of sexual assault arising out of one act of sexual intercourse." He says similar piling on occurs "every day," usually involving poor defendants, and "the Legislature has never had any concern about it."

And whatever claim to unjust treatment Burke might make is undercut by his blustery "I haven't done anything wrong" response and the delay-at-all-costs posture of his attorneys. In addition to claiming that the state constitution makes Burke immune from criminal prosecution – in essence an assertion that the people who make the laws are entitled to special treatment – Burke's lawyers have filed 15 motions for dismissal. These range from the preposterous to the thought-provoking to the truly troublesome.

One contends Burke cannot be charged with misconduct in office since "candidate for attorney general" – the capacity in which he was acting – "is not a public office." Another says only the Legislature, not the courts or executive branch, can regulate what happens in legislative meetings or between lawmakers and their staff. A third says no law was broken because no one sought contributions from the lobbyists; they merely asked the lobbyists – allegedly – to seek contributions from their clients.

But however the criminal cases against Burke and others play out, former aide Ashenfelter sees the possibility of some positive outcomes: "I hope over time that this will be good for the institution. I know it's hard right now for Brian and his family. We're going to look real bad for the next couple of years. But I hope that it causes the state Legislature in the next few sessions to pass really significant, nationally groundbreaking campaign finance and ethics reform laws."

FEBRUARY 2003, MILWAUKEE MAGAZINE

Brian Burke ultimately pled guilty to one felony count of misconduct in office; he was sentenced to six months in jail and ordered to pay fines and restitution totaling about $89,000. His license to practice law was revoked in January 2006 and reinstated in October 2008. The caucus scandal led to a host of other criminal convictions and the creation of a new oversight authority, the Wisconsin Government Accountability Board.

Gordy Sussman in court, 2004. Photo by Mary Langenfeld

The Trial of
Gordy Sussman

"While it is your duty to give the defendant the benefit of every reasonable doubt, you are not to search for doubt; you are to search for the truth."

– STANDARD JURY INSTRUCTION

I t was a very small moment in a very big trial. At the end of a long day of testimony, Dane County Assistant District Attorney Jac Heitz and Madison Police Det. Bruce Frey were exiting the courtroom, pushing a cart bearing computers seized from the business and home of the defendant, Gordon Sussman. These were the machines that provided the basis for the 16 felony charges against him for possession of child pornography, and which shored up the prosecution's case on the remaining four counts, two for allegedly repeatedly molesting a young boy and two for exposing him to porn.

As Heitz and Frey reached the courtroom's outer door, the wheels of the cart jammed against a metal strip along the floor. Sussman, who was talking to me in the hall, without hesitation darted over to give the pair a hand, lifting the cart so it could clear this obstacle.

Why would Gordy Sussman go out of his way, even slightly, to help his adversaries? Was this a spontaneous act of kindness, or just oddly impulsive behavior? Similar questions would arise the next morning, when Sussman, despite repeated warnings against parties having contact with jurors, said "Good morning" to one arriving to court. Heitz called it "an outrageous breach of this court's rules" and "an obvious attempt to ingratiate himself to the jury"; Sussman said it was "reflexive" and apologized.

Such minor moments invoke the case's major questions: Did Sussman, a prominent area businessman, involve himself in a young boy's life because he was a generous and caring mentor? Or was he seeking to exploit a troubled lad's loneliness for the purpose of sexual gratification?

Late last week the jury, after nine days of trial and nine hours of deliberation, decided it was the latter. It rendered guilty verdicts on 18 of the 20 counts, curiously declining to convict Sussman for allegedly displaying pornographic material to his victim – charges that, like the two parallel counts of repeated sexual molestation, hinged largely on the credibility of his accuser, identified in court papers by his initials, SJB.

Did the jury get it right? Having sat through these proceedings, seeing the evidence presented to the jury and some that was not, and having regular access to Sussman and his lead attorney, Stephen Hurley, I can honestly say: I don't know.

It was a case of almost unmanageable complexity, with matters of fact and law that were subject to constant contention. Both sides believed firmly in their (mutually exclusive) positions. Hurley and defense co-counsel Erik Guenther considered Sussman innocent on the child-molestation charges and technically not guilty on the porn-possession charges. And Heitz and the police obviously saw SJB as a true victim and Sussman as a threat to society who needed to be locked up for a very long time.

How long? Sussman faces a maximum sentence of 180 years on the charges for which he was convicted. The actual sentence, to be imposed in several months, will certainly be shorter than that but possibly longer than the remainder of Sussman's life.

SUSSMAN, 53, WAS CHARGED WITH MULTIPLE ACTS OF SEXUAL CONTACT involving SJB, whom he had volunteered to mentor at West Middleton Elementary, which Sussman's two children also attended. The assaults allegedly occurred over two periods: May 1998 to January 2002, and April 11, 2002 to May 13, 2002. During these times, the boy was between the ages of 9 and 12.

In July 2002, two months after he returned to Indiana to be with his mom, SJB came forward with his allegations of abuse. He spoke to several officers in Indiana and Madison, and gave a videotaped interview at Safe Harbor, a local facility designed for child victims and witnesses.

On July 16, police executed search warrants on Sussman's Monona workplace and Verona home, seizing a computer from each. Initially, they found evidence of child porn on just the work machine, which led to seven criminal charges. Early this year, similar images were found on Sussman's home machine, resulting in nine additional counts.

The founder and former owner of Rutabaga paddle shop (he sold the business in 2002), Sussman was a respected businessman with no criminal past. Recently, he led efforts to erect a memorial in Blue Mound State Park honoring four World War II airmen killed in a 1944 plane crash. He has steadfastly asserted his innocence.

As Sussman put it in one of our early conversations, more than a year ago: "I don't fuck little children." He said he had gotten into a mentoring relationship to help SJB, but began to back away in early 2002, after learning that the boy had falsely accused his own father of sexual abuse. In retaliation, said Sussman, SJB turned on him.

I asked Sussman about the child-porn charges, and he replied, "I'm not into pornography." I asked how the images described in the criminal complaint – for instance, a photo "depicting a pre-pubescent youth engaged in an anal sexual act" – came to be on his work computer.

"I've seen pornography on there," he told me. "I can tell you where I've seen images." He said that while searching for the term "rutabaga" for reasons related to trademarks and copyrights, he happened upon a newsgroup containing hardcore porn. His implication was that this was fleeting and accidental.

Sussman went on to admit he accessed other materials of this nature while looking into attacks on United Way funding to the Boy Scouts. He felt these attacks originated from "militant pedophiles," supposedly because they're mad at the scouts for squeezing them out. It was not an explanation that made a whole lot of sense.

In many ways, Sussman comes across as essentially adolescent: impulsive, incautious, spontaneous to a fault. At one point during trial, when I asked him to talk, he suggested that, at day's end, we go canoeing. I didn't take him up on it.

Indeed, Sussman owes being in Madison to an act of impulse. A native of New Jersey, he decided at age 19 to bail on his studies at American University in Washington, D.C., and hitchhike to Boulder. He ended up hanging his thumb on Highway 151 outside of Madison, and, when he had a hard time catching a ride further west, caught one into town. He transferred to the UW–Madison, and began selling canoe paddles on the side. Rutabaga, begun as a basement business in 1974, now employs 60 people and annually sponsors Canoecopia, "the world's largest paddle sport expo."

Sussman, who the day before trial learned his father is dying from rapidly metastasizing cancer, appeared throughout to be jittery and disconnected, his thoughts fluttering from one place to another like butterflies. He has attention-deficit disorder, though he jokes that he does not suffer from it – the people around him do. He compares this disorder to looking at psychedelic posters while stoned and experiencing a shift in perception, adding, in his stream-of-consciousness style of conversing, that he has little experience with drugs.

But a quirky personality is not an indicator of guilt, and Sussman's protestations of innocence have been emphatic and unequivocal. Being charged with this crime, which has cast his life into chaos and caused him to spend hundreds of thousands of dollars on his defense, has made him angry.

More than once, Sussman has vented to me about "the incredible effort the District Attorney's Office puts into suppressing and withholding exculpatory evidence, instead of trying to find the truth." Even after the verdicts, in a call from Florida while on a court-approved visit to his dying dad, he declared: "They know I'm innocent, and they've done this anyway."

THE STATE OF WISCONSIN V. GORDON E. SUSSMAN BEARS INEVITABLE

comparison to the prosecution of Michael Jackson on similar charges. In both, the defense attacked the alleged victim's credibility, suggesting he was being manipulated by a conniving mother eager to shake the money tree of a post-trial civil suit.

A sizable number of witnesses pegged Sussman's young accuser as a cunning and habitual liar. And it's hardly a stretch to believe SJB's mother, an alcoholic who fobbed him off on a series of relatives and others while she went into a tailspin of attempted suicide, institutionalization and incarceration, has her eyes on the prize of a civil judgment, as others alleged and she denied.

The Jackson verdict, rendered on June 13, likely worked against Sussman, as jurors absorbed a full dose of irate reaction to yet another celebrity acquittal and fortified themselves against being duped. But there's nothing to suggest they did not base their verdicts on the evidence they were allowed to see, and the arguments they heard.

The trial was more frustrating than riveting. Originally slated for one week, it dragged on for two. Circuit Court Judge James Martin's 10-minute breaks usually ran closer to half an hour, and the proceedings were frequently interrupted by objections that led to protracted bench conferences. Whispered one courtroom spectator, referring to jury members, "They've got to be just dying up there."

And yet, whether they realized it or not, the jurors got to see two of the state's best trial attorneys at the top of their form. Prosecutor Heitz, with a bullet-like build and crop of Chia hair, exuded an almost palpable aura of rage. He expressed open disdain for Hurley, occasional annoyance with Judge Martin, and at one point bullied to tears one of his own witnesses, an elementary school teacher, over her lack of preparedness. ("How does one know what one is going to be asked?" she sobbed.)

But Heitz's bulldog demeanor was matched by his equally intimidating command of the law. He regularly bested Hurley in evidentiary disputes, even managing to shut down one of the defense's intended main prongs – that SJB had made prior false accusations of sexual assault – by arguing after the trial began that Hurley should have brought a pretrial motion to get this in, accusing him of "a willful and tactical decision to ambush the state." As a result, Hurley never called several potentially key defense witnesses – including SJB's father, who has said his son once threatened to report him for sexual abuse when he refused to let the boy ride his bike in the street.

Hurley, stately and cooler of temperament, did better at working the jurors. He certainly made fewer demands on their time, wrapping up his case in a day and a half after Heitz put on five and a half days of testimony, followed by another half day of rebuttal. In all, the state called 23 witnesses to the defense's 13, though both sides spent roughly equal time asking them questions.

Sussman himself never testified. The day after telling Judge Martin he was "knowingly and voluntarily" relinquishing this right, Sussman told me he disagreed with his attorneys and considered this a mistake. But, Sussman added, in reference to Hurley, "he's the expert." He then veered off into an analogy about which is the best kayak for certain customers, presumably to show the limits of lay versus expert knowledge.

The jury, which ultimately consisted of 10 women and two men, was drawn from a pool of 50 in a day-long selection process designed to prune out anyone whose background or personality suggested bias or aptitude. A former law enforcement officer who had investigated child-porn cases and was now a law student ... gone. A muscular man with a buzz cut who looked as though he might leave testosterone stains on any surface he touched ... gone.

Several jurors were dismissed for having prior knowledge of the case from media attention or because of personal experience with sexual assault. But notably, while potential jurors were asked repeatedly – by Heitz, by Hurley and by Judge Martin – if having to view explicit pornography involving children would be too upsetting, not a single one answered in the affirmative.

As is typical, the lawyers used the selection process to prep jurors, with Heitz asking, "Do you believe that a child who comes from a troubled family is unworthy of belief?" and Hurley countering, "Is there anyone who believes a child who makes an allegation of sexual assault couldn't possibly be lying?"

Throughout the trial, the jury remained remarkably jovial. They chatted pleasantly with each other during bench conferences and returned from breaks – during which loud peals of laughter emanated from the jury room – in obvious good cheer. This was true even for the break after the first showing of the hardcore child porn, with the bailiff trumpeting the chuckling jury's return with the words, "Judge, they're having way too much fun back there."

THE MOST SERIOUS CHARGES AGAINST SUSSMAN WERE BASED ON SJB'S allegations. Prosecutor Heitz, in his opening statement, said SJB's absent father and troubled mother left him so starved for attention he was "willing to endure humiliating sexual abuse" in exchange for Sussman's role in his life, which by all accounts included bike rides and paddling excursions, help with his school work, day trips and occasional gifts.

Before bringing SJB to the stand, the prosecution called Anna Salter, a nationally recognized expert on pedophiles and their victims who had never met either Sussman or SJB. She talked about how child molesters engage in "grooming" behavior to win the trust of victims and their families, but admitted this could not automatically be distinguished from the actions of someone who just cares about a child. She said it was common for child victims to "test the waters" by revealing only part of the abuse, and for their stories to contain inconsistencies.

This was damaging testimony, made more so by Hurley's aggressive and largely unsuccessful efforts to get Salter to yield to his view that inconsistencies are a sign of untruthfulness.

In fact, Sussman's accuser was wildly inconsistent. Initially, SJB told police there were just four or five instances of sexual contact, later that there were 50, then "at least 100," then back to about 50. He said at first there were no instances of anal intercourse, later that there was one. SJB also initially reported that he and Sussman occasionally engaged in oral sex, later that he never gave in to Sussman's overtures in this regard. Do victims test the waters with things that are false?

There was testimony about how SJB was caught viewing pornographic websites at Rutabaga. But the jury never heard about SJB's personal computer, obtained in 2004 from his Indiana residence, which contained images of child porn, adult porn and bestiality. The defense had hired an agent to acquire this machine through the use of deceit, prompting Dane County District Attorney Brian Blanchard (who sat in on some of the trial) to file a complaint against Hurley, still pending, with the state Office of Lawyer Regulation. [This complaint was later soundly rejected, with arbiters affirming that Hurley had an ethical obligation to employ such strategies.]

An even more glaring inconsistency concerned whether or not Sussman, whose penis SJB allegedly saw and touched on dozens of occasions, was circumcised. SJB, who knew the difference and had once met with a physician regarding his own uncircumcised state, told Det. Frey and the Safe Harbor interviewer that Sussman was not circumcised, repeating this at a preliminary hearing in September 2003. But SJB changed his story during a meeting with Frey and Heitz on Feb. 18 of this year, saying Sussman was circumcised and any prior representations to the contrary were incorrect. This is also what he said at trial.

Hurley suggested that the detective and prosecutor prompted this change, perhaps inadvertently. SJB, he said, was smart enough to surmise, when asked if he was sure about something he had repeatedly stated, that he had gotten this wrong. The jury never knew that just days before this Feb. 18 meeting, Det. Frey had obtained medical records from Sussman's personal physician confirming that Sussman was circumcised.

SJB, on the stand for several hours, calmly recounted how Sussman had come into his life as a school-appointed mentor but was soon showing him computer porn – of young boys, young girls, adults with children and "people doing sexual things to horses" – and telling him "about the body parts and what comes out of them." This allegedly led to sexual contact at Sussman's home and office, in parks and in the water during paddling outings, in cars and at a hotel on an overnight trip. All of which SJB endured because "I was embarrassed and I thought it was right."

Hurley, in his cross-examination, got SJB to admit he had accused his father of inappropriate sexual conduct and threatened to report an uncle for physical abuse, although SJB claimed these things occurred. SJB also confirmed that he had never reported Sussman was abusing him to a counselor he visited 65 times during this period, once denying it outright. Finally, Hurley cornered SJB into conceding that the version of events to which he was testifying at trial, and claiming to be true, was different from accounts given to various police officers and at the preliminary hearing, adding acidly, "And we have your word for that?"

BUT WHAT ABOUT GORDY SUSSMAN? WHAT KIND OF MAN TAKES A HUGE
interest in developing relationships with young boys? A parade of educators described Sussman's keen interest in SJB's studies, but this testimony was mostly a wash. For every witness who said Sussman was butting in where he didn't belong, there was testimony suggesting he had SJB's best interests at heart. One teacher had reportedly termed Sussman "the best thing that ever happened" to SJB.

Karen Anderson, Sussman's wife of more than two decades, was subpoenaed by the prosecution regarding her efforts to suspend her husband's mentoring relationships. Anderson, a veterinarian, testified that she merely wanted Sussman to spend more time with her. But she was an uncomfortable witness, and seemed as though she had something to hide. This impression was compounded when SJB's mother took the stand to say that Anderson had called her, crying and "very upset" about the mentoring.

Two Rutabaga employees testified that Sussman's office door was almost always open, and that parts of his office were visible from heavily used common areas. But another (former) employee, who admitted disliking Sussman, said the door was usually closed: "I used to tell my wife, I don't know what Gordy does in there." Further speculation along these lines may have been fueled by crime lab findings of semen stains of uncertain paternity on the mouse pad of Sussman's work machine.

But no witness reported seeing any inappropriate conduct between SJB and Sussman, despite SJB's testimony that Sussman molested him indoors and out with regularity. There was testimony that SJB enjoyed and looked forward to these visits. And jurors got to see a certificate that SJB had given Sussman, thanking him "for all that you have done for me and my mom."

Several witnesses, including a counselor in Indiana who has seen SJB in recent years, averred that he seemed honest and true. Others disagreed. Kim Varian, SJB's cousin, who took him in for several months because his mother "basically needed a break," testified that he was manipulative and dishonest. SJB's uncle called him "a schemer." Barbara O'Connor, a former corrections officer who lived with SJB and his mom for four months last year, said he "lied for no reason at all." And Diane Boles, a teacher at West Middleton Elementary, called SJB "manipulative and precocious" and said things she knew caused her to be "fearful" about the mentoring relationship — for Sussman. Even Judge Martin, in comments made outside of the jury's presence, called SJB's claim that he allowed the abuse to continue because he thought it was right "pretty incredible."

And then there was Suzette Cyr, the *deus ex machina* of Sussman's defense. Cyr, a former lover of SJB's mother and the boy's self-selected godmother, wrote a scathing letter to the mother shortly before trial, accusing her of stealing and rampant dishonesty. In it, she threatened to reveal, unless a debt was repaid, what SJB had supposedly confided to her last summer, when he was staying at her Dallas home. SJB's mom turned the letter over to authorities, and it was provided to the defense.

"It never happened!" Cyr testified that SJB had blurted out, saying his mother had put him up to it. "This thing with Gordy, he never did it."

The prosecution later produced two rebuttal witnesses, including Cyr's stepsister, to impugn her character and attack her credibility. SJB, in his own testimony, denied making these statements. And Cyr herself said she did not report what SJB had told her in part because she wasn't sure if it was true.

THE PROSECUTION'S STAR WITNESS — IN ALL, SHE WAS ON THE STAND about 10 hours — was Madison Det. Cindy Murphy, who specializes in investigating computer crimes. Murphy said her analysis of the hard drives of Sussman's work and home computer turned up more than 1,000 images of child porn. Most were recovered as temporary Internet files from unallocated space.

During Murphy's testimony, several dozen of these images — including the 16 that led to criminal charges — were projected on a screen visible to the jury but not courtroom observers. Jury members viewed them with dazed looks on their faces. Det. Murphy painstakingly documented that Sussman had accessed such images "repeatedly and over a long period of time," through recurring visits to newsgroups with names like "asparagus" (a term for little boys' penises), "teen male" and "teen fuck."

Murphy also described how Sussman's computers were used to download hundreds of (legal) seduction stories containing graphic descriptions of sex between boys and boys, and boys and men. And to conduct Google searches for terms like "grab boys boner." A chart prepared by Murphy tracked this Internet activity on numerous days on both computers, at all hours of the day and night. She said the user tried to conceal his activities, by deleting and hiding information.

Hurley, in his cross-examination, got Murphy to admit there was no evidence Sussman ever saved, manipulated, organized or disseminated this material – or, for that matter, that he even looked at it. All she could say for sure was that he had clicked on certain newsgroup files and Web pages to open them.

According to Murphy, modern-day child-porn aficionados tend to simply view online material, to minimize the risk of getting caught. The defense's computer expert, Will Docken, formerly a U.S. Customs agent who specialized in investigating child porn, disagreed, saying most users store and sort it: "It's almost like they're compelled to."

Docken testified that none of the child-porn images on the Sussman computers were intentionally saved, and that one set of seven photos that led to seven separate criminal charges against Sussman took just one click and "a little over a second" to download. But Docken also affirmed that the person accessing this material on the home and work computer was Gordy Sussman.

Heitz, on cross-examination, got Docken to make a series of damaging admissions. Yes, Sussman had visited child-porn sites, on both his home and work computers. Yes, he intentionally sought out this material. Yes, most of the porn on these machines involved children.

Hurley, in his opening remarks, claimed Sussman had "a curiosity, not a penchant" when it came to kiddie porn. But the evidence seemed to show it was actually a penchant, if not an obsession. Indeed, child porn had apparently been accessed on both computers within hours of their seizure by police in July 2002.

On two occasions during the trial, I confronted Sussman, saying I thought he had been dishonest with me in claiming only nominal contact with child porn. Sussman basically stuck to his story, denying any intention to mislead.

"I've seen child porn fairly minimally," he told me, again explaining that he initially stumbled on these sites by accident and did some additional searches out of concern over "activist pedophiles" who had it in for the Boy Scouts. "I never accessed a lot of files. I have been there on a handful of occasions."

As for the seduction stories involving boys, he admitted downloading maybe 50, "not hundreds or thousands" as was stated in court. He called such visits "a fraction of a percentage of things" he looked at online: "I've seen this stuff, but it's not like I go there on a regular basis." He added, explaining what drew him to this material, "It's like coming up on a horrible auto accident. You just want to stare at the gore."

BEYOND A DOUBT, IT WAS THE CHILD-PORN EVIDENCE THAT SEALED Sussman's fate. Whatever concerns jurors may have had about SJB's credibility must have run smack dab against the thought: What were the chances he had falsely accused a man who just happened to download stories and pictures of boys having sex?

Both Heitz and Hurley gave masterful closing arguments. Heitz waved away the various discrepancies in SJB's statements, saying, "the one consistent thing" was that "he maintains it happened." He called the evidence that Sussman possessed child porn "overwhelming," stressing that each of the boys in the photos the jury had seen had been sexually abused because there is "a market for this kind of material."

Hurley, in his closing, said the many inconsistencies in SJB's statements and numerous witnesses who considered him untruthful made it impossible for the jury to find guilt beyond a reasonable doubt. He noted that child molesters commonly have huge numbers of victims. Yet Sussman's only accuser was SJB: "Where are the others?"

With regard to the images of child porn, Hurley turned to his client and admonished, "Shame on you, Gordy." But he insisted that Sussman's accessing this material did not meet the legal definition of possession, since there was no proof he knew these images were being stored in his machines.

As the verdicts were rendered last week Friday, at about 1 a.m., Sussman showed no emotion. Neither did SJB and his mother, who were present in court. Five sheriff's deputies were on hand as Sussman was placed in handcuffs and led off to spend his first night behind bars.

At a bail hearing the following afternoon, Sussman appeared in court in handcuffs and jail garb. He appeared shell-shocked, staring straight ahead.

Hurley, who promises an appeal, asked the court to let his client remain free on bail until sentencing. He noted Sussman's strong roots in the community, close ties to his two children, and volunteer work on a project to restore a cemetery in Rock County. He also urged that Sussman be permitted to make a prearranged trip "to say goodbye" to his dying father in Florida. Heitz opposed this, noting that Sussman was now a convicted felon facing up to 180 years in prison, "a significant motive" to attempt to flee.

Judge Martin denied the request for bail, but agreed to release Sussman from jail for a shortened trip to see his father. Sussman was allowed a two-and-a-half-day visit early this week, perhaps the last moments of freedom he will ever know, after which he returned to jail. During this time, the judge imposed a number of strict conditions, including that he have no contact with children and no use of computers. Just to be sure, he ordered that the computers in Sussman's residence be disconnected.

JULY 8, 2005

Sussman was sentenced to a total of 13 years in prison. His initial appeal was denied. His wife divorced him, and SJB in May 2009 filed a lawsuit against him, still pending.

Supreme Shift

N o one watches the Wisconsin Supreme Court with more interest than Forest Shomberg. And what he's seen in recent months has filled him with hope.

"There's been a major shift in the way the justices define fundamental fairness as it relates to the law," writes Shomberg, citing a spate of recent cases in which the court has uncharacteristically affirmed the due-process rights of criminal defendants. "It seems like the collective conscience of the court is changing, that they're doing everything they can to prevent wrongful convictions."

For Shomberg, these matters are hardly academic. The 41-year-old former Madison resident is assessing the state's highest court from within the confines of its harshest prison – the Wisconsin Secure Facility Program (formerly Supermax) in Boscobel. Shomberg is serving a 12-year prison term for the sexual assault of a UW–Madison student in 2002, a crime for which he has always professed innocence. (He has several alibi witnesses and passed a lie detector test.) The state Supreme Court is now deciding his case.

Shomberg's appeal hinges on whether his Dane County judge erred in disallowing an expert witness who would have challenged the process through which Shomberg was picked by two eyewitnesses, virtually the only evidence against him. At oral arguments in late September, the prosecution agreed this testimony should have been allowed, but said Shomberg's attorney failed to establish its relevance. That's mighty thin grounds to keep a possibly innocent man in prison.

About a mile from the state Capitol where the Supreme Court convenes, Jim Pugh is also eager to discuss some of its recent rulings, especially a trio of cases sympathetic to the liability rights of injured parties.

"We're raising a cry throughout Wisconsin telling people their jobs will be at risk due to the Wisconsin Supreme Court," says Pugh, spokesman for Wisconsin Manufacturers & Commerce, the state's largest business lobby. The group is running an ad in business publications showing a sports car passing a billboard with an outlined map of Wisconsin and the proclamation, "Hello, Trial Lawyers! Good-bye Jobs!" The ad claims "America's personal injury lawyers are racing to Wisconsin" due to recent court rulings that "send a clear signal to every CEO and top executive in the U.S. that Wisconsin will be a risky state in which to operate."

Pugh, not given to understatement, says the court's "bizarre anti-business rulings" have created a "dangerous litigation climate" in which Wisconsin will be "flooded with frivolous lawsuits by trial lawyers seeking to get rich and killing jobs in the process." He predicts a "long, slow decline" in the state's economy, as businesses avoid locating here, refuse to expand, or move to greener pastures – all options the WMC campaign seems to affirm as reasonable.

Others offer softer interpretations, noting that each of these decisions is limited in scope and potential application. But there's no doubt the court's recent rulings in both the civil and criminal arenas have been surprising, in the alignments they revealed and arguments they employed. In several key cases, Justice Patrick Crooks, once a darling of state conservatives, has joined the court's newest justice, former Milwaukee judge Louis Butler, to create a 4–3 majority. Butler, a reliable liberal, was appointed last year by Gov. Jim Doyle, eroding the court's rightward tilt.

Crooks, who is up for reelection next April, is emerging as the court's most significant swing vote, a majority maker who is as likely to side with the court's liberal faction (Shirley Abrahamson, Ann Walsh Bradley and Butler) as with its conservative one (Jon Wilcox, David Prosser and Pat Roggensack). According to an analysis by the *Wisconsin Law Journal*, Crooks joined the majority in 87 of 91 cases decided in the court's 2004–05 term, including 16 of the 19 cases in which the final tally was 4–3. As Patrick Crooks goes, so goes the court.

The shift suggests a triumph of sorts for Chief Justice Abrahamson, by far the court's longest-tenured member. For the first time in years, she's not the most frequent dissenter, a distinction that now falls to Wilcox. Moreover, the court is now relying more on the state (as opposed to federal) Constitution, as Abrahamson has long urged.

In criminal cases, the court seems more mindful of the justice system's capacity for error and defendants' rights. In civic cases, it has put the interests of individual litigants who have been harmed ahead of the protestations of powerful interests seeking to protect their bottom line.

"It's an interesting court to watch now," says Susan Steingass, a law professor at the UW–Madison. "Nothing's for sure."

MICHAEL YOVOVICH REMEMBERS HOW IT USED TO BE. DURING HIS 28 years in the appellate division of the state Public Defender's Office, he tried to avoid ending up before the Wisconsin Supreme Court. Often when he did, it was because he prevailed at the appellate court level and the prosecution asked the Supremes to get involved.

"I win, I'm scared," recalls Yovovich, who retired earlier this year. "Will the Supreme Court take it and reverse?"

Overall, Yovovich perceived the court as being "very uniformly against the defense and individual rights. At times, they would acknowledge the rights but find some way to deny the relief." Most of the time, the court simply refused to accept cases appealed by the defense.

For instance, one of Yovovich's colleagues tried, without success, to get the court to hear an appeal on behalf of Steven Avery, a man convicted of sexual assault. In 2003, after serving 18 years in prison, Avery was freed when DNA evidence conclusively demonstrated his innocence – at least for that particular crime. (Avery was just charged with the recent murder of a woman in Calumet County, based largely on DNA evidence.)

But Yovovich says things are better now: "It's not going to be a dead-bang loser just because it's a criminal case."

In several cases this year, the Supreme Court has shown concern about possible wrongful convictions. It ordered a new trial for Ralph Armstrong, convicted of a 1981 rape-murder in Madison, based on new DNA evidence. It opened the door for overturning the conviction of former Green Bay police detective John Maloney for the 1999 killing of his estranged wife.

In *State v. Knapp*, the court ruled 4–3 that evidence seized due to a deliberate violation of a suspect's Miranda rights could not be used against him, saying, "It is not too much to expect law enforcement to respect the law and refrain from intentionally violating it." In *State v. Dubose*, another 4–3 decision, it took a stand against "show-up" identifications, where victims are shown a single suspect and asked, in essence, if this is the guy.

Jovovich is especially heartened by the court's ruling this July in *State v. Jerrell* that a juvenile suspect's confession could not be used because of the coercive way it was obtained. (Milwaukee police handcuffed a 14-year-old boy to a wall for two hours, then questioned him for five and a half, denying his requests to call his parents.) "This sends a clear message to the [lower] courts that those standards must be applied," he says.

But *Jerrell* went further, to the dismay of conservatives who see it as an example of legislating from the bench. The court ruled, again on 4–3 split, that in-custody interrogations of juvenile suspects must be recorded. (The three dissenters agreed with suppressing the confession but not with this new requirement.) Police across Wisconsin scrambled to find ways to record these interrogations. And the ruling gave a boost to legislation that grew out of a state commission appointed in the wake of the Avery case.

"It helped accelerate this," says Rep. Mark Gundrum (R-New Berlin), chair of the Avery Task Force (a name it would not have if formed today), whose bill requires the recording of all juvenile interrogations, and any involving adults suspected of felonies. Until the Supreme Court ruling, "there was a reluctance toward any kind of mandate coming down from the state." Afterward, there was broad support for the bill, which creates rules and exceptions and helps agencies pay for recording equipment through a 1 percent hike in the state's criminal-penalty surcharge.

The bill, which also sets new standards for eyewitness identification and use of DNA evidence, unanimously passed both houses of the Legislature on its way to becoming law.

THE AVERY TASK FORCE – MADE UP OF AN IDEOLOGICALLY DIVERSE ARRAY

of prosecutors, judges and advocates – may have played a even larger role in shaping the Supreme Court's approach to criminal cases. In late 2004, the task force presented findings at a Madison seminar on wrongful convictions attended by lawmakers, attorneys, judges ... and all seven members of the Wisconsin Supreme Court.

"They were very attentive," recalls Gundrum of the justices. "There's no question in my mind that they are more focused on the issue of wrongful convictions than perhaps at any time."

Justice Crooks, in an interview, concurs: "I thought the seminar was very helpful in spotlighting some of the rough spots in the criminal justice system." For instance, he notes, the court's ruling in *Dubois* "reflects current thinking in regard to eyewitness identifications." Once considered highly reliable, they are now seen as highly fallible.

The *Shomberg* case may present another opportunity for the justices to set higher standards for the lower courts. One recommendation of the Avery Task Force is to avoid simultaneous lineups, in which several suspects are presented all at once. Studies show these are twice as likely to produce false identifications than if suspects or photos are presented one at a time. Says Gundrum, "What happens is people tend to make a relative judgment."

Shomberg, who has a long history of property crimes tied to his heroin addiction, was placed in a group lineup based on his resemblance to a police sketch of the assailant. The victim agreed at trial that she picked Shomberg because he seemed "the best of the six," even though she wasn't sure. Dane County Judge Patrick Fiedler, having refused to hear testimony from an expert witness knowledgeable in this area, remarked, "The record, which is what I must rely on, has not established to me that a sequential lineup is better than a lineup all at once."

Importantly, in both the *Dubois* and *Knapp* cases, the court relied on the state's own constitution to give defendants greater protection, a concept championed by Abrahamson since she joined the court in the mid-1970s. In *Knapp*, the court suppressed the evidence despite a U.S. Supreme Court ruling in the same case allowing it in. Justice Crooks wrote a concurring opinion "to emphasize that the majority opinion serves to reaffirm Wisconsin's position in the 'new federalism movement' of states going beyond the protections afforded by the U.S. Constitution and U.S. Supreme Court."

This movement has gained strength nationally over the last three decades, because it speaks to both conservatives' concern with states rights and liberals' concern with safeguarding individual liberties. Says Crooks, "People are waking up to their own state constitutions."

Abrahamson, in an interview, explains that federal law serves as a floor, not a ceiling, when it comes to basic rights. While the federal law aims to meet the needs of all 50 states and the federal government, she says, "the state constitution was created by the citizens of this state and adopted by the citizens to fit Wisconsin conditions."

IT IS THE COURT'S RULINGS IN THREE BIG LIABILITY CASES THAT HAVE stirred the most (over)reaction.

The Miller Stadium decision, rendered in March on a 5–1 vote, overturned an appellate court that torpedoed a $94 million punitive damage award – the largest in state history – against the operators of the Big Blue crane that collapsed in 1999, killing three workers. The appellate court ruled that the defendant had not acted with malice or intent to harm. The Supreme Court deemed this standard too narrow, saying all that's needed is a finding that the defendant acted with intentional disregard for the workers' safety.

"This is a very big decision for individual plaintiffs holding large companies responsible for their reckless behavior," says Milwaukee lawyer Walt Kelly, who ran unsuccessfully against Wilcox in 1997. But the threshold for punitive damages is still quite high, much higher than for simple negligence.

"Punitive damages are rarely asked for," notes Steingass, the UW law professor, who served nine years as a circuit court judge handling civil cases. "You have to be acting with reckless disregard for the rights of others, and that's a high standard." She says the perceived phenomenon of sky-high civil judgments is largely a myth. A national analysis of cases from 2000 showed the median tort award was $31,000. And most cases that go to trial are won by the defense.

Moreover, in the crane case, the Supreme Court avoided deciding whether the $94 million award was excessive. Crooks, in a concurring opinion, expressed his view that this was something the court should have done – signaling to both parties some discomfort with this amount.

In *Ferdon v. Wisconsin Patients Compensation Fund*, decided on a 4–3 vote in July, the court struck down the state's cap on non-economic damages in medical malpractice cases. The case concerned a boy left partially paralyzed with a deformed arm due to an injury at birth. A jury awarded him $700,000 in non-economic damages; the judge reduced this to $410,322, to comply with the caps.

The Supreme Court found "no rational basis" for the caps, and deemed them to violate the Wisconsin Constitution's equal protection clause. Crooks, in a concurring opinion, affirmed that the Legislature could pass a constitutional cap on non-economic damages, but that the one in place had been "set arbitrarily and unreasonably low." He says he does not want a cap so low that it "offends the right to a remedy in Wisconsin."

Justice Prosser, a former state Assembly speaker, wrote a stinging dissent accusing the majority of aspiring to become a "super-legislature." He also faulted his colleagues for relying on the state constitution, possibly to insulate the ruling from U.S. Supreme Court review.

The Wisconsin Association of Trial Lawyers notes that the old cap, in place since 1995, affected just nine jury awards, and that malpractice-related expenses account for less than one-half of one percent of state health-care costs. But state physicians have been screaming bloody murder, and the state Legislature acted quickly to restore the caps, at just $5,000 higher for adults and $105,000 higher for children.

On Dec. 2, Gov. Doyle vetoed this bill, saying it did not go far enough. Likely, Justice Crooks would have agreed.

THE THIRD AND MOST CONTROVERSIAL CASE, REGARDING LEAD-PAINT liability, was decided in July on a 4–2 vote. The court ruled that a young man who allegedly suffered retardation from eating paint chips in Milwaukee as a toddler could seek to recover damages, even though he wasn't sure which of several companies made the paint. His lawyers still must prove the chips caused the injury, no easy task. [In the end, the case was lost when a jury decided they had not met this burden.]

Attorney Kelly says this "enormously important and path-breaking decision" affirms protections for "individual citizens who are harmed by products." Pugh, of Wisconsin Manufacturers & Commerce, spins things differently.

"It's crazy, absolutely crazy," says Pugh, envisioning lawsuits against "every dairy farmer in Wisconsin" based on claims that someone who ate cheese ended up with high cholesterol. "If we have a system where you're guilty even if you're innocent, nobody's going to put a job in this state."

Crooks shakes his head at such statements. "To portray this in the way it's been portrayed is a real exaggeration," he says, noting that the court simply applied its own precedent of "risk-contribution" from a 1984 case involving DES (diethylstilbestrol), an anti-miscarriage drug blamed for birth defects. "If this was such a horrible decision, where was the outcry [in the earlier case]?" He adds that the circumstances at hand are exceedingly rare: "It's not a case that's going to be applied over and over again."

Bob Habush seconds that opinion. The famed Milwaukee lawyer, on the winning end of the Miller Park case, says the DES and lead-paint cases are the only two he can think of in which the "risk-contribution" theory could be applied. "It's such an unusual and unique fact situation where you can't identify the offending product."

Justice Butler, who wrote the lead-paint majority opinion, says the court actually "applied the precedent [in the DES case] but narrowed it," ruling that the plaintiff must prove the companies knew they were making a dangerous product. "We didn't just extend risk-contribution to every situation."

So why is WMC sounding an all-out alarm? Crooks and Butler just smile and decline comment. Habush takes the bait: "They are trying to use this hyperbole, this hysteria, to forward their political agenda." Former Justice Bill Bablitch, who along with Steingass is one of Crooks' campaign co-chairs, adds a chorus from the same hymnal: "This is an opportunity for those interests to froth up their constituents, raise some money, and perhaps elect some candidates favorable to their positions."

IN AUGUST, A NATIONAL REPUBLICAN GROUP LED BY DICK ARMEY, THE former majority leader of the U.S. House of Representatives, announced it was prepared to spend $2 million to help oust Justice Crooks due to his votes "in support of frivolous lawsuits" which had turned Wisconsin into a "Tort Hell Tundra." Trial lawyers, he said, "used to avoid Wisconsin, but now may swarm to the state like a scourge of mosquitoes, replacing the doctors who leave because they can't afford medical liability insurance."

Wisconsin Assembly Speaker John Gard followed up by labeling Crooks "an activist judge" and encouraging people to run against him. But with less than a month until the filing deadline, no challengers have stepped forward, attesting to the difficulties of ousting a sitting Wisconsin Supreme Court justice. (This last happened in 1968, when Chief Justice George Currie got the boot, partly as backlash over a court ruling that upheld the Milwaukee Braves' right to move to Atlanta.)

Pugh says WMC has no interest in trying to take Crooks out. He cites an analysis by a national consultant which found that Crooks voted in favor of "restraining the spread of liability" in 56 percent of relevant rulings since 2001. And a challenge from the right, he says, could make Crooks more vulnerable to some "extremely liberal activist judge."

Mike McCabe, executive director of Wisconsin Democracy Campaign, thinks the Supreme Court has become "noticeably more partisan" in recent years, as candidates' campaigns are increasingly bankrolled by partisan interest groups. Not only are the justices more likely to fall clearly into a conservative or liberal camp, they frequently find themselves compromised by their political affiliations.

For instance, three of the seven justices recused themselves from a case decided earlier this year in which former legislative leaders were seeking dismissal of felony misconduct charges. The three justices all had ties to the leaders. But so did Crooks, who did not recuse himself; one of the defendants, former Assembly Speaker Scott Jensen, ran Crooks' last campaign and funneled thousands of dollars into his campaign coffers.

"He had a flagrant conflict of interest," fumes McCabe. "He had no business ruling on that case." The four justices who did vote deadlocked 2–2, preserving an appellate court ruling that the cases could move forward. Crooks voted to reverse the appellate court.

Most of the people whose cases come before the court – and the many more whose lives are affected by its rulings – are not politically connected. They aren't looking for special treatment or ideological bent. They just want a fair hearing, a chance to prove that the law ought to work a certain way because that's what makes sense, and serves the interest of justice.

Take Forest Shomberg, who awaits the court's ruling on his fate (a decision could come any day) from within his 8-by-12-foot cell. He writes in one letter: "The court understands that mistaken identification is the primary cause of the conviction of innocent people in the United States, [and that] expert testimony to the scientific principles of perception and memory is essential to the truth-seeking process."

Or so he hopes.

DECEMBER 9, 2005

This originally appeared as a much longer article in Milwaukee Magazine. *The Supreme Court in January 2006 rejected Shomberg's appeal in a 5–2 decision; Shomberg was freed in November 2009 after his trial judge set aside his conviction based on new evidence unearthed by the Wisconsin Innocence Project. Crooks was reelected to the court in 2006 without opposition. None of the deleterious litigation consequences predicted by Wisconsin Manufacturers & Commerce have come to pass, but the criminal and civil rulings discussed in this article have been issues in every Supreme Court election since, including the one in 2008 that ousted Justice Butler from the court. In that race, Wisconsin Manufacturers & Commerce spent heavily.*

Wisconsin's Ethical Crisis

Shortly after former Assembly Majority Leader Scott Jensen was convicted on multiple felony charges for misconduct in public office, Douglas King penned an opinion column lamenting the erosion of ethics in Wisconsin government, which both the *Milwaukee Journal Sentinel* and *The Capital Times* of Madison saw fit to print.

"Wisconsin once had a proud tradition of nonpartisan, independent, professional civil servants," wrote King, a former 30-year state employee with agencies including the Department of Natural Resources, University of Wisconsin System and state Department of Administration. But now, "It has become a politicized system of cabinet appointments with direct lines of political influence all the way down into the heart of agency staff...."

King gave examples of behavior he purportedly witnessed that show just how far the state's ethical standards have slipped. One was of "an agency head who chewed out staff because they could not find personal information about officials that could be used to influence their votes on legislation." Another was having "watched administrators being directed to hire the relatives of politicians rather than the most qualified applicants."

Wow, those crooked government officials in Illinois have got nothing on us. But when I called King, who now runs a consulting firm, he was reluctant to name the officials who had engaged in this baldly unethical behavior, and seemed genuinely aggrieved that his essay had, on any level, cast aspersions on the integrity of Wisconsin public servants.

"Ninety-five percent of state employees don't behave this way," says King, who retired in 2001 and recalls his decades on the state payroll with pride. "The overwhelming majority of people in the public service are honest, hard-working, trustworthy, ethical." He's dismayed by the headlines used to present his essay. The *Cap Times* called it, "Personal integrity rare amid political corruption"; the *Journal Sentinel* ran it under, "Whatever happened to clean government in Wisconsin?"

"That implies that government is not clean now," protests King. "I never said that." His point, rather, is that the misbehavior of a few have tainted the good deeds of the many. Indeed, King now says, "I feel more strongly about how good Wisconsin functions than I am offended about the conduct I described."

If that's so, one wonders why King wrote his incendiary column in the first place, but I'm inclined to cut him a break. His view of state government is properly complex. Yes, there are bad things that happen today that may not have happened 50 or even 20 years ago. In the late 1980s, the state Capitol was rocked by revelations that a lobbyist gave legislators gifts, tickets, trips and meals. That seems pretty small potatoes compared to the conduct that's led to the criminal convictions of five former legislative leaders, including Republican Jensen and Democrat Chuck Chvala, once Majority Leader of the state Senate.

But in assessing and decrying this change, we run the risk of overstating the case, and presenting too bleak a picture. Contrary to what some reform advocates and even some politicians would have us believe, corruption is not rampant. Most public officials work hard and play by the rules. But the public doesn't see it that way. The public's view of the situation is anything but complex.

A survey conducted last fall by the Wisconsin Policy Research Institute tells the story. It found that only 6 percent of respondents believed elected officials primarily represent the public's interests; 88 percent felt they mainly served special interests or their own. Nearly half thought the standard of ethics in Wisconsin government has declined over the last 10 years, with just 9 percent perceiving improvement. And the percentage of those who say the state's ethics have taken a turn for the worse was appreciatively higher than in years past.

There is no reason to doubt that this survey gives a true picture of public attitudes. Go to any bar, ballpark or bowling alley in Wisconsin and you can find people who think politicians and other public servants are all a bunch of crooks. But are these attitudes more jaundiced than the situation merits? And, if so, whose fault is that?

LEE SHERMAN DREYFUS, WHO BEFORE HIS STINT AS REPUBLICAN

governor of Wisconsin from 1979 to 1983 was chancellor at UW–Stevens Point, observes sagely that scandal has always been with us.

"Even Madison as a capital is the result of one whale of an ethical lapse," notes Dreyfus, referring to how land speculator James Doty greased the skids for this selection by dispensing buffalo robes and choice lots to territorial legislators. There was also much scandalous behavior by the railroad companies in the late 1800s, which helped trigger the righteous backlash known as the Progressive Movement, led by "Fighting Bob" La Follette. And beginning in 1910, as city attorney and later mayor, the Socialist Daniel Hoan cracked down on what Dreyfus calls the "hotbed of corruption" that was Milwaukee.

The upshot was that, for much of that last century, government in Wisconsin was pretty clean. "What was called a scandal when I was in office wouldn't make it on the radar screen today," says Dreyfus. "Now we have people trading votes for campaign contributions."

Dreyfus thinks he knows where things went wrong. Once lawmakers served a term or two and got on with their lives. Now the Legislature is dominated by career politicians for whom winning is everything. "The whole purpose is to stay in the job, stay in the Legislature, stay in power," says Dreyfus. "You need to be reelected. And when that verb becomes 'need,' then you're in the hands of the money guys." Dreyfus sees the current political milieu as "absolutely ethically troubled, all the way down the line, both parties."

He'll get no argument from Jay Heck, executive director of Common Cause in Wisconsin, who adds the words "or lack thereof" when I tell him my focus is on the state's ethics. Heck says the caucus scandal that brought down Chvala, Jensen and other former legislative leaders eliminated the caucus system and made public officials much less likely to campaign on state time. But it did nothing about what he sees as a larger and more pervasive problem: the extent to which the state's political process is driven by campaign contributions.

"If anything, the money's worse now," he says. "It's an even bigger problem because there's more of it." He thinks it's only a matter of time before a fresh scandal breaks, over ethical lapses tied to politicians' all-consuming need to raise campaign cash.

That said, Heck concedes the public has a harsher view of public officials than is warranted. "Not every member of the Legislature is corrupt. Not everybody is engaged in unethical activity." He blames the caucus scandal for tainting people's perceptions, especially since it involved the Legislature's top leaders. "There's no question it's easy to see Scott Jensen being charged and [former state senator and attorney general candidate] Brian Burke being charged and just write off the entire institution."

QUESTIONNAIRES WERE USED TO WEED OUT SOME; OTHERS WERE GRILLED in court. That's how the initial pool of 131 prospective jurors for Jensen's trial got narrowed down to 15 – a dozen jurors and three alternates.

The respondents were asked whether they voted and whether they or a family member had held elected office. They were asked if they belonged to groups like Common Cause, and what they thought about politicians and state government.

"There were a number of negative comments about public officials," recalls the prosecutor, Dane County District Attorney Brian Blanchard. "A number of people said, 'I don't trust any politicians, they're all in it for themselves.'"

But what "surprised all of us," says Blanchard, was the large number of prospective jurors who knew nothing about the case – the biggest state political scandal in decades, one that had already led to criminal convictions of four former state lawmakers. "There were a whole bunch of people who didn't read the newspapers," he relates. One woman explained that her husband would read the paper and tell her if it contained anything she needed to know. The caucus scandal, evidently, did not rise to this level of importance.

Such barely aware citizens, I suspect, make up a sizable share of the respondents of surveys that show overwhelming majorities think public officials are either in it for themselves or else are beholden to special interests. You don't have to know a lot about politics to have a low opinion of politicians.

But even close observers of the caucus saga might feel justified in taking a dim view of people who hold public office. Indeed, Jensen's many defenders – including state Supreme Court Justice David Prosser, a former Assembly Speaker – have been quite vocal in asserting the "everybody did it" defense, which holds that Jensen's criminal ethical lapses were commonplace.

"Why punish him and not the parade of others?" demands the blogger Jessica McBride, who refers to "literally hundreds of others who did or were involved in doing the exact same thing."

Blanchard balks at such statements, saying he is unaware of any lawmaker besides Jensen who abused the rules to this extent. He calls the "everybody did it" claim "a convenient cop-out for people charged," but essentially false. Sure, other public officials made some use of state resources to advance political campaigns. But, says Blanchard, "the evidence at trial is that Scott Jensen took this to a whole new level."

Blanchard suggests that Jensen and others made this leap because others failed to exercise due diligence: "The Legislature itself never investigated the facts here. The Ethics Board took no interest. The Elections Board took no interest." People did what they did, transgressing farther and farther, because they were pretty sure they could get away with it.

Still, Blanchard says it's important to put Wisconsin's caucus scandal into perspective. Lawmakers here made illegal use of state resources for political ends. That's different, he stresses, than the criminal conduct of which former Illinois Gov. George Ryan was convicted this spring: trading favors for personal gain.

"Corruption is incremental," reflects Blanchard, "and what happened here was a decision to take advantage of public resources." It wasn't the worst conduct imaginable, but it was serious enough that "we had to charge the cases," lest continued non-enforcement lead to even greater abuse.

OF COURSE, THE LEGISLATURE'S PERENNIAL FAILURE TO PASS MEANINGFUL reforms regarding how campaigns are financed feeds into negative public perceptions of the institution. Heck calls the perpetually recurring pattern – finger wagging, calls for reform, legislative proposals that go nowhere – the Legislature's "dirty little secret."

"Republicans and Democrats don't want to do much to change the status quo," he says. "They just want to talk about it, to use it to political advantage, to smear the other side."

Heck's comment points up another key reason that huge majorities of Wisconsin residents view their public officials as ethically challenged if not utterly corrupt. It's what the public officials are constantly saying about each other.

Take, for example, the current race for governor. Both the Democratic incumbent, Jim Doyle, and Republican challenger Mark Green are hoping to get elected by milking accusations that the other is unethical. Indeed, the candidates and their partisans seem to relish the current scandals that have cast a pall over the state's erstwhile reputation for clean government, not because it presents opportunities to pursue reform but because it provides them with slop buckets full of mud to hurl.

"Once again Jim Doyle was caught with tainted campaign dollars," begins a typical press release from the Republican Party of Wisconsin, responding to reports that the governor voluntarily returned $10,000 in contributions from executives of an Illinois firm accused of corrupt business practices. "The only reason he returned this cash is because he got caught."

The governor, pegged by his critics as a pay-to-play operator, is in a no-win situation. When a bill relaxing regulations on rent-to-own companies arrived on his desk, speculation was rampant that he would sign it because of industry contributions to his campaign. When he vetoed it anyway, the buzz was that he backed down to avoid embarrassment. The idea that Doyle may have done what he thought was right regardless of these contributions seems not to have occurred to anybody.

Republicans are also fond of using the word "corrupt" to describe the state's electoral system, accusing Doyle of blocking reforms. In fact, an investigation by Republican-appointed U.S. Attorney Steven Biskupic found no evidence of widespread or systemic voter fraud, and the few instances in which convicted felons may have voted illegally would not have been prevented by the photo ID requirement the Republicans seek.

The Democrats, of course, are playing the same game, just as dirtily. "Mark Green was at the center of the caucus scandal," declares state Democratic Party chair Joe Wineke in one release, which goes on to assert: "As former Caucus Chair of the Assembly Republicans, Green and his legislative staff were at the center of the caucus scandal, illegally campaigning on state time, according to documents and testimony in the Jensen trial."

Blanchard, a Democrat, says it ain't so: "It would not be fair or accurate to say that documents and testimony in the Jensen trial proved that Mark Green was at the center of misconduct." He says Green "was not described by anyone" at Jensen's trial in these terms.

But in the state's current political climate, the mere fact that an allegation is hyperbolic or even untrue is, to people like Joe Wineke, no reason not to make it. When I asked him about these public claims, Wineke admitted that placing Green "at the center" of the caucus scandal "might have been a touch strong," explaining that the role of political parties is "to push the edge" regarding such statements.

That said, Wineke defends his party's efforts to link Green – who was caucus chair of the Assembly Republicans, not the now-defunct Assembly Republican Caucus – to the caucus scandal. He points to various tangential links involving former and current Green staffers. And he finds Green's claim that he was unaware of any illegal activity incredible. "He was a buddy of Jensen's!" Wineke shouts. "He was in the Republican leadership! Of course he was aware of this!"

Elsewhere, the Democrats have hammered Green for his alleged close ties to convicted former lobbyist Jack Abramoff and indicted former House Majority Leader Tom Delay. In this, state Dems appear to be following a script set by the national party. As *Newsweek* noted, the Democrats' "midterm campaign strategy is to use the Abramoff scandal to portray all Republicans as corrupt money-grubbers."

Apparently, that's easier than coming up with actual ideas.

DREYFUS, WHO AFTER HIS QUINTUPLE BYPASS SURGERY LAST YEAR USES a respirator and is often short of breath (the worst thing that can happen to a politician, he jokes) is saddened by the state of electoral politics in Wisconsin. He says the type of campaign he ran in 1978 – low cost and relatively free of mudslinging – would be impossible today.

And while Dreyfus laments the need of candidates to engage in negative campaigning, he says "they'd be crazy if they didn't." Politics, he believes, has ceased to be a contest of ideas; now it's about blowing the other guy out of the water. "We live it a totally divided society where everything is conflict."

Unfortunately, the constant bombardment of the body politic with conflict-based political sales pitches – vote for me because the other guy's a crook – is having an inevitable corrosive effort. Citizens no longer trust politicians because politicians advance their careers by painting each other as untrustworthy. Public officials ruthlessly attack one another's integrity, then bristle when their own integrity comes under attack.

The media and citizens like Douglas King are quick to join poll respondents in drawing sweeping conclusions that Wisconsin has lost its ethical bearings. They don't split hairs between who is and who isn't genuinely corrupt because public officials don't either. Politicians are now popularly regarded as they regard each other: with contempt.

It's a tragic situation, right down to the fact that they have only themselves to blame.

SPRING 2006, WISCONSIN INTEREST

Gov. Doyle was easily reelected to a second term. Scott Jensen managed to have his conviction overturned and to delay being retried. This was one of former Gov. Dreyfus' last interviews; he died in January 2008.

Eric Hainstock at Green Bay Correctional Institution, 2008

Free at Last

Eric Hainstock's first letter to *Isthmus*, dated April 15, 2008, got right to the point: "When I was 15 years old I shot my high school principal. I never meant for this to happen. He grabbed me from behind and I got scared. I was already pretty stressed, so that freaked me out even more. Please don't get me wrong, I am not blaming Mr. Klang for grabbing me. But I am blaming him, the teachers, social services and the school as a whole for never listening to me.... No one ever listened."

Like other communications to follow, the letter is a plaintive appeal for understanding, with a heavy dollop of self-pity. "No one ever listened"? Perhaps it felt that way to Hainstock.

"I want my story told," wrote Hainstock, now 17, who picked *Isthmus* on the recommendation of his "celly," a former Madison resident. "I want all the social service agencies to listen, the schools, parents all over the state." He pegged his purpose as altruistic – to make sure no one else would ever have to "live in the hell that I did."

On Sept. 29, 2006, Eric Hainstock brought a shotgun and pistol to his school in Cazenovia, about 80 miles northwest of Madison. A janitor wrestled the shotgun away, but Hainstock proceeded down a hall, to be confronted by principal John Klang. A struggle ensued, and Klang was shot three times, in the head, leg and chest. The 49-year-old husband and father of three died later that day.

Hainstock, a high school freshman, was charged as an adult; his lawyers tried but failed to waive his case back into juvenile court. A year ago, on Aug. 2, after a weeklong trial in which he was alternately portrayed as a screwed-up kid and coldly calculating killer, Hainstock was convicted of first-degree murder and sentenced to life in prison. His first parole eligibility will be in 2037, when he'll turn 46.

Despite the trial judge's recommendation that Hainstock begin his sentence in a juvenile facility, he was sent to the Green Bay Correctional Institution, a maximum-security adult prison. I wrote him back there, saying *Isthmus* was interested in doing a story but is "NOT on your side." I also warned that media attention might generate "more outrage than sympathy." (For presumably similar reasons, Hainstock's appeals attorney urged him not to cooperate with this article; he rejected that advice.)

Hainstock, in reply, said he knows it's easier for people "to hate me and move on," but this is not the whole story. There is a context for what happened. His 10-page letter and accompanying psychological reports detail a lifetime of abuse and neglect.

In fact, wrote Hainstock, "I face less abuse in prison than I did at school or at home." He's made dramatic gains in his reading and math skills and is working toward his GED. He regards his cellmate as a mentor and protector.

"How does someone do better in every area of their life in prison?" he asks. "Easy. No beatings. No name-calling. If someone were to hit me or call me a name, they would be immediately punished. Yet, at home or school, no one was held accountable."

ON THE DAY OF THE SHOOTING, HAINSTOCK TOLD POLICE HIS GOAL WAS to confront Klang and "make him listen" to his concerns about bullying. Fellow students, he said, called him "fag" and "faggot" and rubbed up against him.

Other details soon emerged. Eric's father, Shawn Hainstock, was charged in 2001 with felony child abuse for kicking Eric and other punishments. Family acquaintances said Shawn would berate Eric, calling him names like "retard," or make him stand in the corner, his nose touching a wall and holding one leg in the air, for long periods. Not long before Klang's death, Hainstock clashed with his stepmother and ended up with human bite marks.

But these indicators of turmoil pale in comparison with Hainstock's self-description of the abuse he endured.

"My home life was a prison," he writes from his cell at Green Bay. "A nightmare. Can you imagine being a kid and hating, fearing, your parents and your home? My dad was charged, then let go on abuse. The community and family knew he and my adopt[ive] mom beat me and tortured me.... They all knew. The school and social services and family."

Eric Hainstock's former home is about four miles northwest of Cazenovia; it's a winding, hilly jaunt through some of the most gorgeous land in Wisconsin. There are vehicles in the front yard and horses on a farm next door. Weston Schools, where the shooting occurred, is five miles from Cazenovia in the opposite direction, on a hill overlooking the countryside. Both places are lovely but feel remote, isolated, detached from their communities.

Hainstock, in his letters, which his cellmate helped him write, sums up his family life as follows: "The only place I actually felt at home was anywhere but." He thrived when, after the abuse charges, he was removed from his father's home to live with his paternal grandmother. "There I felt safe, wanted, loved." His behavior and grades markedly improved. But eventually his father regained custody.

At the home of his father and stepmother, says Hainstock, he was treated like a slave, made to do all the cleaning, sometimes until late at night. He had to eat peanut butter and jelly sandwiches while his folks "would eat steaks in front of me." He was often hungry at school, because his dad wouldn't pay the 30 cents a day for a reduced-price school lunch. His dad also took him off Ritalin, a drug that had a huge positive impact, because "he didn't want to spend the money."

Hainstock says both parents beat him, kicked him, slapped him and threw things at him. His dad made him hold hot sauce and peppers in his mouth, which burned so bad "I couldn't breathe or swallow," and run laps in the yard, sometimes for hours. The clothes and shoes his father bought didn't fit. He was only allowed to shower once or twice a week, which made him stand out at school: "Not one other kid smelled like that." There was never a word of comfort or praise. "I would accept all the beatings if I could have just heard one 'I love you' or 'Good job, Eric.'"

When I phone Hainstock's father and start to explain my purpose on the answering machine, the call disconnects; on second try the hang-up occurs after one ring. But he eventually does respond to a letter asking to talk.

Shawn Hainstock knows he's not a perfect parent but suggests Eric is exaggerating: "What teenager doesn't think they're getting a bad deal?" Making kids run as punishment is what gym teachers do, he notes. As for the peppers, "All I did is take a dried jalapeño pepper when he got a filthy mouth and raked it across his tongue," much like the "half of America" that uses soap on kids' mouths.

Aside from having kicked his son, Shawn says, "I don't think anything I did was wrong." He remembers good times, camping and fishing, working on demolition derby cars. "He was a really good boy," he says of Eric. "He'd just go through really rough streaks."

Eric Hainstock doesn't have any good memories of life with his father and stepmom, Priscilla. He thinks authorities should have "had the courage or even just did their job and got me out of that home. I wanted to die. I tried to die. I wanted to be somewhere else. I would dream about laughing and being loved like I saw other families. Never came true, and now it never will."

AT THE TIME OF THE SHOOTING, HAINSTOCK WAS STARTING HIS FIFTH year at Weston Schools, a K-12 facility with about 350 students. He transferred there in sixth grade, which he repeated due to behavior problems and poor test scores. Earlier, while living with his grandmother, he had attended school in Wonewoc, where he did much better.

"There was never, not once, a good day [at Weston]," he writes. "It was hell and misery every single day."

Hainstock, who identifies as bisexual and by his own account "acted like a girl," says he was constantly called fag, gay boy, girlie boy, punk and sissy. "Every day the same thing. They would call me names in the hall, in class, at lunch, before school and after. The teachers all knew this." But they wouldn't protect "the smelly gay kid."

It got physical: "I would be slapped, hit all over my body, pushed in bushes or thrown to the ground, my head was stuck in dirty toilets, sometimes three times a day." In his letters, Hainstock lists a half-dozen school officials, including Klang, to whom he purportedly complained. "I told them two, three, four times a week every week every year. NOTHING was ever done."

Shawn Hainstock backs up this part of Eric's account, saying his son regularly got "beat up" at Weston. "I complained to that school so many times I was to the point of getting a disorderly conduct – and nobody did nothing."

One student told a newspaper that Hainstock was picked on more than anyone else at school. But other news accounts and web postings from former classmates allege that Hainstock also engaged in bullying and obnoxious behavior. He broke school rules and was often disruptive. Two weeks before the shooting, police were called after he threw a stapler at a teacher. The day before, he got a disciplinary warning from Klang for having tobacco at school.

A few letters into our exchange, I take Hainstock to task. Wasn't his own behavior a problem? Isn't he exaggerating the extent to which he was a victim (head flushed in dirty toilets "sometimes three times a day") or how often he complained to school officials?

Hainstock, in reply, clarifies that he meant to say that, during one single day, his head was flushed three separate times, not that this was a daily occurrence. He admits he bullied two other students, which was "wrong." And when hit or called names, he would respond in kind: "I wasn't a complete doormat."

But he says he only acted out at school "because I was a mess. Not so kids could react or further torment me. That would be insane." He insists there were "at least 25–30 kids at Weston who bullied me." Two of them "lied plain and simple" when they denied this at his trial.

And Hainstock is adamant that he repeatedly importuned school officials. "I asked Klang at least three or four times a week to have students leave me alone," he writes. "I am not in any way overstating the case. I hated it. I wanted it stopped. For crying out loud, I brought a gun to school so it would stop."

Weston officials seem oddly uninformed on this score. Neither Terry Milfred, who was superintendent when the shooting occurred, nor Tom Andres, who was hired afterward, knew enough to say whether Hainstock frequently complained about being bullied.

Milfred recalls that Hainstock had expressed "specific concerns," but doesn't know details. His impression is that Hainstock had a hard time fitting in: "Eric was the type of student who tried to relate in maybe somewhat of a clumsy way that didn't always sit well with [other students]. He tended to irritate people more than befriend them."

Andres, who became superintendent in January 2007, has heard from students that "Mr. Klang was probably one of [Hainstock's] biggest advocates."

He says that on bullying, the district is now more vigilant: "Anytime someone comes in with a complaint or a concern we deal with it pretty seriously."

But Andres believes the underlying issue is not bullying but "the whole thing of respect. Bullying can be handled. To subvert it, to push it under, is not helpful either. Then you can no longer deal with it."

ON THE MORNING OF SEPT. 29, 2006, HAINSTOCK WOKE UP FEELING WHAT he later called "anger and rage at everybody. Everyone who picked on me. Everyone who wouldn't help me."

He took his father's .22-caliber revolver and a 20-gauge shotgun. Having missed the school bus, he siphoned gas from lawnmowers for the family truck. He drove to school for the first time, not knowing how to shift the gears.

In his letters to *Isthmus*, Hainstock says he brought guns to school "to tell them all to stop it." After the shotgun was taken from him, he went to see Klang. The pistol was inside his jacket, under his armpit. When Klang grabbed him, "I freaked out. The gun just went off again and again."

Hainstock says he accepts responsibility for what happened: "Not a day goes by that I don't think, cry and dream about what I did to Mr. Klang. I have to live with it every day. It is a hell unto itself. He didn't deserve that."

But he also feels "I am not to blame for everything. I was 15 and never lived a day of peace or hope." No one got him out of his parents' house. No one stopped "the torture" at school. If they had, he writes from prison, "I would not be here today, and Mr. Klang would not be dead."

There was never any question that Hainstock's actions caused Klang's death, and that he would be punished for it. But under what system and how severely?

Hired by Hainstock's public defenders, Middleton psychologist Michael Caldwell spent a total of seven hours with Hainstock on three occasions, and reviewed voluminous records from his past. He diagnosed attention deficit hyperactivity disorder, as well as depression and borderline personality features, including "intense emotional instability." Hainstock had a negative self-image and engaged in self-mutilating behavior, cutting his skin.

Caldwell cited studies showing that adolescents lack control of impulses and emotions due to their level of brain development. He argued that the extreme high stress of Hainstock's entire life further retarded this development, rendering him "substantially less mature than his chronological age."

Hainstock "is particularly weak in his ability to plan, to generate realistic potential future outcomes of various courses of action," wrote

Caldwell. "As a result, he is likely to show poor judgment and generate grossly irrational plans, more characteristic of a preteen."

Another psychologist, Marty Beyer of Virginia, similarly found that Hainstock was "emotionally delayed and depressed because of untreated traumas." She saw much of Hainstock's misbehavior as a cry for help: "He desperately wanted someone to pay attention to how unhappy he was at home and school and do something about it."

Beyer quizzed Hainstock about the likely consequences of bringing guns to school. "Eric said he had not thought about it, but now realizes he would have been arrested for having a gun in school. It was apparent when he considered my question [that this] was the first time it had dawned on him that because he carried loaded guns into school, he would have been arrested and expelled, so the point of being listened to would be lost."

WHEN THE REV. JERRY HANCOCK TALKS ABOUT THE CRIMINAL JUSTICE system, it is with knowledge and authority.

Before being ordained in January 2006 and starting a prison ministry through the First Congregational United Church of Christ in Madison, Hancock worked within the system for almost 35 years. He was a public defender, a deputy prosecutor under Dane County District Attorney Jim Doyle and an administrator in Doyle's Justice Department. He capped off his career as head of the state's office of consumer protection.

Now he spends his time "speaking truth to power" in pursuit of reform. His prison ministry project has about 60 volunteers who visit inmates throughout the state. He was asked to visit Hainstock in the fall of 2006, shortly after his arrest. At first, at the Sauk County jail, he came once a week. Now, at Green Bay, it's about once a month. Hancock won't discuss the content of these "pastoral visits," but Hainstock does, saying they pray, talk about God, and work on forgiveness.

Hancock, who attended much of Hainstock's court proceedings, challenges his claim that school and social service officials turned a blind eye to his mistreatment. "Lots and lots of people in Sauk County, some who happened to be at Weston high school, cared and still care about Eric," he says. "They tried to help him. But his family life was in such chaos that it was impossible to meet his needs."

He assesses that Shawn Hainstock, who'd also attended Weston, had an "adversarial" relationship with school officials. So "Eric didn't get the help that everybody – except maybe his father – thought he needed."

Even the violence was anticipated. Ruth Willis, the wife of Hainstock's pastor, testified in court that she told a Weston Schools official "if he didn't find help for this boy, he was going to have another Columbine on his hands." According to Hancock, "Everybody saw this coming. They saw that Eric was a deeply needy kid who nobody could quite get to. But people really tried."

Still, Hancock thinks Hainstock's view that nobody helped him is "a perfectly valid way to see it," especially for an adolescent. "The adult perspective is that we tried. The kid perspective is you abandoned me." And, in fact, those who did try to help him failed: "Every adult in his life let him down."

So did the justice system. At the hearing to waive Hainstock back into juvenile court, at which the two defense psychologists testified, Hancock says "it was clear to everybody that Eric needed treatment," due to his lifetime of abuse. And the treatment he needed – "integrated, consistent and intense" – was not something the adult prison system would likely provide.

But the juvenile system doesn't allow confinement or supervision beyond age 25. And so, says Hancock, the judge affirmed Hainstock's status as an adult, perhaps throwing away his chances of rehabilitation but at least ensuring that "the public would be protected."

Hancock is angered by this: "What kind of crazy system is that? In a rational and humane system, you wouldn't have to choose" between rehabilitation and public safety. "Eric's case is a failure of the justice system."

Hainstock also mines the irony: "I would never have been allowed, regardless of how grownup I acted or sounded, to go to war, drink at a bar, vote. But when a mistake happens, then I am old enough to be treated as an adult."

At trial, the prosecutor depicted Hainstock as a habitual liar with a violent temper who resented adults telling him what to do. A school guidance counselor said he "enjoyed playing the role of victim." One student said Hainstock "would push people more than he got pushed."

The jury heard that Hainstock, in the days before the shooting, had made threats about Klang and invoked Columbine. They heard he came to school announcing his intention to "kill somebody." They did not hear from the psychologists who concluded he was emotionally immature and unable to think through the consequences of his actions. The jury found him guilty of first-degree murder.

Rhoda Ricciardi, one of Hainstock's two veteran public defenders, was devastated. After the verdict she took six months off. Then she asked to be reassigned job duties that did not involve criminal cases. As she puts it, "If this is the justice system, I don't want to be part of it anymore."

IN SENTENCING HAINSTOCK TO LIFE IN PRISON WITH THE POSSIBILITY OF parole, Sauk County Judge Patrick Taggart remarked, "I believe you can be rehabilitated." If there was reason to doubt that statement then, there is less now. Hainstock, in prison, has thrived.

He's gained 50 pounds, filling out his scrawny frame. He no longer has issues with hygiene or personal care. He's gone from a fourth- to a 10th-grade reading level, and is on track to get his GED next year, about when he would have graduated had he stayed in school.

"For the first time, he's had stability and predictability in his life," says Hancock. "He's benefiting from having a consistent environment."

Hainstock agrees. "I have it much better in here than I did out there," he writes. "I am happy." He doesn't want to be in prison. He misses people he knew. He misses fishing and being outdoors. But no one picks on him – the older inmates see to that. No one abuses him. He gets enough to eat. His clothes and shoes fit. "It is sad, but yes, prison is an improvement."

In prison, Hainstock says he doesn't need to be on any medication. Records show his conduct at Green Bay is nearly perfect, save for two minor write-ups for missing class.

Hainstock's days are tightly regimented. Breakfast is at 6:30, school starts by 9 and runs until 4, with a few breaks. In the evenings, he and his cellmate, 37-year-old Brannon Prisk, play games and talk. He recently read *How to Be a Successful Criminal*, about a former Wisconsin inmate who turns his life around.

Bill Pollard, the warden at Green Bay, wouldn't know Hainstock "if he walked right in front of me." The prison, designed for 750 inmates, has 1,100, including eight under the age of 18. Pollard says Green Bay ends up with younger inmates because it has one of the largest schools, with 20 teachers. Pollard agrees that strict rules can be welcome.

"There's some people who, due to their previous environment, find this setting to their liking," he says. "They like the structure. I wouldn't, personally."

Hainstock says Prisk is like a father to him. "He listens to me. When I get a good grade he puts it on the wall. He tells me how good I am and can be. He doesn't hit me or call me names like my parents did." Prisk, who is straight, knows Hainstock is bisexual and is okay with that. "My dad said gays would go to hell. Brannon said God loves me the same as anyone."

Prisk reminds Hainstock to brush his teeth. He helps him with his schoolwork. "He talks to me and lets me talk to him" – about politics, music, whatever. They play word games to build Hainstock's vocabulary. Prisk, serving a sentence for aggravated battery, will get out in May 2010. Says Hainstock, "I don't know what I will do without him."

In one letter, Prisk pops in to offer his thoughts. "It breaks my heart that he is here," he writes of Hainstock. "He is a great kid."

Shawn Hainstock is impressed with Eric's educational gains but feels he's having "a rough time" in prison. He says his son seems consumed with anger and is "sucking up a lot of the garbage" he hears in prison. Recently, Eric wrote a letter telling his father off.

The state Department of Corrections refused to let me visit Hainstock at Green Bay. DOC spokesman John Dipko says "a close family member of Mr. Klang" voiced strong objections. State law permits denying media access when this would "jeopardize or be detrimental to ... the welfare of the victim, victim's family or the community."

This decision upsets Hainstock. "Once again, they are attempting to not hear the truth," he writes. "Why can't my story be told? I was a victim, too."

Hainstock, in his letters to me, becomes increasingly familiar, at one point signing off with "talk to ya later gator." He scrawls an elaborate signature he says is a bunny. Later, he sends me a drawing of Sylvester the Cat.

When we finally do speak, it's via collect calls from prison. He sounds older than I expected, and more mature.

Hainstock says some people in prison have told him he's "cool" for having killed his principal. He corrects them: "No, I'm not. I took a life. He can't go to his daughter's wedding. He can't walk her down the aisle."

He thinks about the Klangs every day. "I hope someday I can see them, talk to them, tell them how bad I feel. And I hope they can forgive me. I know it ain't easy." (Klang family members, through the DOC, declined to be interviewed for this article.)

Hainstock says that with Hancock's help he's forgiven the students who picked on him. He's working on forgiving his father. But that's a tougher task.

"I love my dad because he is my dad," he says. But he's still plenty angry. He says his father never lifted a finger to help him. He hasn't given him a single item for his cell. At one point Hainstock implores me, "I hope and pray you have no mercy on him."

And yet, in Hainstock's life, this is the parent who has stood by him. Shawn and Priscilla make the 160-mile trek to Green Bay about twice a month. Eric's birth mother isn't even on his visitor's list. When he was a little boy, he remembers, "She would promise to pick me up for a visit. I would pack my little bag and sit at the front step waiting for her. She would never come." She still doesn't.

Shawn Hainstock, telling the same part of Eric's story, begins to cry: "I don't know how anybody can turn their back on their own child."

LOOKING AHEAD TO HIS FUTURE, HAINSTOCK WANTS TO TAKE A vocational class in masonry, to learn a skill. After he gets his GED, he plans to take college classes. Someday he hopes to visit schools, cautioning students against bullying. "I want to help kids," he tells me. "I don't want this to go on no more."

But what he wants most of all is to someday have a family. When I ask if he thinks he'd be a good father, he laughs softly. "I believe I would be. I wouldn't screw up like my dad. I'd try to tell my kid the mistakes I made."

I ask the Rev. Hancock what *he* hopes the future will bring. It is the longest wait for an answer in my reporting career.

"First and foremost," he says at long last, "I would hope for all the love and compassion in the world for the Klang family. And I would hope that we as a society will meet our responsibilities to Eric Hainstock."

What responsibilities are those? I ask. Again, the pause seems interminable. More than a minute. I can see that Hancock is not just trying to formulate his response, he's trying to channel it – from his life, from his ministry, from his soul. When he does respond, there are tears in his eyes.

"They're the same responsibilities that society has to all children – to allow them to grow up safe and secure with a sense of self-esteem."

AUGUST 1, 2008

After this article was published, the Wisconsin Department of Corrections separated Hainstock and Prisk. Prisk protested this decision, to no avail, saying Hainstock's prison behavior subsequently took a turn for the worse. Hainstock's appeal was rejected by his trial court judge but is pending at the appellate court level. In the fall of 2009, Sue Klang, John's widow, emerged as a prominent supporter of a statewide school curriculum designed to help educators combat bullying. Hainstock has never again communicated with me from prison.

RO4040 at the National Primate Research Center, 2009. Photo by Bill Lueders

My Monkey

The first entry, for April 26, 2004, sets the tone for much of what follows: "Born today, rejected by mother, male infant."

Thus begins the life story and paper trail of r04040, a rhesus macaque monkey at the National Primate Research Center in Madison. He's one of the center's nearly 1,500 "nonhuman primates" used for experimentation and research that draws $46 million a year into the UW–Madison.

But he's not just any monkey. He's – and I know this is an odd thing to say – my monkey. I was there on the day he was born, getting a tour of the facility for an *Isthmus* article, "Inside the Monkey House," published in June of 2004.

Back then, my tour guides brought me into a bright and sterile room in which r04040 lay in an incubator. At first he looked dead. Then he slowly opened his tiny eyes and looked at me. I may have been the first person he ever saw. (And what a sight I must have been, in the lab smock, mask, shower cap and clear plastic face shield all visitors must wear!)

In the five years since, I've often thought about r04040. What kinds of studies and experiments was he being used for? Was he even still alive? Would knowing what his life was like support the arguments made by the center's proponents, that it does vital research under the most humane conditions possible? Or would it bolster critics, who say these animals are pointlessly abused?

Some things I knew: R04040 had never had anything like a normal or natural monkey life. He'd never seen the sky or sunlight or grass or trees. He'd never foraged for food. The only living things he'd encountered were other monkeys and humans covered head to toe in odd garb.

His life was expropriated to serve human interests because humans have decided they have that right. He was conscripted by birth into a place where, to quote Arlo Guthrie, "you get injected, inspected, detected, infected, neglected and selected!"

As the five-year anniversary of my visit neared, I asked for records regarding the use and care of r04040. The UW ultimately gave me 25 pages of entries that collectively told the story of my monkey's life.

For several years, r04040 was housed in a pen with other juveniles. Now fully grown, he lives with another monkey in a tiny cage in a roomful of other similarly paired monkeys. It's common for monkeys in captivity to develop neuroses and even psychoses. They may engage in repetitive behavior like pacing, or self-mutilate. My monkey seems to have spent much of his life suffering from chronic diarrhea and being injured by cage mates.

But the most shocking thing was the experiments r04040 has been used for during his first five years – almost none at all. That prompted me to ask further questions of my monkey's keepers, and ultimately brought me back into contact with him, face to face.

THE NATIONAL PRIMATE RESEARCH CENTER AT THE UW-MADISON IS ONE

of eight such centers in the United States, all funded primarily by the National Institutes of Health (NIH). It is home, at last count, to 1,186 rhesus macaques, 212 marmosets and 75 cynomolgus (a.k.a. crab-eating) macaques. The Harlow

Center for Biological Psychology, located a stone's throw from the Primate Center, has an additional 500 rhesus macaques.

In 2007, the last year for which numbers are publicly available, Wisconsin led the nation in the use of monkeys for research. The total reported by the U.S. Department of Agriculture, which oversees animal research, was 8,559 monkeys, including 7,313 at Covance Laboratory on Madison's northeast side. More monkeys are being experimented on in Madison than any other place in the nation, perhaps the world. (Some other states have more monkeys, but the above numbers report only those used in experiments.)

For the current year, the Primate Center is receiving $42.7 million in federal funds, mostly from NIH, and about $3.5 million in nonfederal support, from foundations and industry. The UW's share in the center's costs, through the state's general fund, is nominal, about $250,000 a year.

The center's monkeys are housed in two large buildings near Regent Street. The UW has a master plan to double the size of its Primate Center facilities, to where it could house upwards of 2,500 primates. The center is optimistic it can snare some of the money the Obama administration is making available for such purposes.

About 150 monkeys a year die at the center, some as part of experiments, some from natural causes. About the same number are born.

Center director Joe Kemnitz and head veterinarian Saverio "Buddy" Capuano are generous with their time and remarkably open in their dealings with me. They seem proud of their role at the center, though both have been vilified over it. Kemnitz has twice had protesters show up at his home, in 2005 with a giant video screen showing ghastly images of primate research. Capuano has encountered "anger and ambivalence," even from within the veterinary community.

When the NIH office to which he referred me ignored my request for the center's annual report, Kemnitz gave me a copy, with nothing blacked out. Reports given by the feds to research critics redact the names of all researchers.

MOST OF THE PRIMATE CENTER'S RESEARCH FOCUSES ON AIDS, AGING

and stem cells. There are more AIDS-related studies than any other kind; the UW is a world leader in stem cell research; and the center's studies on how restricting calorie intake promotes longevity have recently been featured on "60 Minutes" and CNN's "Vital Signs."

Other studies concern bone loss, kidney transplants, movement disorders, stress and Parkinson's (funded in part by the Michael J. Fox

Foundation). One recent study found that marmoset fathers exposed to a whiff of their own infants experienced decreased levels of testosterone. Now we know.

The center's annual report for the period ending Feb. 28, 2009, lists 26 core scientists engaged in research, and more than 200 affiliated scientists at the UW and other institutions. Over the last year, these efforts yielded 101 published papers, 88 of which mentioned the center.

That the center tracks such things is grist for its critics.

"Outside funding gives the school a reputation as a research institution," says Rick Marolt, a local opponent of primate research. "Researchers get labs, employees and can publish articles that will help them get professional recognition, tenure and promotion."

A native of the Twin Cities, Marolt moved to Madison in 1992. Eight years later, a local controversy over zoo elephants prompted him to attend a meeting of the local Alliance for Animals. "For the first time, I heard there were monkey labs in Madison," he recalls. "I instantly felt this was the most heinous thing in the world."

He still does. Marolt, 47, who teaches management courses at the UW–Madison and Edgewood College and does business consulting, sees primate research as a great and unnecessary evil, one in which UW officials, researchers and members of the press are complicit.

Animal experimentation, he says, is unreliable: "According to the FDA itself, 92 percent of the drugs found safe and effective in animals are not safe or not effective in people." Some are even harmful. Yet the agency insists that drugs be tested on animals first.

As for research into human pathology, adds Marolt, "The case is just overwhelming that nonhuman animals have not been good predictive models of human disease." And he questions the use of monkeys for AIDS research, since "monkeys do not even get HIV."

Marolt's main objections are not scientific but moral. As he puts it: "If researchers have proven that monkeys are very similar to people in cognition, emotion and social relationships – so similar that they are viewed as functional replacements for people in research – then why should monkeys not get similar ethical consideration?"

Moreover, Marolt disputes that one species ought to dominate another. He says that as recently as 30,000 years ago, three hominid species (including neanderthals) coexisted. Had they all survived, he asks, "Would the most powerful one have the right to experiment on the others? And what if you're not the most powerful one?"

LISTED ON THE PRINTOUT I RECEIVED FROM THE PRIMATE CENTER ARE hundreds of events in the life of r04040. It catalogs the chronic diarrhea and repeated injuries. But aside from routine DNA profiling and one brief placement in 2008, my monkey has apparently not been used for any research.

The animal welfare advocates I show the report to find it appalling.

"R04040's life, taken as a whole, has to be balanced by the purported claim that using him is helping us," says Rick Bogle, Madison's best-known opponent of primate research. He sees no evidence of that. "So far, in his five years of life, it seems likely that he has been miserable. And for what?"

But Kemnitz and Capuano, who pair up for two interviews with me in Kemnitz's spacious office, see it differently. They think r04040 has had it pretty good.

"This animal has not had a difficult life," says Capuano. "He's healthier and happier than a lot of animals without being obese." The traumas he's experienced are "the normal things you're going to go through growing up."

Like chronic diarrhea and attacks by cage mates? Absolutely.

They say r04040's diarrhea, now less frequent, is not necessarily stress-related, even though his lab record speculates that it was. They say monkeys who live in the wild – which Capuano suggests is actually more stressful – experience diarrhea. As for the injuries from other monkeys, he adds that this is "exactly what happens when they live in the wild."

Rhesus monkeys, males especially, engage in aggressive play and establish dominance hierarchy. Capuano says no monkey has been killed by another in the more than four years he's worked at the center (after prior stints at primate labs in Philadelphia and California). Kemnitz allows that "We've had animals who lose fingers and body parts in fights." But the center is a relatively safe environment due to how closely the animals are monitored.

"We had more serious fights among animals at the zoo than here," says Kemnitz, referring to the time when the center lent its animals for this use. "In this setting, they'd be separated right away."

Yet r04040's record shows he was reported for injuries 20 times in 2008 alone, apparently without the culprit(s) being identified or removed. It wasn't until Jan. 26 of this year that r04040 was removed from the group setting and paired with another male.

According to Kemnitz, the median life expectancy of primates at the center – excepting those used in lethal research – is 26 years, longer than typical in the wild. (Marolt is unmoved by this line of contention: "We could put people in the same environment, keep them free of normal risks, give them medical attention, and maybe they would live longer too. So what?")

My hosts explain that it's not unusual that r04040 has not been used for experiments. Most researchers want to wait until the animals are young adults. "Very few get used before they're five years old," says Capuano. In fact, r04040 has just been assigned to a pending project for infectious disease work. It's been determined that he lacks natural resistance to infections, which makes him an ideal subject.

I press the pair on the sentience of monkeys. These are highly intelligent animals who can count, problem-solve, discriminate between types of music, even empathize (one study found that rhesus monkeys will go hungry if getting food means shocking another monkey). Isn't it sad to see them spending their whole lives in cages?

Kemnitz and Capuano refuse to concede the point. "If you watch the animals, they don't look chronically depressed or sad," says Kemnitz. "They were born here. They're fed and cared for." And the center tries "to make their lives as enriched as we can."

Capuano agrees. "I'm a veterinarian," he notes. "I took an oath to protect animals."

What about sanctuary? It's been suggested that, if animals are needed for research, it should be for limited periods, after which they can spend the rest of their lives in a more natural environment.

Several such sanctuaries operate around the country. Amy Kerwin, a former UW primate researcher, has been trying to create one here. And the UW recently found new homes, including sanctuaries, for a colony of 75 cotton-top tamarins deemed no longer useful for research.

Kemnitz and Capuano regard my question cautiously.

"I understand where they're coming from," says Kemnitz of sanctuary advocates. "I'm sympathetic."

But there are difficulties. For one thing, a "major focus" of the UW's work is on aging, for which it needs geriatric animals. Then there's the issue of cost: Who will pay for these sanctuaries? Who will buy their replacements ($5,000 per rhesus)?

"Philosophically, I'm not opposed [to sanctuary]," says Capuano. "Financially, that's another story."

Besides, who says a walk-on part in a sanctuary beats a lead role in a cage? As Kemnitz puts it, "Just because animals are living in a different environment doesn't mean they're better off."

EARLY ONE MORNING IN APRIL, I ARRIVE AT THE PRIMATE CENTER TO take another tour. As in 2004, I've had to get a two-doctor-visit tuberculosis test; what's new are the 30 pages of rules to review and sign.

The security guard summons Capuano, who leads me to a room where I meet some animal-care staffers at the start of their shift. The center employs about 100 people, half of whom have regular contact with monkeys.

Capuano warns me about some of the primate behavior we may observe: "These animals don't even know me very well. They may respond to us aggressively and show off."

We head to a locker room to strip to socks and underwear, then dress in official garb: full-coverage scrubs, mask, shower cap, face shield, a double layer of latex gloves. On the elevator ride to our destination, one worker tells Capuano, "The guys you're looking at are getting big for their cage."

It's true. R04040 and his cellmate, r04060, are both nearing 10 kilos (22 pounds). The federal Animal Welfare Act requires that monkeys between three and 10 kilos each have 4.3 square feet of floor space (that's 25 by 25 inches). But at 10 kilos they must get six square feet.

We enter a room with about a dozen double cages, each less than four feet in any direction. R04040 and r04060 are the only two monkeys in the room, in an upper-tier cage. Capuano says the room is going to be hosed down later that day, as is done every two weeks. These two were left behind for now, pending our visit.

Both monkeys react with alarm to our intrusion, pacing quickly back and forth and on several occasions throwing their bodies against the side of the cage, making a crashing sound. I try to take some photos, but it's difficult.

Capuano asks if I'd like r04040 put into a smaller enclosure nearer the floor. This will require the assistance of one of the staffers I met a few minutes ago.

While we're waiting for her to arrive, Capuano shows me a pair of larger, vaguely zoo-like rooms across the hall, joined by a transit hole. Both are also empty, due to renovations. Here, I'm told, is where r04040 spent most of his life, housed with about 10 other rhesus macaques.

Capuano also shows me a room like r04040's that happens to be full of monkeys. They dart about and make a lot of noise. Each cage contains a red plastic ball, one of the "enhancements" provided by the center to keep the monkeys occupied.

For a minute I am left alone by the doorway of this room. Suddenly one monkey, a 10-year-old male, leaps onto the cage wall, clutches the wire with all four limbs and pulls his body violently into it, eight times in rapid succession: *bam, bam, bam, bam, bam, bam, bam, bam!*

In the hallway are two large cages, each containing about 10 tiny marmoset monkeys. They're perched shoulder-to-shoulder on the top rung, as though posing for a family portrait. We make our way back to r04040's room.

The staffer, whom I hardly recognize in her getup, holds a transfer cage up to r04040's enclosure and creates an opening. Like a shot he rushes in, hitting the far wall.

"See how fast he did that?" asks Capuano, explaining that the monkeys are taught this, for when they must be moved. R04040 exits the transfer cage into the smaller enclosure just as swiftly.

I make mostly unsuccessful attempts to photograph my monkey as he darts nervously around his strange new environs. He regards me warily, opening his mouth in an obvious threat. Even when he adjusts to our presence – becoming, says Capuano, "more comfortable" – there is still fear in his eyes.

I wonder what I'm doing here, taking his picture, using him. Is the trauma my visit causes justified because I plan to write about it?

MAY 15, 2009

Part Three

GETTING PERSONAL

Lorenz F. Lueders

Farewell to Dear Old Dad

Daddy what was I supposed to do?
I don't know why it was so hard to talk to you.
I guess my anger pulled me through.

– JACKSON BROWNE

I was at the hospital the night my dad died. He barely knew I was there. The last thing I remember him saying was "I'm going to sleep now." The last thing I told him was "Goodbye." It was typical of the conversations we had.

My dad and I got along, but there was always something awkward between us, some sense that we were just too different, too much in our own dissimilar worlds. The truth, I think, is that we were too much alike.

We had almost nothing in common. He was into cars and I was into books. He could fix almost anything and I was a mechanical nincompoop. He was the blue-collared Everyman and I was the college-educated radical. Yet he taught me everything that made me who I am. He was my mentor, though I never told him so.

His name was Lorenz Frederick Lueders. My mom and older friends called him Lorry; people he met later in life knew him as Larry. He went to Milwaukee's St. Anne's grade school and Messmer High, served in the Philippines during World War II, fathered four children, worked as a route salesman for Adelman laundry, and belonged to the Model A Club. He liked beer and smoked cigarettes. He died of lung cancer on Oct. 28, 1985, two weeks before his 63rd birthday.

My dad had lots of friends, many of whom he met in grade school. He loved playing cards and fishing and going on family vacations. But most of all, he loved to work. He used to leave home at 5 a.m. for his job at Adelman and work till about 3 in the afternoon. Until about 10 years ago, he had to work six days a week.

For most of the years I spent growing up, he also had a second job, doing nighttime custodial work at various office buildings. Still, he barely made enough to get by. He never went to ballgames or bars. I can't remember him ever buying anything for himself.

In his spare time, my dad worked. For him, keeping busy was an addiction. He always had some project in the works. Around the house he built a patio, a driveway, storage cabinets and a two-car garage. Inside he added a recreation room (ceiling and floor tile, lighting, paneling, cabinets and bar), a second bathroom, a third bedroom and – his favorite – a workroom.

Most impressive were the two Model A cars he put together in his garage. The first, a 1929 Roadster, was literally in boxes when he brought it home. Each part had to be sanded by hand, rustproofed, repainted, and fitted together in whatever relation constituted a car. My brother, Rick, worked with him. Together, it took them seven years.

The Roadster was a masterpiece of restoration; it won an award and lots of admiration. The second car, a 1930 Model A Sedan, also took the better part of a decade to complete and it, too, was a beaut. But by that time he was too sick to show it off.

AS A YOUNG MAN, MY DAD WANTED TO BE AN ARTIST, A VOCATION FOR which he showed considerable promise. But his hopes of going to art school were dashed by the necessity of going to work. Still, the artist lived and brooded within him.

A few years ago he completed what is perhaps his greatest work: an elaborate dollhouse for his granddaughter, Jill. For more than six months he disappeared into his workroom for hours every night, painstakingly constructing sturdy miniature furniture to perfect scale. The final product was beautiful beyond a young girl's dreams.

There was almost nothing that my dad couldn't build or fix. He seemed to instantly understand the inner workings of things, the relationship of one to another part. He always knew what went wrong and how to make it right.

For instance, when I was 10 I dropped a coat hanger into a lightbulb socket to see what would happen. There was a big flash and, afterward, the light wouldn't work. That evening he took one look at it and said, "You dropped a coat hanger in here to see what would happen, didn't you?" Ten minutes later it was fixed.

As a kid, I used to imagine that my dad would die with a hammer in his hand. There was almost never a time when he wasn't working. To this day, I suspect that if he hadn't gotten sick, that's how he would have gone: pounding away at this thing or that.

My dad, like me, was stubborn and short-tempered. But he was a good man. He never hit me or lectured me or tried to prescribe my destiny. He taught by example and by example alone. I'm only now realizing how much I learned.

My dad took pride in everything he did. There was no "good enough" in his book. He was a perfectionist – even in how he serviced his customers. There was no better route salesman on the Adelman staff.

He lived what people said was a full and happy life. Still, I can't help but think of him as a victim. A hapless victim of forces – work, capitalism, cigarettes – far more powerful than him. His death makes me angry. I will avenge it if I can.

MY DAD WAS 62 YEARS OLD AND HE WORKED LIKE A FANATIC ALL HIS life – for what? He never even got a chance to retire.

Of course, it was his own fault. Nobody told him he had to smoke. Not the U.S. Army, which included a pack of cigarettes in each day's ration. Not the thousand advertisements with carefree, happy smokers who'd walk a mile for a Camel. Not the tobacco industry, which under the law has every right to kill people for profit.

My dad quit smoking on the same day he quit work – October 28, 1983 – two years to the day before he died. That was the day his left lung collapsed and he was rushed to the hospital.

From there it only got worse. Surgery, chemotherapy, the oxygen tube, the pills, the wheelchair, the portable potty, the spit-up tray, the needles. At first he complained that he couldn't walk from the front room to the kitchen without pausing to catch his breath. Later it was all he could do to walk three steps. In the end he needed help lying down from a sitting position.

And yet he never stopped fighting. I don't think he ever lost his will to live. He fought like hell to make it to my wedding, last May, and he was fighting even harder to live to see our baby, yet unborn. Living was so dear to him. He breathed life into the poet's words:

Do not go gentle into that good night.
Rage, rage against the dying of the light.

In the end, there was relief. It was so hard for those who loved him to see him suffer so, fighting for every breath. When he finally let go, it was as much for our sake as his own.

Yes, I learned a lot from him. Mostly, that life is much too precious to waste. And love too important to harness.

Goodbye, Dad, I'll miss you. I'll fight like hell for you until the end.

DECEMBER 1985, THE CRAZY SHEPHERD

Letter to a New Arrival

When you were born, Jesse, I held your mother and cried. I recognized you the moment your head popped out: Even before the rest of you appeared, I knew you were a boy. I loved you immediately – not just as a cute little baby but as a human being, my son.

We named you Jesse, Hebrew for "gift of God," because it sounded gentle and strong. Our choice proved controversial. "Whenever I hear that name," one relative complained, "I think of Jesse James or Jesse Jackson" – as though a bank robber and a civil-rights leader were equally to be despised.

Finally, your mom put her foot down. "There's nothing wrong with that name," she insisted, and, of course, there isn't.

Your middle name, Lorenz, German for Lawrence, was my dad's first name. The day he died he asked me once again about what your mom and I had told him. It was hard for him to talk then, his lungs were so far gone, but he cradled his arms as if he were holding a baby. "Yes," I reassured him, "if it's a boy, we're going to name him Jesse Lorenz." He shaped his thumb and forefinger into an "OK" sign. It was the last thing that ever made him happy.

How your grandpa would have loved you, little one! Just to have seen you, so tiny and cuddly and full of life, would have melted his heart. He would have wanted you to have the best of everything – to grow up strong and happy and healthy and proud. I want all that for you and more.

I want you to be free – freer than your mom and I – to shape your own destiny. People everywhere will try to sentence you to a future based on the limits of their imagination: Go to school, get a job, work hard, look right, fit in, move up, roll over, play dead. Tell them to go to hell!

Being at peace with the world is boring and wrong. It's better to be a rebel, a dreamer, a malcontent. Treat people with respect but never let them put you down. Sometimes the only honorable thing to do is fight: not with your fists – that's always dumb – but with all your heart and soul.

Be a kid as long as you can. Most folks force themselves to grow up before they need to, only to find out too late what a lousy deal it is. It's better to fight it every step of the way – you'll still have to grow up but maybe it won't be as bad.

I'm getting way ahead of us, though. Right now, all you want is to be fed and to have your diapers changed. There will be plenty of time for lectures later, when you're old enough to not want to listen.

SOMETIMES I'VE WONDERED WHETHER IT WAS RIGHT TO BRING YOU INTO the world. That's a terrible admission, but it's true.

When you were born, the president of your country was engaged in an illegal campaign to provide military aid to a group of mercenaries, called Contras, bent on overthrowing the elected government of another country, Nicaragua. Thousands of Nicaraguans have already been killed for the crime of supporting their own government. Thousands more will die if our president has his way.

One official of our government advanced the notion that members of Congress who refuse to support these killers are in league with communism.

The president backed him up. Will this tactic work? It always has; the people of this country are conditioned from birth to have an intense fear and loathing of anything labeled "communist." Presidents and other liars merely need to utter the word to get what they want: more money for weapons and military involvements; less money for schools and the needy; tighter controls on what people may see, hear and read.

Every day they build more bombs. Every day they tell more lies so they can build more bombs still. Every day it becomes more likely that the bombs will be used.

The day you were born it occurred to me that you might be able to do something about the problems of the world. Perhaps, if we taught you to be a humanitarian and a fighter and.... Then I realized the problems of the world can't possibly wait that long.

No, the responsibility for making this a better world is ours, not yours. And your arrival is, at the very least, a beginning – an expression of confidence that life is good enough to spread around. Is there hope for the future? No one who looks into those big, calm eyes of yours could doubt it.

JUNE 1986, THE PROGRESSIVE

Jesse Lueders was homeschooled by his mother and me, after our divorce, until the fifth grade. He went on to graduate from East High and the UW–Madison, with a degree in philosophy. In August 2010 he began his first year of law school at UCLA.

The author does the deed. Photo courtesy of Seven Hills Skydivers

Skydive!

That Rick Carlson and I ever met is really just a freefall of fate. He called one day in February to say he had some photographs of himself and two other people falling hundreds of feet per second with the Capitol building in the background. Would *Isthmus* be interested?

In the course of routing his inquiry to the right people (the photo eventually ran on the cover of our annual guide to Madison), I mentioned to Carlson that jumping out of an airplane was something I'd always wanted to do. I didn't mention that I get dizzy looking down from the second story at shopping malls. He told me his club, Seven Hills Skydivers, let newspaper writers have a free first jump.

Carlson, the manager of Hardee's in Sauk City, said one option would be to make a tandem jump – leaping from an airplane at 10,000 feet strapped to the front of an experienced diver, known as a "tandem master," presumably wearing stain-resistant clothes. The freefall lasts about 45 seconds; the experience (sampled by a 76-year-old grandmother at the club last year) usually costs $100.

A second, more popular way to go involves taking an eight-hour course and then jumping at 3,000 to 4,000 feet with a chute that opens more or less automatically. This usually costs $110, or $100 per person for groups of five. (The price for subsequent jumps drops to $21.) The only problem, said Carlson, was that I couldn't do this kind of jump until April, then still two months away. I told him this sounded like the better option.

How dangerous is it? I asked. Not very, claimed Carlson, who besides jumping out of planes likes to plunge scores of feet underwater wearing scuba gear and taking pictures of sharks. He did say, however, that there were about 30 deaths a year in the skydiving community. "By coincidence," he added, "all involved newspaper writers." I said I would get back to him.

About a month later, I got a call from Sue Meseberg, who handles publicity for the club, asking if I wanted to set a date for my first jump. I said I would call back the following week. About five weeks later Meseberg called again: How would I like to just visit the club, watch people jump and see "how nice they land"?

That Saturday I visited the club. Everyone I saw come down, Carlson included, landed very "nice."

Everyone I met also seemed very nice. It was a nice day. Overcome with complaisance, I agreed to take the first-jump class two weeks hence.

I didn't get a lot of encouragement. "There may be reasons to not do some of the things we don't do in our lives," mused one of my *Isthmus* colleagues. A friend remarked: "I think you're smarter if you don't do it." And my 4-year-old son, Jesse, made it known that jumping from an airplane wouldn't win me any points with him: "If I did that, I would be really brave about it. I wouldn't be scared at all."

The only exception was Kathy Bailey, *Isthmus'* administrative director, who made the plunge a few years back. "Do it!" she exhorted. "It was one of the best experiences of my life."

Driving to the Seven Hills clubhouse in northeastern Dane County at 7:30 a.m. on the prescribed Saturday in May – after a fitful and mostly sleepless night – the question occurred to me: Why then, dear Kathy, did you never do it again?

It was too late to ask. First-jump class was about to begin.

THERE WERE 16 PEOPLE IN MY CLASS, AND IT LOOKED AS THOUGH I, AT AGE

30, had a good 10 years on every one of them. Even as a videotape accompanying the signing of the disclaimer insisted "You must realize that people have been killed or injured," they just sat there, chomping their gum nihilistically. I was the only one to ask how dangerous it was.

Bob "Goldie" Payne, the club's director of training, noted that before the introduction of the square (as opposed to round) parachute, "we used to break six legs a year out here." In the half-dozen years since, there have been just three or four sprained ankles and one broken leg – the latter involving a person who didn't heed instructions.

"All of the injuries I know of," added Payne without a trace of irony, "occur on landing."

But skydiving class is not about convincing people how safe it is. The purpose is to prepare them to survive the worst. As Payne – who has made more than 4,000 jumps – later told me: "We make it sound harder than it is so you have a healthy respect for it."

Seven Hills Skydivers has 60 members, about half of whom are active. The club trains about 300 first-jump students per year, only about a third of whom come back for a second jump. A Seven Hills pamphlet proclaims: "We actually feel sorry for the earthbound people who only dream about skydiving but never take that first step."

The classroom training lasts five hours, with another two hours of exercises outdoors. Students are taught about equipment and rules (no drinking until after the last jump of the day). You're taught how to do the deed: You have to crawl through the airplane door in 100-mph wind onto a narrow platform; push off so that you're hanging from a bar under the wing; let go on command ("Skydive!" the jumpmaster yells), throw your body into an arch and begin a countdown that leads, if the parachute doesn't open after five seconds, to a decision to initiate emergency procedures. And you're taught how to steer the parachute ("canopy") and how to land – even in power lines or trees.

"You will become very apprehensive," said my instructor, Jerry Lehnherr. Skydivers seek to turn that apprehension into "high awareness" – to control one's fears and not to be controlled by them.

Lehnherr, who holds part of a world record for the largest configuration of falling human bodies (144 in 1988 over Quincy, Illinois), explained why skydivers keep coming back for more: "Adrenaline is the most powerful drug in the world, and we all are addicts."

There is among skydivers a powerful appreciation for "the first time." Meseberg, a medical billing secretary who since 1984 has made about 500 jumps, says her first time was the most frightening. When the plane door opened to the roaring wind, she remembers thinking "Oh my God, I'm going to fall!"

Then she realized: "That's the purpose of this whole thing."

Carlson, who made his first jump at age 27 four years ago, says the terror turns to thrills and the thrills to enjoyment, "and eventually it's just something you want to practice and get better at." (Experienced divers usually jump at about 10,000 feet and pull their own chute after about 45 seconds of freefall. Many practice "relative work" – formations involving a number of skydivers.) Carlson jumped four times on my first jump day; in-between he tried to keep my spirits up.

"It's definitely something you'll remember for the rest of your life," he said, adding wickedly, "however long that may be."

BY THE TIME I BOARDED THE SINGLE-ENGINE CESSNA PLANE, I HAD ENOUGH nervous energy to make cocaine obsolete. There were five of us – a pilot, three students and a jumpmaster – packed into a plane barely large enough to hold us. I was in position to jump second. The ride was bumpy, the view sickening.

"I can do this," I was saying, again and again. When the plane door opened and the first guy jumped, I began to really panic. I became suddenly convinced that my radio wasn't working properly because I couldn't hear the instructions the first guy was getting from the ground. I screamed this fear into the jumpmaster's ear. He screamed back: "It's quieter once you leave the plane."

The door swung open again. I looked down on the fields below. We were at 3,500 feet, two-thirds of a mile in the air. The jumpmaster, 57-year-old John Frederickson, told me to get into position. The wind was blowing furiously. It was a struggle to plant my foot on the platform. On command, I grabbed hold of the bar beneath the wing, pulled myself onto the platform, and pushed off.

There I was, hanging in a 100-mph wind from the wing of an airplane. I looked back to the jumpmaster. I was supposed to say "Check in!" I didn't say a thing. The jumpmaster yelled "Skydive!" I couldn't believe what he was telling me. "Skydive!" he yelled again.

I am convinced that moment of decision – that letting go – is a metaphor for something much larger in our lives. Oh how we hang there, holding on in fear – to relationships that don't work, jobs we hate, lifestyles that injure us. And yet all the time within us is the capacity to ... well, to fly.

Or at least to fall.

When I let go of the airplane the front part of my body went into an arch; the back part, my legs, began kicking like crazy. I had expected that the time it took the chute to open – supposedly three to five seconds – would seem roughly twice as long as *Gone with the Wind*. Instead, it seemed only an instant – an instant long enough for me to forget to count, forget my name, forget everything except my own boundless terror.

When the chute finally opened, it was ... a relief. I looked up, grabbed the toggles I needed to steer with, and cautiously followed Lehnherr's instructions from the ground. When I did the exercise called a flare – pulling down sharply on both toggles to break speed – I stopped dead in the air. Never in my life have I heard such silence. I understood what Meseberg meant when she called it peaceful.

By the time I remembered to look at my altimeter and orient myself – one of the first things you're supposed to do – I was at 1,500 feet and completely disoriented. I spent much of the trip down trying to locate the clubhouse. I never did. It wasn't until I was about 50 feet above the ground and saw the faces of my classmates that I had any idea where I was. I flared on command and landed on my feet, falling forward to my knees, right in front of the clubhouse.

It's hard to describe the way I felt then. Immediately I burst out laughing. I had scored an adrenaline high that would last for hours. My hands shaking uncontrollably, I walked back into the clubhouse with Carlson and told him "Thanks."

The next weekend I went back and made my second jump.

JUNE 1, 1990

Second and last jump, I should say, at least so far. A few months after this article appeared, instructor "Goldie" Payne shattered his leg on a tandem jump. And not long after that, Rick Carlson jumped to his death.

In Search of the Perfect Pet

t began with me the way it does with most people: that feeling, I guess you would call it a void. Something was missing in my life. Not just fame, fortune, serenity, a lime-green Ferrari Testarossa, the editorship of *The Capital Times*, a clear reason for living, etc. – I had reconciled myself to those absences long ago. What I needed was something to care for; something that would depend on me. I needed ... a pet.

During my three decades on the planet, I have had an array of pets. Most recently, I had tropical fish, which I neglected badly. After my young son, Jesse, poured a whole container of fish food into the tank, I pretty much let things go. Months later, I emptied the 10-gallon cesspool after it had evaporated to the halfway point and discovered to my horror that one hearty Danio was still alive and flipping.

Tropical fish make good pets, colorful and peculiar, but frankly, they're not real affectionate. The most affectionate pets, of course, are dogs – the only best friend a man can have that can sleep with his wife and not strain the relationship (between the man and dog, I mean).

My family had two dogs while I was growing up. My dad was dead-set against the idea at first, until my sister brought Pepper home as a puppy. That dog would go crazy with joy when my dad came home from work, the only member of our family to have this reaction. It broke my dad's heart when Pepper – 14 years old and too wracked with arthritis to walk – had to be taken to the Humane Society and be put to "sleep."

A few months later, just before Christmas, I went back to the Humane Society and rescued a year-old border collie from Death Row. Snoopy, which is what my dad named him, was an amazing dog. He couldn't do any tricks – if you threw a ball he'd just look at it – but he could walk on his hind legs just like a person, which is obviously what he thought he was.

My dad loved that dog, too, but this time he died before the dog did. Eventually, my mom moved someplace where she couldn't have a dog. My sister took Snoopy, then seven years old and in perfect health, to the Humane Society, and ... well, no one in my family has mentioned him since.

My experiences with cats have been similarly mixed. I like their independence and their longing for adventure – both qualities that increase their odds of ending up pregnant or dead. The first cat I had in Madison was run over by a car – nine times, apparently, since it didn't come back. Another one is still part of my family, and just had a litter of the most darling kittens imaginable. (Of course, it's morally wrong to let a cat go unspayed, and because I participated in this negligence, I know I'm not responsible enough to take one of the kittens.)

But cuteness in a pet isn't everything. Rabbits are cute, but I know from experience that they are dirty and evil. One rabbit I had – a Dutch bunny named Bunky – used to excrete an average of 15 pellets a minute, which made him real fun to play with on the couch.

SO DOGS, CATS, RABBITS AND FISH WERE OUT. I CONSIDERED BUYING A bird. I've always liked canaries, and saw a beautiful orange one in the shop – too beautiful, I soon realized, to be locked in a cage crapping on a newspaper for the amusement of a tropical-fish abuser like me.

We also looked at reptiles. Jesse, who is 4, was about to attend a Ninja Turtle party, so we set out to find the real thing. It wasn't easy. At a place called Aquarius Pets in Monona, we learned the sale of turtles smaller than four inches was prohibited under federal law (enacted, the salesperson said, because people were getting salmonella poisoning after putting turtles in their mouths). I also learned that turtles larger than four inches are too large for a 10-gallon tank, and that, anyway, turtles stink.

That same day I drove to Fur, Fin and Feather on the west side; there I encountered what I thought would be a perfect pet: the chameleon. I watched in fascination as the unearthly creatures shifted from green to brown, and as the throat of one of them suddenly flared out into what I later learned was his dewlap. They scampered across the aquarium with dazzling speed.

There is something about lizards that is so strange and horrifying I suspect a person cannot come to terms with it and not be changed ("You must ackzept ze leezard in yourzelf"). Some of the larger varieties – iguanas for instance – pack more cold, reptilian reality into their gaze than I can stand. But chameleons, at first glance, seemed safe enough. Then I asked the clerk what they eat.

"Crickets and meal worms," she said. Ah, isn't there some food you can just take out of a jar? Nope: "The chameleon will only eat it if it's alive and moving." Gulp.

Later, I told Jesse about the horrible things chameleons eat. He was all for getting one. A few days later I went to another pet shop and looked at some meal worms. They were alive and moving. The clerk said you're supposed to keep them in the refrigerator.

Clearly, these were not creatures with whom I wished to share my living space – much less my refrigerator. But I resolved then and there I wasn't going to let worms keep me from having other living things to care for, that would depend on me.

I decided to plant a garden.

JUNE 1, 1990

The Horrors of Fitness

Two years ago, seeking glory and a byline, I jumped from an airplane at 3,500 feet. Going to the Madison Athletic Club, I can honestly say, took more guts than that – about 10 pounds more guts, to be exact.

I resisted. I put it off. A MAC-member friend offered me a free pass for 12 visits between Dec. 15 and Jan. 15; that was in 1990. This past year, I accepted her offer, but it was almost Christmas before I finally slunk through the door to encounter firsthand the horrors of physical fitness.

I was sweating before I even suited up. All the men looked like Gaston, the big bully in *Beauty and the Beast*. ("As a specimen, yes, I'm intimidating.") All the women I imagined agreeing with the fitness buff on "L.A. Law" who wondered whether people like me ought to even be allowed to live.

The club is bathed in the soft glow of blue and pink neon lights. There are mirrors everywhere, so people can be constantly reminded of how marvelous they look. The music is almost always awful – worse than Top 40; worse than All Oldies All the Time; worse even than the music my parents listened to. The usual staple is syncopated dance-beat stuff with stunningly inane lyrics: "Mu-sic takes you round and round and round and round and round. Hold on to love. Hold on to love. Mu-sic takes you...."

I first heard this particular anthem while pedaling round and round and round and round and round holding on to one of the club's exercise bikes – a.k.a. Life Cycles. The Life Cycle, like most of the so-called aerobics equipment, allows the user to simulate a fun activity without actually having fun. Other machines offer joyless simulations of rowing, skiing and walking. Another popular contraption, the Stairmaster, simulates an activity – climbing stairs – that isn't any fun at all.

Most of the machines have electronic digit counters showing how long and how far you're able to bike, row, ski and walk without ever leaving the basement of the AT&T building. They also calibrate caloric output – a demoralizing function that proves you can't possibly burn up as many calories in one hour of exercise as you can easily consume in one moment of weakness. (Of course, after a good workout, the very thought of ever eating anything again is enough to make you want to blow chunks.)

The club also has a vast array of weight-lifting equipment. This and the consumption of steroids allow you to accumulate grotesque clumps of muscle all over your body. One of the club's terrifically nice instructors showed me the basics of a total body workout – a circuit of weight machines that allows you to direct pain to every major muscle group. Soon I was grunting with the best – okay, the rest – of them.

I ONCE READ ABOUT A FELLOW WHO WOULD REPEATEDLY WHACK himself in the head with a two-by-four because he liked the feeling when he stopped. That's kind of my attitude toward working out. The good feeling of stopping keeps me coming back.

In fact, after my first several visits, I began having big MAC attacks – a craving to subject my innards to physical strain. I began to take pride in the fact that, even though I'm not in as good shape as most people at the club, I sweat more than any of them. Usually I go through three or four sweat towels, two shirts and a half-inch of carpeting. This output looks awesome in the mirrors, and helps boost my confidence.

My basic workout has remained consistent: I bike until I can't stand it anymore; use the Stairmaster (a.k.a. Sweatmaster) until I can't stand it anymore; row or ski until I can't stand it anymore; do situps until I can't sit up anymore; and lift weights until my arms are so tired I can barely pick up my sweat towel when it falls to the floor.

When I first started going to MAC, I could accomplish all this in about 20 minutes. But almost immediately, I had to work harder to reach the same level of exhaustion. By the time my month-long pass expired, I had used up all 12 visits and brought my total workout time up to nearly two hours. I signed up for a six-month membership.

Now I actually look forward to my thrice-weekly workouts. It's promoted a much healthier lifestyle, as when I now say no to that ninth beer: "Thanks, but I have to go to the gym tomorrow." I've even grown to like the atmosphere, rank as it is, at MAC.

It's true, many of the club's 1,650 members are vacuous, narcissistic brats with annoyingly perfect bodies. But these people are not really intimidating. Most are so self-absorbed you hardly know they're there. Some are just plain crazy.

There's one fellow who works out until his muscles bind up in knots that he relieves with violent thrashing, including throwing his whole body against metal equipment and walls. My friend saw another guy doing backward push-ups on the benches in the steam room, where the temperature easily tops 700 degrees. Then there's the walking mass of muscles I watched shave his chest. He was noticing how much harder it was to maneuver the razor into the narrow crevice between his two huge pecs since the last time he did this. "I guess that's a good sign," he said. And I should worry what these people think of me?

For me, fitness is still something to aspire to – not, as it says on the club's "complimentary courtesy sack" for wet clothes, "A Way of Life." But maybe someday I'll come round (and round and round and round and round) to achieving this level of addiction. I hear it's all done with mirrors.

FEBRUARY 21, 1992

I went to the club for a few more years before deciding to throw in the sweat towel.

The cover of the September 1982 issue

How I Helped Kill
The Crazy Shepherd

We didn't spend a lot of time figuring out what to call it. One night a group of us were in the Gasthaus, the student union bar at the University of Wisconsin–Milwaukee, plotting a new student paper and drinking to excess, and Jim McCarter suggested naming it after some line from Allen Ginsberg. I thought for a moment, then blurted from the epiphany of "Howl": "Holy the vast lamb of the middle class! Holy the crazy shepherds of rebellion!"

Thus, at that moment in the spring of 1982, *The Crazy Shepherd* was born. It was the perfect name for the kind of paper we had in mind: bold, radical, resonant, uninterested in respectability, willing to court misunderstanding. The kind of paper that was not afraid to piss people off. Hell, that was the whole idea.

In May 1982, the premiere issue of our new paper, *The Crazy Shepard*, rolled off the same Port Washington presses that once printed *Kaleidoscope* and the *Bugle American*. Who would have guessed that, alone among these legends of Milwaukee's underground press, the *Shepard* would survive into its second decade? Who would have thought that, a few name changes down the line, it could became a dynamic alternative weekly picked up by people of all ages all over town?

Probably no one who saw that first issue.

Our debut offering – eight pages, no ads – is mainly memorable for putting the *Shepard* on record as being quite possibly the only publication in human history to unintentionally misspell its own name. It wasn't until we were hawking copies from the student union steps that someone broke the news: "Shepard" was the name of an East Side street, not the bucolic archetype.

The *Shepard* billed itself as a "Free Expression Magazine" and vowed in a front-page editorial – winningly entitled "Sheep Dip and Shepard Defiance" – to provide an outlet for opinion holders ("even convicted felons or Young Republicans") and a tonic to the pretended objectivity of the mainstream press.

"One thing the *Shepard* won't try to be," its founders promised, "is a newspaper." Having perused my private archive of *Crazy Shepherd*s (and one *Crazy Shepard*) for the first time in years, I am struck more than anything by this assertion: We didn't mind being called crazy, but we didn't want to be a newspaper.

Today, I'm news editor of Wisconsin's largest weekly newspaper and as such have attained a modicum of respectability (although I still do love to piss people off). McCarter is now publisher of an established community weekly in Minnesota. A third co-conspirator, Petr Kotz, is the managing editor of a small daily in Illinois. The *Shepherd Express* is now "Milwaukee's weekly newspaper" – certainly a step up from our original motto, "Not Just Another Cult Magazine."

But back then, we harbored few ambitions. We just wanted a forum for free expression – by which we meant expression of the sort no newspaper we knew of would allow. Looking back, I realize ... our spelling was atrocious, but our instincts were correct.

AFTER THAT FIRST AWFUL ISSUE HIT THE WASTEBASKETS 10 YEARS AGO
this month, the *Shepherd* took the summer off. It returned to launch its first
full season of monthly publication in September 1982. Unlike the folks
behind *USA Today*, which made its debut that same month, the *Shepherd* staff
knew next to nothing about newspapering and cared next to nothing about
making money off it. (Irony overdose: Which of these two has since lost
more than $800 million?)

The paper came together in McCarter's modest apartment, always
fragrant with the aroma of cigarettes and Jim's roommate's socks. Jim, a
jack-of-all-trades whose past vocations included working as an auto mechanic,
a carpenter, a roofer and a short-order cook, turned the rat-level enclave
on Murray Street into a fully functional newspaper office.

Still, all we could ever afford to pay for was printing and cardboard
ashtrays. Our technical resources were astoundingly crude. In the beginning, we didn't even have a typewriter. About three days before each issue
went to press, we would borrow an IBM Selectric from someone's mom,
type up the whole issue in columns and get them reduced to 77
percent at a nearby Kinko's. We had to return the typewriter before the
September issue went to press, so all corrections were done on a different
borrowed typewriter with strikingly different type.

For the first two years, all headlines, including those in ads, were done
by hand from plastic sheets. Each letter was individually lined up and
scratched off. It was crazy. We picked wildly diverse fonts to suit the mood
of different stories, and freely lifted photos, drawings and other graphics
from other published sources, without so much as a passing thought to copy-
right law. The results were issues that looked and felt completely original.

We treated our bodies harshly, like there was no tomorrow – or, more
precisely, like tomorrow was not something for which one should sacrifice
a single moment of hedonistic excess in the here and now. There was always
lots of beer and cigarettes and late night trips to Axel's, a campus bar a few
blocks away. Yet the staff was not a bunch of slackers. Some deadline nights
we'd still be working as the sun came up.

I remember pursuing typos as though they were brush fires raging out
of control; more of them sprang up than we could ever get to. Twice we
forgot to put a date on the front cover; once a typo caused us to skip an
entire volume year (which explains why the *Shepherd* is now celebrating its
10th anniversary while publishing Volume 12).

Everyone had to sell ads. Everyone had to collect money for ads –
which, believe me, is a whole other task. As the only staffer with a car,

a '78 Buick Opel, I delivered most of the 10,000 copies printed. You might call it a labor of love; at the time it seemed like a love of labor.

FROM THE START, THE SHEPHERD WAS A MAGNET FOR DISSIDENTS AND malcontents – okay, for middle-class kids who happened to be attending University of Wisconsin–Milwaukee – contributing their diverse talents to a common cause. Some of the people who flocked to the paper were brilliant; and some, as our name invited, were just plain crazy. Usually it was hard to tell the difference.

McCarter, no question, was the *Shepherd's* driving force. It was his vision and personality that sustained the paper through its leanest and most creative era. He was smart, funny, at times hard-nosed and domineering – a natural leader. He built layout tables and a darkroom and finagled enough money from our friends in student government to ride the paper through its first two years. Plus, he always had good pot.

Kotz, whose official masthead designation was "Plastic Lawn Animal," penned well-researched articles like "Bobby Kasten: Portrait of a Corporate Whore." Petr (whom I blame for our inability to spell our name) pushed the paper's predilection for irreverence. If something made him laugh, then it was okay to put it in the paper. It was Petr who, from the depths of his own private hell, hatched the great Brewtown slogan: "Milwaukee: Where you wait for buses and then die."

Kurt Buss was our resident philosopher, a guy who'd suddenly say things like "Just balling that jack toward the vortex of all parallel lines" and then give his pleasantly deranged laugh: *heh-heh-heh-heh.* Karen Gerrity, who would later marry Kurt (their second child is due in July), was the paper's ambassador, spreading good will all over town.

There were so many people! If I started to name them, this would read like a genealogy from the Book of Numbers. Karen Haegerl drew the stunning front-cover portraits of our protean mascot, the shepherd. Jeff Worman, in words, art and deed, established the paper's iconoclastic credentials. Chris Deisinger's straightforward reportage pointed us toward the future; Eddie Emerson's anarchy As, scribbled on layout pages before they went to press, kept us grounded in myth.

My original title was poetry editor, which meant that I handled the "Poetry Pasture," in those days a sprawling spread. I also cranked out reams of copy; sometimes my stories ran in smaller type so I could fit in even more of what the *Milwaukee Journal* once called "harsh, long-winded social commentary."

When Jim's roommate with the smelly socks moved out of the apartment, me and my smelly socks moved in. For a time, pages of the paper were pasted up in my room. I remember coming home to our never-locked apartment after closing Axel's and there'd be people I didn't know congregating in the *Shepherd*'s front office, my living room. It was crazy.

The *Shepherd* anchored my existence, and winked at my refusal to conform. Back then I didn't have much of a plan in life, other than to vent my anger at the way it is. I didn't anticipate a career in journalism, or anything else. But neither was I nihilistic or aimless. "My primary ambition," I once told *Milwaukee Magazine*, "is to avoid selling out."

HOW CAN I MAKE SENSE OF THE CRAZY SHEPHERD? THE WHOLE
undertaking was an exercise in impulsiveness. The *Shepherd* was created by people who wanted to print what no one else saw fit to.

We were quite completely serious about the "free expression" part. The *Shepherd* staff was staunchly pro-choice, but ran a number of articles by a member of the anti-abortion Feminists For Life; when another pro-lifer challenged our decision to run graphic photos of Salvadoran death-squad victims by sending us a graphic photo of an aborted fetus, we ran that, too. We rejected offerings that were too poorly written, but never just because they might offend. (Our credo: "Foul language is fine, but watch the libel.")

Once we got into a bad odor with the attorneys for United Feature Syndicate, which didn't see the humor of "Penis," our cartoon takeoff on Charles Schulz's famous "Peanuts" characters. We were sued, unsuccessfully, in student court over my extensively researched article on the Unification Church – which ran with our in-house drawing of a guy with his head shoved completely up his ass and the words, "Looking for God? Try Rev. Moon."

The *Shepherd*'s first taste of notoriety came in April 1983, when it published an article by a fellow named Bob Breen about Channel 12 news guy Jerry Taff. Breen betrayed the assurances he made to Taff that the sordid details of their conversation – including Taff's confession that he never voted and his impudent put-downs of his broadcast news peers – would never see print. The *Milwaukee Sentinel* branded the resulting article "a hideous display of journalistic ethics" – a slam we proudly emblazoned across our next front cover.

Many of our early issues revolved around a central theme: nuclear war, gun control, right-wing extremists, Central America, poverty, Milwaukee, work. The gun issue featured a story about how I successfully arranged to buy handguns at a half-dozen Milwaukee-area outlets reeking of beer and dressed like a revolutionary communist, including a Chairman Mao hat and "Smash the State" button. The poverty issue included a two-page board game called "The Poverty Game" that just so happened to be impossible to win. The issue on Central America contained never-before-published poems by people in Nicaragua.

We ran a lot of spoofs in those early days, parodies of other papers and back-page posters like "Are You a Chic East Sider?" My personal favorite: a spread called "Fall Fashions" in which (truly) ordinary people modeled mud-caked work clothes. We also engaged in more serious mischief, such as printing the home address of police chief "Hal" Breier and photographs of undercover members of his infamous Red Squad.

What made the *Shepherd* special was its willingness to break the rules. We were not frothing-at-the-mouth revolutionaries, but neither did we subscribe to anyone else's notions of what a publication should be. The *Shepherd* was born in the wilderness of our youth, and suckled by the she-wolf of our imaginations. Like Karen's drawings of the shepherd, the paper was ever-changing. It was, like all of us, unique in the world.

IN 1988, I MET MICHAEL MOORE AT AN ALTERNATIVE NEWSPAPER convention in British Columbia. Moore was then editor of *Mother Jones* magazine. Later he directed the delightfully devious documentary *Roger and Me*. I mentioned to him that I got my start in journalism at a Milwaukee paper called *The Crazy Shepherd*.

"*The Crazy Shepherd!*" exclaimed Moore. "That's one of my favorite papers!" Turns out he'd been reading it for years.

By this time, of course, the *Shepherd* was no longer Crazy. It abandoned that identifier in March 1986 – the same month I left the paper for a real job in Madison. This name change, a deliberate attempt to make the paper more viable, was not especially controversial. We all knew it didn't make sense to call ourselves crazy anymore.

It wasn't that the *Shepherd* (later the *Milwaukee Shepherd* and then the *Shepherd Express*) decided to stop taking risks or breaking rules. But something fundamental changed. The *Shepherd* evolved into the very thing it once pledged to never be: a newspaper.

Looking back, I know that I am largely to blame. During my internship at *The Progressive* magazine in the summer of 1984, I was introduced to the ancient art of editing – actually changing copy to improve readability! – and busily plied my newfound ability when I returned that fall as the

Shepherd's first editor. We had a new office – an old house in a recovering neighborhood on Wright Street – and two new Apple IIc computers. The paper's slide down that slippery slope to professionalism and technological sophistication had begun. And nothing or no one could stop it.

I'm not saying that what happened is a bad thing. Today's *Shepherd Express* is by almost any standard a better publication than *The Crazy Shepherd*. But something about the paper back then was extraordinary, and it did get lost.

When Karen Gerrity left the paper in July 1985, she wrote a farewell letter that recalled those early days: "We were the picture of youthful exuberance, rebels with a cause. We were going to take on the world in a cultural revolution and win."

Yes, we believed that; and yes, it was crazy. But some days I'd trade all the respectability I've since achieved just to feel that way again.

MAY 28, 1992, SHEPHERD EXPRESS

This article ran in the paper's 10th anniversary issue. The Shepherd Express *remains a successful weekly in Milwaukee.*

The author reads "Howl" at the University of Wisconsin-Milwaukee, 1982

A Howl for Allen Ginsberg

Allen Ginsberg is the only man – my father included – I've ever kissed on the lips. It happened in March 1982, at the end of a two-day Milwaukee visit by Ginsberg that I helped arrange. The kiss was just a friendly gesture, but emblematic of the way that Ginsberg touched my life – how he broadened the boundaries of the permissible and made the radical real.

Ginsberg died last Saturday at age 70, soon after being diagnosed with liver cancer. For four decades, he was the poet laureate for a succession of Beats, hippies, yippies, yuppies and Generation Xers. Ginsberg, in his words and life, confirmed the transformative power of language. At least for me.

I got turned on to Ginsberg in the mid-1970s, when I was in high school. My favorite English teacher had read Ginsberg's poem "America" to the class. I loved the energy of it, the anger, the wit. So, too, with Ginsberg's classic 1956 poem "Howl," which I stumbled into adulthood reading aloud, thrilling to its cadences, its celebration of pushing the boundaries of human experience. "Howl" is about "angelheaded hipsters burning for the ancient heavenly connection to the starry dynamo in the machinery of night." It's about people who, among a great many things, "howled on their knees in subways and were dragged off the roof waving genitals and manuscripts."

Two months before Ginsberg's Milwaukee visit, I mostly shouted this poem into a microphone in the union of the University of Wisconsin–Milwaukee amid the caterwauling of my friends' electric guitars – a performance-art piece that was met, I swear, with apples hurled at us by students from the second-floor balcony.

Ginsberg's Milwaukee visit was the crowning achievement of my student activist days. Three friends and I had started (and constituted the entire membership of) a student group called the Society for a Better Society (SBS). Our pals in UWM student government helped set us up with $2,000 to bring Ginsberg to town.

On our banners and flyers for the event, we billed Ginsberg as "America's greatest living poet"; he found this out and objected, asking us to include a program note stating that he disavows this distinction. Privately, he told me he was worried that such an appellation might get him assassinated. He also felt that Gregory Corso deserved top-dog honors.

FROM THE TIME I PICKED GINSBERG UP AT THE AIRPORT TO THE TIME WE kissed goodbye, the visit was packed with activity. This week, after learning of Ginsberg's passing, I retrieved a mildewed folder from a box in my basement. It contains posters and press releases from this 1982 visit, and a handwritten note from Ginsberg agreeing to a full slate of activities spread over two days: "Just leave me free before noon daily to write & meditate."

We visited Woodland Pattern bookstore, toured the Milwaukee Art Museum (with Kenosha writer Michael Schumacher, later the author of a well-received Ginsberg biography) and went to a dank downtown bar for a spirited interview with Joel McNally of *The Milwaukee Journal*.

The night before the main event, Ginsberg rehearsed with the Blackholes, the Milwaukee "power punk polka band" that agreed to be part of the show.

At the rehearsal, Ginsberg proudly played an original tape of a performance he'd done a few weeks earlier with The Clash. The next day, Ginsberg spoke to a class of creative writing students at UWM. I recorded the encounter on my portable recorder – only to later discover that I had taped over Ginsberg's treasured Clash session.

The public performance itself took place before a standing-room-only crowd in the UWM Ballroom. When the campus cops started fretting about the too-packed room, Ginsberg personally smoothed things out. He read for more than an hour, and then brought the band on stage as he sang from his most recent book, *Plutonian Ode*. (The collection was published just two months earlier, and Ginsberg painstakingly scrawled changes to my first-printing copy.) I remember thinking he was a bit like the Greek god Dionysus, leading revelers to the insights that intoxication brings.

Ginsberg stayed with some local poets and brought a different lover to bed both nights he was in town. He casually discarded the gift of the youngest man, and gave his hostess strict instructions on how to do his laundry. But he also gave constantly of himself to unending streams of people who wanted a piece of him. It was the first time I really grasped the demands of celebrity.

I'll probably hold on to that mildewed folder in the basement for a good many years. But, for me, Allen Ginsberg's essence resides in my tattered copy of *Howl and Other Poems*.

This weekend, as a promised bedtime story, I'm going to read "America" to my son. He's 11, and it's been several years since I last read it to him. Then, as always, I'll kiss him goodnight.

APRIL 10, 1997, SHEPHERD EXPRESS

Waiting for Wood

Not long ago, while biking to work, I passed a pile of old floorboards on a curb in front of someone's house. That evening, as I returned with my car to load the boards into my already filthy back seat, resting the ends on a back window that won't open all the way, hoping the glass wouldn't shatter but willing to take the chance, I told the owner that I had seen the boards that morning and couldn't stop thinking about them all day. "I know," I added, sensing her concern. "It's pathetic."

Oh, the thrill of it, the gathering of wood! To come across an orderly array of oak, a bevy of birch, or even a lowly pile of pine. Wood, progenitor of fire, giver of warmth, reducer of heating bills. You complete me.

Gathering wood is one of my favorite activities. I've gone camping about five times a year for more than 20 years, and never once have I either brought or bought wood. Yet invariably I have roaring fires, and often a woodpile left behind for the next happy camper. Armed with a backpacking saw, I set forth into the wilderness, returning with oak and hickory and black walnut, filling my trunk until it takes two bungee cords to hold the load in place. I cut, stomp and crack the wood into firepit-sized logs, arranged according to size and quality. Add a little white gas, and it's burn, baby, burn.

Then there's wood splitting, which is to wood gathering what intercourse is to foreplay. I was a late bloomer, having split my first log sometime in the middle of the Reagan administration. Initially, I missed a lot, and broke quite a few ax handles. Now I use a heavy maul with a fiberglass handle, and my aim is true.

The first thing I did after I bought a house a few years back was to install a wood stove. But I soon discovered it's a lot harder to find wood in the city than in a state park. (I also learned that dumping hot ashes in a plastic compost bin is a good way to set one's house on fire, but that's another story.)

Since then, my need for wood in winter has turned into a four-season obsession. I scout the curbs for trees and wood piles. My west-side pal and I patrol the woods near his home, chainsaws wailing like the souls of the damned. Once, I even went after a deadfall alongside a city bike path. It was in the late fall, and no one was present – until, that is, I drove my car onto the path and whipped out my chainsaw. Suddenly, a plethora of passersby appeared. "Need wood," I explained.

I've asked city and county officials if they ever let people take wood from public parkland. The answer is no. City recycling guru George Dreckmann says the city once let people pick through log piles from trees it cut down, but ended this practice after a fight broke out among rival oak gatherers. "We actually had two guys face off with chainsaws," he says. Now everything is churned into wood chips. Bummer.

And so I am left to my usual devices – calls and letters to people who have felled trees in their yards, tips from friends who see "free firewood" signs, bags of scrap wood saved by my brother from his woodworking projects. A wood junkie depends on the kindness of others, but also must be vigilant. Recently, in a moment of folly, I nearly threw out about 20 wooden chopsticks I had accumulated over the years. Snapping back to my senses like dry kindling beneath a boot, I put them in a bag by the wood stove, for when cold weather comes.

OCTOBER 1, 1999

Where the Winners Aren't

It's just after noon on a Monday as I arrive at the Ho-Chunk Casino near Wisconsin Dells. The only empty stalls near the entrance are those "Reserved for Tribal Elders."

I walk through a row of doors, past a pair of security guards and into the casino, which opens to either side like vast butterfly wings. It's a massive facility – 94,000 square feet of gambling space – with several dozen gaming tables and more than 3,000 video slot machines. It takes me about a half-hour just to walk through. I figure there's at least 1,000 people inside. And it's nowhere near full.

I'm here to get a sense of what the Ho-Chunk have in mind if voters approve a Feb. 17 referendum authorizing a casino on Madison's southeast side. The tribe has said it wants the new casino to be smaller – just 1,000 gaming machines, and 10–18 tables – but there are no guarantees. The DeJope bingo hall building occupies about 80,000 square feet.

About 20 tables are in active use, mostly for customers playing poker or blackjack. The blackjack tables on the floor have $5 or $10 minimums, with a separate "High-Stakes Blackjack" room for people who want to wager $25 to $500 per hand. The various poker games – three-card poker, seven-card stud, Caribbean stud poker – were added last fall, on the casino's 10th anniversary. There's also a couple of craps tables, with roulette soon to come.

But the vast majority of people here today and every day – the casino is open 24 hours a day, seven days a week – are playing the video slot machines. They range from two-cent machines to ones than can burn $20 a turn. They come in countless varieties: "The Three Stooges." "The Honeymooners." "Kenny Rogers' 'The Gambler.'" Some riff off favored activities: "Fishin' for Luck," "Reelin' 'Em In." Some appeal to greed: "It's Money Time." Others to magic (or is it desperation?): "Break the Spell."

These machines are much faster, much more efficient at extracting money, than slot machines of old. All accept paper money, up to $100 bills.

Players don't pull levers; they push buttons. The few machines with levers on the side have them just for show.

The Ho-Chunk refuse to say what payout levels their machines are set at, other than that it's at or above the state-mandated 80 percent – that is, 80 cents paid out for every dollar wagered. Gaming experts tell me the actual percentage is probably between 90 percent and 94 percent, less than the 95 percent to 98 percent ratios offered in Las Vegas.

But these are per-play averages, and today's machines allow hundreds of "games" per hour. Even if set at 98 percent, these machines are guaranteed to separate players from their money. And that's what's going on all around me, even as the casino sound system periodically exclaims the Ho-Chunk slogan, "Where the winners are!"

THE FEW TIMES I'VE TRIED MY HAND AT CASINO GAMBLING, IN LAS VEGAS and Reno and the St. Croix casino at Turtle Lake, I've always played black-jack, which I fancy to be a game of skill. Of course, that's only partly true: You do get to make choices, and when you leave the table with less money than you sat down with, which is usually what happens to me, you kick yourself for not making the right ones. But the odds are always in the house's favor.

It's the same with gaming machines, only more so. If you play long enough, they're going to get the better of you. Everybody knows this, either as imparted knowledge or through personal experience. And yet people – lots of them – still come to play. Sometimes all day. And even if they lose, as most do, they come back for more.

What's the appeal? I wonder.

One guy about my age with a cigarette dangling from his lips – smoking is allowed throughout the casino – is playing a $1 slot machine, wagering $3 per play. He began with $100. The counter says he has $61 left. Make that $58. Er, $55.

"So you can lose $100 in just a few minutes?" I ask. "Yeah," he replies. He also says, lest I conclude he's an idiot for throwing his money down this rat hole, "I won $1,000 playing Keno once." That's not among the games they offer here. Yet.

"How you doing?" I ask an older man playing, incongruously, a machine themed on rock music. "I'm out $40," he replies. "How long did you get to play?" "About 30 minutes." He frowns, disgusted, perhaps at the machine, perhaps at himself.

I chat with a pleasant woman who has a casino-issued Player's Card stuck in her machine, a common sight. The card accumulates points – kind of like frequent flyer miles – that can be redeemed for cash, meals and merchandise. (It also gives casino management detailed data on individual gamblers' habits.)

While we're talking, her machine jams; she can't leave because she has about $20 of credit inside, but she doesn't even try to flag down a casino employee. She just sits and waits till a repair person comes, in response to the glowing bulb atop her machine. Sometimes, she says, she's waited as long as 45 minutes. She doesn't seem to mind.

I start with a five-cent machine. That doesn't mean it's five cents a play, although this is possible. To maximize your chances and qualify for the jackpot, you must make the maximum bet. So a five-cent machine can cost up to two dollars a play. Each play takes about two seconds.

Playing conservatively – and, dare I say, wisely – I quickly turn a $10 bill into $13 on the credit counter. Unlike other gamblers, I tell myself, I know the secret: Walk away while you're on top.

And so I cash out, getting 13 $1 tokens, and walk away. Then I deposit three tokens into a $1 machine and erase my ill-gotten gains on a single play.

I can't resist approaching a guy who is playing a machine called "Winning for Dummies." "Are you winning?" I ask him. "No," he replies. "That should tell you something," I say. We both laugh, but I can tell he's not amused. A moment later, when I make a fifth attempt to insert a $20 bill into another "Winning for Dummies" machine that's rejected it four times, I realize that we share a common bond.

Giving up, I invest my $20 in a machine called "Free Parking Monopoly." I play a few turns at 45 cents each and watch my credits dwindle. Then the image on the screen changes, telling me I've won a chance to buy some parking stalls. I buy five of them and the game sends cars reeling into the parking lot, awarding me credits every time they pull into one of my stalls.

By the time this bonus round is over, I have about 750 credits, more than $35. I decide to stick with my strategy – walk away when you're ahead. I press the cash-in button and 750 nickels pour into the tray. I scoop them in a cup to cash them in. My strategy is working.

I WALK AROUND SOME MORE, WATCHING PEOPLE. JUST ABOUT EVERY-
one here – players as well as employees – is white. I see just two African Americans and three people I think may be Ho-Chunk. Most of the players are older, in their 40s, 50s and 60s, although I'm told that a younger crowd comes out at night. Along the walls are ATM machines and places to cash

checks. There's an area where people can sit at a bar drinking alcohol while playing video poker machines. Somewhere in this gambling complex is a child-care center where parents can drop off their kids to play what are billed as "graphically stunning games."

Then it's back to Free Parking Monopoly, a game that actually calls out enticements: "Come on over and park yourself in front of Monopoly"; "Get your engines warmed up, 'cause it's time to play Free Money Monopoly." It takes about 10 minutes for the machine to free me of all of the money I've won from it – and then some.

I also play a game called Atlantica, which emits a mesmerizing musical sound as aquatic-themed images blur past. As with other machines, I have no idea what constitutes a win other than when a line snakes through images on the screen and credits get added to the digit counter.

It's not just gambling foes who refer to these modern gaming machines as "the crack cocaine of gambling." This term is also used by people in the gaming industry. And no wonder: These machines whirl and whiz and seem to reward, even as they kick your hinder. It's only later, as I'm heading home, that I reflect on how I kept playing without any positive reinforcement, thinking: I've lost eight turns in a row, the next one must be payday. Make that nine turns.

No, the secret of gambling is not to walk away when you win. Everybody does that. The secret is to walk away when you're losing. The secret is in learning not to hope that you can beat the odds. The house wins – always – by preying on people's natural impulse to hope for the best.

I leave after two hours, about half of which was spent gambling. I've lost $31. Atlantica, having whisked away the last of my credits, flashes a parting message: "Game over. Insert money."

FEBRUARY 6, 2004

The Dane County referendum on the Ho-Chunk Madison casino was defeated by a margin of nearly two to one.

Farley and Me

n grade school, I read every book I could get my hands on by a now-forgotten and probably forgettable science-fiction writer named Lester del Rey. In high school, I fell for John Steinbeck; in college, I turned to Twain and turned on to Kerouac.

These were authors whose work, I came to realize, was dependably excellent beyond the one or two titles for which they're best known. One book led to another and to another still. I wandered deep into their literary canons.

In recent years, I've been a big fan of Jon Krakauer and Michael Pollan – but each has written only a small pile of books. The latest writer I've become obsessed with whose body of work makes obsession a real commitment is Farley Mowat.

The "Who?" that usually follows mentions of this name is almost invariably answered with, "The guy who wrote *Never Cry Wolf*." Mowat's publishers are as guilty as anyone of this association, splashing mention of this 1963 tome, later a classic Disney film, on the covers of his other books. But *Never Cry Wolf* is only a wee piece of the Mowat oeuvre. One of Canada's most revered writers, Mowat has written 40 books over the last five and a half decades. His most recent was published in 2006; he turned 86 this spring.

A few years back, at the urging of a fellow animal lover, I read *The Dog Who Wouldn't Be*, Mowat's funny and heartwarming 1957 tribute to his childhood dog. It's one of my all-time favorite books, but somehow it didn't stir my curiosity about his other work. I just assumed its brilliance was a fluke.

Then, last fall, I picked up an old paperback of *A Whale for the Killing*, Mowat's chilling 1972 account of how an 80-ton fin whale trapped in a Newfoundland lagoon was executed by local yahoos who blasted it with rifle fire and ripped open its back with boat propellers. It's a tale filled with anguish and outrage, one that severed Mowat's ties to a place and people he and his wife Claire had come to love.

That set me on a Mowat binge. Every other book I've read over the last few months has been a Mowat. I've now finished nine Mowat titles, plus a 2002 biography written by James King. With each book I find his work and legacy richer and more compelling. He's had an amazing life, which he's deftly fashioned into enduring art.

THE FARLEY MOWAT BOOK THAT MOST ASTOUNDED AND HAUNTS ME IS

the first one he published, back in 1952. *People of the Deer* tells the story of the Ihalmiut, a tribe of inland Eskimo living in one of the most inhospitable regions on earth – the Barrens of northern Canada, west of Hudson Bay.

In the latter part of the 19th century, the Ihalmiut numbered in the thousands, getting everything they needed from vast rivers of caribou making twice-yearly migrations. By the time Mowat visited, between 1946 and 1948, they were on the verge of extinction, due to over-hunting and other changes wrought – sometimes callously, sometimes unwittingly – by Europeans.

Mowat learned the Ihalmiut's language and writes with nonjudgmental authority about their history, religion, mythology and culture. It's a portrait etched in sadness, for despite Mowat's appeals to his fellow Canadians it's pretty clear things will not turn out well for the tribe's remaining members.

Much of Mowat's writing has this in common – it opens up a window to worlds few people ever get to see. That's what fascinated me about *The Siberians*, Mowat's 1970 book about his travels, as a celebrated author, to the Soviet north country. King, his biographer, dismisses this as a minor work. But it mines the richness, complexity and (oddly enough) progressivism of a part of the world about which people often have cartoonish impressions, if they think about it at all.

Never Cry Wolf, in a similar vein, confronts the ignorance that underlies humankind's murderous impulses toward wolves. You come away from this book, as with *People of the Deer* and *The Siberians*, with fresh understanding and full admiration for its subjects.

Same too with *The Snow Walker*, Mowat's collection of short stories about northern peoples. One tale – about a pilot saved by the ingenuity of a young Inuit woman he initially regarded with casual disrespect – became a fine 2003 film of the same name. The longest story is a true account of an infamous murder trial, its point being that white society is ill-equipped to pass judgment on native peoples whose culture it has thrown into upheaval.

Mowat is as witty and self-deprecating as he is insightful and perceptive. In *Born Naked*, his 1994 memoir of his idyllic childhood, he tells of his disastrously successful teenage dalliance with making explosives: "It did not seem impossible to me that Mr. Nobel might soon have to look to his laurels."

IN MUCH OF HIS BEST WRITING, MOWAT DRAWS FROM HIS OWN LIFE experience. *Born Naked*, worth buying just for its title and cover photo of young Farley with a critter, recounts his years spent on the Saskatchewan prairies, pursuing what Mowat came to call the Others – creatures great and small. These included Mutt, the hero of *The Dog Who Wouldn't Be*, who climbed trees and ladders, wore goggles on road trips, and spit pits from cherries; and his two pet owls, Wol and Weeps, the stars of *Owls in the Family*.

There is something touching and sad about how Mowat views his childhood as the best years of his life. The line that ends *The Dog Who Wouldn't Be* – I won't quote it all – about heading "into the darkening tunnel of the years" is among the most moving I've ever read.

What's striking about Mowat's autobiographical writing is its candor. He acknowledges his father's infidelities (he has a whole book on his dad, 1993's *My Father's Son*, high on my must-read list) as casually as he relates how, at age 12, a neighborhood lad "introduced me to bestiality, onanism and homosexuality all in one fell swoop by first masturbating his dog, then himself, and finally me."

The Mowat book I found hardest to read is one that he, according to King, struggled mightily to write. *And No Birds Sang* is Mowat's 1979 account of his experiences in Sicily and Italy during World War II. It's as jam-packed with battles as any John Wayne film, and Mowat and his fellow Canadians were undeniably heroic, outfighting and outwitting seasoned German troops.

But Mowat bleeds war of any trace of glory, leaving only its searing intensity and senselessness. The most shocking atrocity he describes – fittingly enough, given his lifelong affinity for the Others – is that of a German sniper shattering the legs of a donkey, one by one, with rifle fire, for chuckles.

In the thick of his war experience, Mowat writes a letter home, a cry of pain that the passage of six decades has done nothing to mitigate:

> "I could try to tell you how I really feel deep down inside, but that wouldn't do either of us any ruddy good. The damnable truth is we are in really different worlds, on totally different planes, and I don't know you anymore. I only know the you that was. I wish I could explain the desperate sense of isolation, of not belonging to my own past, of being adrift in some kind of alien space. It is one of the toughest things we have to bear – that and the primal, gut-rotting worm of fear."

MOWAT'S LATEST BOOK, RELEASED TO CRITICAL ACCLAIM LAST YEAR, IS
Bay of Spirits: A Love Story. It details his travels along the rugged coast of Newfoundland in a boat named "Happy Adventure."

In 1957, on the tiny island of St. Pierre, Mowat met and fell head over heels for Claire Wheeler, a 27-year-old Toronto artist. Together they explored places and ways of life that, like much of what has drawn Mowat's attention, teetered on the edge of unsustainability.

The same might be said for his relationship with Claire, which was complicated by the fact that Mowat was, at the time, married to someone else, with two small children. But their relationship would survive this, as well as Mowat's own eventual infidelity and emotional distance, as King relates. Claire and Farley remain together, splitting their time between Port Hope, Ontario, and a farm in Nova Scotia.

Bay of Spirits may be Mowat's best book. It's one of several he's written about Newfoundland, and his descriptive powers and narrative skill have never been stronger. Here's a taste:

> "At dusk we cleared for home with one of the lads at the wheel while Skipper Alf and I repaired to the forepeak for a noggin of my rum and a feed of his dried capelin toasted on the hot stove top. Afterwards all four of us crowded into the small wheelhouse where the skipper played his accordion. We sang Newfoundland songs and old sea shanties while our wake spread astern like phosphorescent milk spilled from the rising moon."

Maybe it's strange that Mowat's writing has such a hold on me. My childhood was nothing like his, yet I feel a connection. I never went to war or sea or lived among native peoples, yet he makes these experiences real to me. I share his love of nature and the world of the Others. These are things I've had to seek out, as did he. And among the places I've found them is between the covers of a few good books.

SEPTEMBER 14, 2007

I sent a copy of this article to Farley Mowat, who wrote me a nice letter, saying "It makes an old fart like me feel good." I've now read a half-dozen more Mowat books, including his memoir about animals, Otherwise, published in 2008. I think it may be his best.

Ken Wulf with the author's bird, 2007. Photo by Linda Falkenstein

To Kill a Turkey

Ken Wulf told me exactly what to expect. I'd hold my bird's head and body down to the ground. I'd put a paring knife in its mouth and cut the back of its throat. Then I'd hang on — "a turkey is a very strong animal," he warned — while its lifeblood spurted out. "You'll be able to feel it," Wulf said. "When the last heartbeat goes, you'll know it's dead."

Wulf imparted this information casually, across his kitchen counter. The local poultry farmer, whom I'd called out of the blue the day before, readily assented to my request to "process" my own Thanksgiving turkey. To him, it made perfect sense. To me, it was a harder sell, despite being my idea.

I knew if I planned to have turkey for Thanksgiving — or on a sandwich for lunch — it was appropriate that I do this. All my life I've been having others kill the animals I eat. I try to buy meat from organic farmers, but I'm not a vegetarian. Animals die to feed me. They die in places I never look and try not to think about.

Once, in a supermarket parking lot, I saw a truck with a bumper sticker that asked, "What's more ridiculous than a meat eater who doesn't hunt?" I trotted after its owner, inspired to make a wise-guy reply: "A hunter who doesn't eat meat." On reflection, I concede the guy's point: If you cause the death of animals through your dietary choices, you ought to be willing to pull the trigger.

But for a nonhunter and self-proclaimed lover of animals, the cognition comes easier than the, er, execution. There's a reason people like me let others do their killing for them: We're cowards and hypocrites.

Not to mention fools. Our urge to look away when someone else kills the animals we eat is so great that our heads stay turned while their genetics are scrambled and their bodies are pumped full of chemicals.

My will to kill was inspired in part by Michael Pollan's great book, *The Omnivore's Dilemma*, where he slaughters chickens and hunts a wild pig. A photo of him beaming proudly over his fallen prey later moves him to revulsion: "I felt that I had stumbled on some stranger's pornography." Yet he eats what he kills, just as he's eaten hundreds of animals killed by others.

And so, for this Thanksgiving, I set out to know the animal that ended up on my table and play a direct role in putting it there – beyond slathering some oil, sprinkling some salt and sticking it in the oven at 325 degrees.

In the process, thanks to Ken Wulf and others, I got an education in poultry farming, organic and otherwise. One thing I learned is that, for most turkeys and chickens raised in America, there are far worse things than death.

IN THE MODERN AMERICAN DIET, POULTRY IS KING BECAUSE IT'S CHEAP.

You can buy whole chickens for about a dollar a pound; turkeys in season are even cheaper. Annually, the United States consumes 10 billion chickens – that's not a typo – and about 300 million turkeys, including 45 million each Thanksgiving.

Wisconsin, it's safe to say, eats more birds than it produces. The last agricultural census, in 2002, showed the state raised just 33 million chickens and six million turkeys. Only 600 of the big birds came from Dane County.

Almost all poultry served in the U.S. comes from huge operations like Butterball, Jennie-O and Tyson. The market for organic chicken and turkeys is minuscule, less than .1 percent of the total. Some years back I drove past a turkey farm in Minnesota. You could smell it from a mile away but there wasn't a turkey in sight. The birds – thousands of them – resided within long white enclosures. You'd never know they were there, except for the odor.

Commercial turkeys live in darkness and filth, with hardly more space than they need to stand. Their beaks and toes are lopped off at birth, with no anesthetic, to keep them from hurting other birds in close confinement. "They're foragers, and if they don't have anything to forage, they end up pecking at each other," explains Karen Davis, president of United Poultry Concerns in Virginia.

The genetically modified birds are given antibiotics to boost growth and prevent disease. It's been calculated that a human baby that grew as fast as a commercial turkey would weigh 1,500 pounds at 18 weeks. Some turkeys get so big they can't support their own weight, and use their wings in pitiful attempts to walk.

All commercial breeding turkeys, Wulf says, are artificially inseminated. That's not just for convenience but necessity. By the time the birds are sexually mature, they're too heavy for normal sex. One article I found said a two-person team can inseminate 600 hens per hour, or 10 per minute. That involves presenting the animal, exposing her oviduct (vagina), inserting a tube and squeezing a trigger. Talk about sex without romance.

The factory farm environment is not conducive to tender treatment of animals. An undercover video taken by PETA (People for the Ethical Treatment of Animals) at a turkey farm in Minnesota shows a man bludgeoning birds with a metal pipe and wringing their necks with his bare hands. The local district attorney declined to prosecute.

I also watched an online video called "Butterball House of Horrors." One memorable clip showed an employee bragging, "I kicked the [blank] out of the mother[blank]er. His [blank]ing eyeball popped out." The words are so ugly I feel the need to hide them. The act is of course even worse – especially from the turkey's perspective.

Other documented acts of cruelty against commercial turkeys include tearing live birds apart, stomping them, punching them, even sexually assaulting them.

Turkeys raised on these farms are slaughtered at 12 to 26 weeks of age, well short of their 10- to 12-year natural lifespan. They are packed into crates and sent to processing plants, where they're hung upside down by their feet on a conveyor belt. Then they're either zapped with a handheld stunner or dipped face-first into an electrified bath. This is done, notes Davis, "to facilitate feather release," not to incapacitate the birds. They remain conscious as their throats are cut, and sometimes still when they are tossed into scalding water for de-feathering. There is a more humane method, approved by the USDA and used widely in Europe, of killing birds in their crates by removing their oxygen. But U.S. food processors have resisted this change.

"No other country raises and slaughters its food animals quite as intensively or as brutally as we do," writes Pollan in his book. "The industrial animal factory offers a nightmarish glimpse of what capitalism is capable of in the absence of any moral or regulatory constraint."

KENNY WULF'S LIFELONG ATTACHMENT TO THE LAND HAS ITS ROOTS IN A tragic industrial accident. When he was six and living in Detroit, his father was involved in a catastrophic tetrachloride spill at work. Twenty-eight workers died. Ken's father, one of just three survivors, sustained extensive damage to his liver and lungs. He was told that the Detroit-area air might finish him off, so he moved his family to Rhinelander, in northern Wisconsin.

The family, which had 11 children, grew much of what it ate in a large garden plot. When Ken was 10, he struck on a scheme that got him started in the chicken business.

It was Easter and the local feed store was giving away brightly colored baby chicks – dye was injected into their shells before hatching – as a promotion. The dye wore off after a few days, and so did people's interest in the chicks. Wulf ran an ad in the *Hodag Shopper* offering to take them. "I ended up with 480 of the 500 they gave away."

His grandmother, impressed by his initiative, helped him build a wattle-and-daub shed and paid for the birds' feed. At 12 weeks, they averaged five to seven pounds. Then he and his grandma butchered them, about 30 a day.

"Since I was eight years old, I could clean any animal on the planet," says Wulf, now 55. He's raised chickens, turkeys, ducks, geese, rabbits, even raccoons. After a stint in the Marines in Vietnam, he became a supervisor at a Tyson plant in Arkansas, a job he left "without regrets."

For much of his life, Wulf worked construction. But wherever he was, he kept critters and had a big organic garden. "There's nothing more good for your soul than to put on your plate food you grew yourself," he says. "That's better than prayer."

Wulf rents land for his chickens from the R&G Miller Farm across the street from his home in East Bristol. He took me on a tour to a barn with hutches, wherein hopped about two dozen rabbits – white, brown, black and gray. Wulf explained how he would stun them with a snap of his wrist, to dislocate their spinal cord, then bleed them to death. At the time, his hand was in a cast from a mishap, so he couldn't demonstrate. I was glad for the cast.

Does it ever bother Wulf to ... you know?

"I started so young, it was just a natural thing," he says. "I was taught you kill animals with respect and you do it ceremoniously. If you kill something, you should have respect for the animal."

When the time comes, Wulf will drape a cloth over the hutches, so the rabbits can't see what's going on.

Wulf – whose name I found in a local directory of earth- and animal-friendly farmers – mistrusts the government almost as much as corporate food producers. He thinks Congress and the federal agencies in charge of protecting the nation's food supply are "on the take." And the nation's food supply is being compromised as a result.

"I don't ever order chicken when I go to a restaurant because I know what's in them, and I don't want it in me," he says. Indeed, one main reason he raises chickens is "for my own self-defense."

The problem with my plan to slaughter a turkey from Wulf is that, when I called, he didn't have any. He wants to branch out into turkey farming next year, but this year stuck to chickens.

Wulf returned to chicken farming in 2004, teaming up with John Miller to form what's now known as J&K Certified Organic Meats. This year he raised 3,000 birds, the last of which were processed in August. His entire operation is certified organic; he buys feed from the Millers and uses pens designed by Joel Salatin, a Virginia-based organic farmer who stars in Pollan's book. (The pens are moved from spot to spot, serving as mobile fertilizing units.)

It's a hard life. Wulf still owes $1,000 to the hatchery that provided his chicks and $5,000 to the plant that processed them. He's in the process of buying out Miller and converting his company to sole proprietorship.

"Everything I've made in the chicken business goes back into the business," he says. "Everybody gets paid but me."

Wulf does not lack confidence in his product, which he proclaims "the best chicken in the world." But it costs much more to raise certified organic chickens in what he calls "the most humane manner possible" than to give them a hellish existence on big factory farms. Wulf sells birds for $2.89 a pound, some directly to restaurants, some to grocery stores. He sets up at several local farmers' markets. He makes cold-call visits to restaurants, urging them to try his product, to see how good it is.

But many restaurants and consumers don't care about anything but cost. About half the birds he raised this year remain in freezers, awaiting buyers. Wulf keeps plugging away, with evident frustration. As he puts it, "It takes a special kind of motivation to get up in the morning and go to work knowing you're not going to get a paycheck."

TO SATISFY MY REQUEST FOR A TURKEY TO KILL, WULF OFFERED ME ONE of six Thanksgiving turkeys he'd arranged to get from Elmer Beechy, an Amish farmer.

Beechy raises Nicholas white turkeys, which Wulf calls "a bird as perfect as any we can get." It's a heritage turkey, meaning it's a product of selective breeding, not genetic manipulation. Its lineage traces to the eastern wild turkey.

In early October, my wife, Linda, and I visited Beechy, just northeast of Hillsboro in beautiful Vernon County. He lives with his wife and 15 children – that's not a typo – in a sparsely furnished home with a large wood stove and small handwritten sign: "Smile, God loves you."

We came upon Beechy riding his horse-drawn buggy to the land he rents to raise turkeys, about two miles away, and met up with him there. He showed us his two flocks, each consisting of 1,500 birds. One flock, in its last 10 days of life, was 15–16 weeks old. The other, to be processed closer to Thanksgiving, was a few weeks younger. The birds are sent off to Minnesota or Iowa for processing.

Beechy and his family moved to Wisconsin from northern Indiana in 1996. He began raising turkeys several years later, originally for Organic Valley, now on his own. He sells his birds under the brand name Tilth Farms; some go to stores, most to distributors who take orders from customers. He has no trouble unloading 3,000 turkeys. Once people taste them, he boasts, "they come back for more."

We were invited to wander around and take pictures – but only of the birds, not of Beechy or his family, per Amish sensibilities. When Linda approached, the turkeys waddled in her direction, curious, making rat-a-tat sounds: "hark-hark-hark-hark-hark, hark-hark-hark-hark-hark-hark-hark." They were clearly happy.

Turkeys are friendly and social. In nature, they'll spend their first five months – longer than most of those raised for meat are allowed to live – glued to their moms. They have distinct personalities and can recognize human faces. Ben Franklin touted the turkey ("a true original native of America") over the eagle as the national bird.

Matthew Smith, a farmer in Blue Mounds, raises several varieties of heritage turkeys, about 250 birds a year, most sold directly to consumers. He starts his flock in May and sends them off to a processing plant in November, just before Thanksgiving. His birds are not certified organic, since Smith feeds them "run-of-the-mill" scraps from grocery stores, not just organic grain.

"You get pretty well attached to them," he says. "I talk to them and listen to them. You can see when they're happy, when they're excited, when they're terrified." They go "bonkers" when he feeds them, emptying a 55-gallon drum of old fruit. At night they sleep in the branches of trees, an age-old protection against predators.

Smith likes and respects his birds. "My philosophy is, I want to make their time here as joyful as possible." He would not buy a commercial turkey, because he knows what they go through: "They can barely stand up. They can't stretch their wings. They don't even see the light of day."

Smith's birds sell for $4.25 per pound, more than four times what it costs to buy a Butterball at the supermarket. And even still, he says, "We're not getting rich off this."

LESS THAN A WEEK AFTER MY FIRST VISIT, I WAS BACK ON BEECHY'S farm, opening the hinged lids of two crates while Wulf and Beechy seized turkeys by their thrusting legs. One by one they inserted the birds upside down into the crates. I held down the lids with my feet, as Wulf instructed.

"These are beautiful birds, Elmer," Wulf remarked. "You did a good job." Beechy was matter-of-fact. "Lot of good eatin' here," he said, stuffing in the sixth and final bird. I fastened the lids with bungee cords and we drove back to Beechy's house. We weighed the full crates on an ancient scale, subtracting what they weighed when empty. It came to 20 pounds per bird.

"Just pay me what you think you can and come out okay," said Beechy, suggesting a price. Wulf topped it, paying $1.80 per pound, more than half what he'll get after processing, when the turkeys will weigh about 20 percent less.

The caged turkeys seemed calm, their snoods changing color from pale pink to bright red to purple/blue. This is done for show, like a peacock spreading its tail. On the way home I watched them through the rear window; some were blinky-eyed, like my dogs when they're tired.

Wulf's cast came off the day we drove to Beechy's farm, but his hand still hurt and he couldn't firmly grasp a knife. I ran into him at the Northside

Farmers' Market near my home, and he suggested we "dispatch" my turkey the following Friday, the last in October.

At 8 a.m., I arrived at Wulf's house in East Bristol. The bird he had picked out for me was in a pen in his backyard, near a table and a pail of water being heated. It was, he said, the biggest and most dominant of the bunch.

Wulf showed me his forearm, marked with deep scratches. My turkey had done this to him the day before, despite all Wulf's experience, when he moved it from the Miller farm to this backyard pen. That's how powerful and unpredictable they are, "20 pounds of muscle and hollow bones."

There wasn't a lot of ceremony. Wulf grabbed the turkey by the neck and it reacted violently, thrashing its wings and jabbing its legs in all directions. He set it on the ground, holding down its neck with his hand and its body with his knee. He called me over to take his place. The bird tried to push upward and I was astounded by its strength. I had to squat on top of it to keep it still.

A moment later, Wulf was back with the paring knife. The turkey's mouth was open and he told me to insert the blade and make the cut, "from ear to ear."

I knew this moment was coming and thought this was where I'd wrestle with my conscience. I'd tell myself this turkey had an uncommonly good life, on a farm in Vernon County. We should all be so lucky. It was raised for one reason – to be, in the end, "good eatin'." And death would come swiftly.

But could I really kill this animal? And for what? So I could have a tasty meal? My son is a vegetarian; so are some of my friends. They manage to eat without animals dying. Why can't I?

None of these thoughts occurred to me. There wasn't time. I started inserting the knife, then hesitated. "Ken?"

He took the knife from my hand and plunged it in, severing the arteries at the back of the throat. "I don't want the animal to suffer," he said, by way of explanation. He gave the knife back to me and I made another pass. Blood was flowing from the bird's mouth. It stopped struggling almost right away, but I could feel its heart beating against my thighs. Seconds later, it stopped.

WE LET THE TURKEY BLEED INTO THE GRASS FOR A COUPLE OF MINUTES, then slung its body on the table, neck hanging down, to bleed some more.

Holding the bird by its feet, I dripped it into the water, heated to 150 degrees. It smelled instantly like turkey soup. Wulf counted out 60 seconds. I flopped it back on the table and we began plucking feathers. They came off easily, but it took a fair amount of time.

We cut off the turkey's head and feet, tossing these into a garbage can. We removed the neck. Next we cut out the anus, being careful not to penetrate the membrane behind it. Wulf had me reach in and pull out the gizzard, which he later sliced open to show me the tiny stones the bird had swallowed to help it digest. With the gizzard came several feet of intestines.

"It's a lot easier going to the grocery," Wulf joked. The notebook I wrote this in is stained with blood.

One by one, we removed the organs: heart, lungs, liver, kidneys, gallbladder. "Look at that liver, it's beautiful," said Wulf. It was deep purple, the color of cooked beets. A commercial turkey, he said, would have a pinkish liver, because of all the starches in its diet. And the heart of a commercial turkey would be five times as large, all bound up in fat. This one was small and lean. Toward the end, we removed the testes, indicating my turkey's sex. He'd been too young – "just a young boy," said Wulf – to identify by external organs.

The last step was dropping the bird into a vat of water, to clean and cool it. Wulf kept the neck meat, liver and giblets, having failed to convince me that these were the best parts. Then we bagged the bird, and weighed it: 18.76 pounds. He sold it to me for $3.50 a pound.

We'll have the turkey at my mom's house this Thanksgiving, with my whole extended family, 14 people in all. I'm sure it will taste good, and mean more to me because of what I did to get it. But the experience left me neither pleased nor proud. And when I saw the photos I took of the prostrate bird, blood dripping from its mouth, I felt sickened and ashamed.

It reminds me of a story a friend told me about her husband, a stockbroker-turned-farmer. He had raised some birds on his farm and slaughtered them, something he had never done before. He didn't like it, and told her so.

She replied in a word: "Good."

NOVEMBER 23, 2007

Ken Wulf liquidated J&K Poultry in 2009 and sold off most of his equipment, but he still raises chickens and turkeys for himself and his family. "I can't do store chicken," he says.

An Excruciating Visit to the Dentist

"**A**re you excited?" she asked me, as I took my place on the reclining dentist's chair. She was young, in her early 20s, very pretty. My mind raced: What would I be excited about? Was this going to be one of those *Penthouse Forum* encounters?

Then it occurred to me. Today is the New Hampshire presidential primary.

Could that be it? It would surprise me that a person so young could be so plugged in. But isn't that what's propelled the candidacies of Barack Obama, Ron Paul and Mike Huckabee – fired-up young people seizing their chance to be involved?

I decided not to leap to any conclusions. "Excited about what?" I asked her. "About getting your fillings replaced!" she answered. Silly me. "The highlight of my year so far," I cracked.

The young dental assistant – let's call her Heather (not her real name but close enough) – asked if I wanted the TV on. I almost said no, then remembered how mind-numbing it can be to have people working on your mouth with no place for your brain to go. "Sure," I said.

She handed me the remote and told me I could pick the channel. Often in the early morning I watch "Fox and Friends," but I didn't know if Heather and the dentist would realize I was being ironic, so I turned the tube to CNN.

The dentist came in and gave me a few injections. Heather had already numbed the area with a cotton swab. He told me I probably wouldn't feel a thing.

As it turned out, the encounter was probably the most painful experience I've ever had at a dentist's office. I say "probably" because there's one memorable occasion in close contention.

When I was a kid, maybe 12 or 13, a dentist drilling a hole for a filling went too deep, turning my mouth into an epicenter of blinding pain. The dentist called over another person – maybe a dental assistant, maybe a student.

"See there," he said casually, pointing to a spot in my mouth. "That's an exposed nerve."

BACK TO MADISON, JAN. 8, 2008.

Everything went well for the first 15 minutes. Roger Clemens was angrily defending his honor against accusations that he used performance-enhancing drugs. There was a story about some creep who led police to the body of a hiker he killed.

Then Bill Richardson came on to talk about the New Hampshire primary. I couldn't see him, because of the way I had to turn my head, and I didn't hear him introduced, because the drill was grinding away at my old fillings – three of them, at a cost to me of nearly $100 each, after my insurance did its part. But I recognized Richardson from his voice and his references to New Mexico.

Heather's grasp of the situation was apparently less acute. "What are they voting for?" she asked the dentist.

He explained that it was the New Hampshire primary. "Oh," she said, not comprehending. "When do we vote for president?" She took a wild stab: "October?"

"November," the dentist corrected.

The thought ran through my head: "The Wisconsin primary is February 19, about six weeks away!" But I didn't say it. For one thing, the dentist had resumed drilling in my mouth. For another, here was a person who didn't even realize the New Hampshire primary had something to do with the presidential election. Did I really want her to find out about the primary in Wisconsin?

"But it's this year, right?" Heather said, processing the dentist's comment. Nothing gets past this woman, I thought.

It turned out that Heather had more to say about the presidential sweepstakes she barely knew was going on. "I don't care who gets elected," she announced, "just as long as there's no more war."

Awwww.

There was more still. "I've never voted," Heather confessed. "But I'm going to vote this time. I'm going to vote for Hillary."

I thought maybe that was the only candidate whose name Heather knew, but I was wrong. She offered this nugget: "Obama annoys me."

Look who's talking, I thought.

The dentist gently encouraged Heather to vote for whichever candidate she liked but by all means vote. My brain began screaming: "NO, NO,

NO, NO, NO, NO, NO! NOOOOOOOOOOOOOOOOOOOOO!!!!!"

Until five minutes earlier, Heather hadn't even been certain this was a presidential election year. Now she was being openly encouraged to vote.

I considered my options. I could ask the dentist to stop drilling so I could lecture Heather on civic responsibility. But that seemed and still seems like a rude thing to do. I thought about asking the dentist to please just kill me, and see if perhaps that would be taken as a cue that I had had enough talk about politics. Again, that seemed somehow not right.

There's nothing I can do about it, I realized. Not until next time. Then I can insist on being anesthetized.

JANUARY 8, 2008, ISTHMUS | THEDAILYPAGE.COM

Election Night with the Dane County GOP

A t least they had sense enough not to call it a Victory Party. The event that brought together a couple hundred Republicans Tuesday night at City Center West, an office park on Madison's far west side, was dubbed an "Election Night Watching Party." The people there knew John McCain and Sarah Palin were not likely to win.

Of course, that doesn't mean they were not delusional.

"The guy has no experience," one of the attendees was loudly proclaiming about Barack Obama as I entered the large conference room with two giant TV screens. The man, a mustached fellow of about 50, was incensed. "The people of this country are so stupid and naïve, they can't see this stuff. They can't see the writing on the wall."

There was writing on the wall all right. It was about 7:40 p.m. and the media had just called Pennsylvania for Obama. I positioned myself within earshot of Mr. Mustache and jotted down as much as I could.

He was talking about how the media were obviously biased in Obama's favor. "I get so sick of that stuff. I can't tell you how sick," he said, launching into a list of things he could not tolerate. One was: "I can't tolerate same-sex marriage. The Democrats are big on that."

I briefly considered asking what he was talking about, since Obama and Biden and the Democratic Party are all opposed to gay marriage. But he was soon on to another topic.

"They're going to throw the Bible away," he announced. "You know, it wouldn't surprise me if the Democrats started using the Koran."

Mr. Mustache was on a roll. "And Pelosi, somebody ought to give her a broom and say, 'Fly away on this thing.'"

The huge TV screens were locked on to Fox News. The sound was just loud enough to hear but few people seemed to be listening. Besides, from my perspective, Mr. Mustache was more interesting.

"They're going to raise taxes," he intoned, invoking the specter of a Democratic president as well as Democratic Congress. "You can't stop them. They're totally unstoppable." The person he was talking to nodded in agreement.

"And then this business about spreading the wealth," Mr. Mustache continued. "What a crock! I don't make a lot of money. He'll probably take what I have and give it to some homeless person on the street."

Later in the evening, Mr. Mustache saw my name tag, which identified me as being with *Isthmus*, and struck up a conversation. Turns out he's a regular reader. Nice guy.

BILL RICHARDSON, THE MEDIA COORDINATOR FOR THE DANE COUNTY
Republicans, encouraged me to talk to the group's vice chair, Dave Baker, if I wanted someone to quote. I asked if the chair, whom I've spoken to in the past but whose name I couldn't remember, was present.

Yes, said Richardson, pointing out a tall, stocky fellow in a blue shirt and tie. Richardson told me the man's name but asked me not to use it. He said the man's business relationships could be imperiled if this information came out.

So I spoke to Dave Baker. It was just about 8 p.m., and Fox News was saying Obama had 200 electoral votes in the bag compared to McCain's 81. I asked why he thought the election was turning out this way.

"Money can buy an election," Baker reflected, referring to the "media blitz and robo-calls" coming from the Obama campaign. I mentioned that I had gotten quite a few robo-calls, but almost all were from Republicans. Baker allowed that there were other reasons for the Democrats' success.

"Obama has an excellent delivery. He has a way of telling people what they want to hear." The economy was hurting, and Obama promised relief.

But Baker, a retired insurance executive, said Obama's plan just did not add up. He's promised to cut taxes for most Americans but, according to Baker, 40 percent of the American public isn't paying taxes anyway. Moreover, "I'm very concerned about his redistribution of wealth, which is contrary to the American tradition. We're a democracy, not a socialist state."

I pointed out that, in fact, Obama merely wants to rescind the tax cuts for the wealthy that John McCain himself once opposed. Baker allowed he didn't know enough about it to say.

By this time, I had again forgotten the name of the Dane County Republican Party chair. I asked Baker, but he refused to say: "I'm not sure he wants that public."

Later, a photographer from a student paper told me he'd been instructed not to take anyone's photo or quote them without permission. He says he was told this was because there could be serious consequences for some people if it were to come to light that they're Republicans.

Just after 8:30 p.m., the chairman whose name is secret made an announcement from the podium: "It's looking to be a little bleak but there's a long way to go." The room was filling with people. There was lots of food. That's one nice thing about GOP events – there's always a good spread. Democrats usually just put out a couple of bowls of popcorn and pretzels.

Isthmus blogger David Blaska was there, remarking dryly that he was "clinging to my guns and my God." There were a group of young women wearing what appeared to be prom dresses with ridiculous high heels. There was a young man with a blond Mohawk strip dyed in his short black hair and a McCain-Palin sticker on his back. I listened in as he was interviewed by WTDY radio. Mr. Mohawk said he was attracted to McCain because he cared about truth, like all of the babies being aborted. He urged people to consider, but for all these abortions, "how much more money would be in Social Security today."

PERHAPS THE MOST ASTOUNDING CONTRIBUTION TO THE FESTIVITIES WAS when Dr. Kenneth Luedke, the chiropractor (now retired), went around the room handing out a four-page printout of an e-mail to everyone. "Something to think about for the future," he said, as he handed one to me. The first thing I noticed was that it was wastefully printed on only one side of the page; the second was that it was utterly insane.

The handout was a transparently fraudulent letter entitled "A German lady remembers and speaks." What this German lady remembered was that Adolf Hitler came to power during a period of economic crisis while promising "change." The next thing you know, the Holocaust. The woman went on to warn that history was apparently repeating itself.

"I have heard what this man Obama says about abortion and the 'mercy killing' of babies who are not wanted," the letter said. "Where are your voices? Where is your outrage? Where is passion and your vote? Do you vote based on an abortionist's empty promises and economics? Or do you vote according to the Bible?"

I looked around the room and saw people reading the letter. No one seemed to think it was out of bounds. When I caught up to Dr. Luedtke later, it was clear I was the first person to challenge him on it. "What's your point?" I asked. "That Barack Obama is as bad as Adolf Hitler?"

Oh no, Dr. Luedtke replied, only that he might bring about something similar, perhaps inadvertently. The letter was just food for thought, something to consider. By the way, Luedtke is also a loyal *Isthmus* reader.

There was a well-known real estate developer who had several empty beer cans on the table in front of him. He was marveling at how well McCain was doing, despite being clearly on his way to losing the election. "I'm surprised he was able to keep it this close," the man told me. "This should have been a regular Reagan-Mondale blowout."

Carl Skalitzke, a failed candidate for state Assembly, gave a little talk about the need to recruit more GOP candidates. "I have a digital camera, and I ran for state Assembly," he said. "If you have a digital camera, you can run for state Senate."

It's hard to argue with logic like that.

I didn't stay to watch the audience respond to John McCain's gracious concession speech from Arizona, so I don't know if the Republicans of Madison booed Obama, as did McCain's audience. I headed home just in time to hear Obama give his stirring victory address from Chicago. Just as I pulled into the driveway, I swear, two deer bounded across my front yard. I'm pretty sure they were Democrats.

NOVEMBER 5, 2008, ISTHMUS | THEDAILYPAGE.COM

Initially, GOP spokesperson Richardson [no relation to the governor of New Mexico] posted a reply thanking me for attending and commending my report, adding, "Yes, we have all kinds of people with close-in and far-out ideas on how the world should go." He later changed his mind, likening me to a guest who comes to a party and leaves "a turd in the punchbowl" and announcing that I was banned from all future Dane County GOP events.

The cabin at dusk. Photo by Bill Lueders

My Cabin in the Woods

For most of my life, it's something I've wanted: a cabin in the woods. Part of that owes to Thoreau's *Walden*, my favorite book, which I first read in my teens. The idea of cobbling together a place to live with boards from the mill, nails from the general store, and know-how passed on through the generations has powerful appeal. It's the ultimate compact between humankind and the natural world: Here, in this spot, I will build a place to live.

My wife, Linda, and I spent four years looking for a suitable piece of land. About a dozen times a year, we'd hit the road with a *Gazetteer* and a list of available properties, culled from want ads and real-estate listings. Most were not right for one or another reason — too much open space or not enough, too hilly or too flat. A couple of rather nice parcels were located smack-dab next to what appeared to be unauthorized junkyards, or hunting camps in which empty beer cans served as lawn ornaments.

We actually found several properties we liked enough to put in offers. At the time, the value of land was rising faster than mist off hot pavement; it nearly doubled during that four-year search. We lost out on more than one piece of property by offering only the asking price.

In the fall of 2005 we found a 13-acre patch of land in Richland County that would become our own. It's an oblong parcel on a north-facing slope, mostly wooded with a couple acres of wetland. A tiny, burbling, spring-fed creek runs along the front of the property; a large rock outcropping juts out imposingly high on a hill.

We offered the seller $200 more than he was asking and he accepted, a bit grudgingly; the deal was sealed at a Richland Center title company in late November. We came to the land the next day to stroll about in blaze orange while the shots of deer hunters rang through the hills. I felt like an intruder.

THE FIRST YEAR WE BUILT A CAMPSITE, AND CLEARED A TRAIL TO IT. Linda and I camped there a few times and spent many a day walking the property. I scoped out several possible building sites, including one right in front of the rock outcropping. I would stand there for long periods, imagining, but somehow it never seemed right. It was just too audacious — to take the most striking geological feature and use it as a backdrop. The gods might have sent the rock walls tumbling down, crushing my cabin and presumption.

The following summer, I cleared the driveway one tree at a time. I picked a route that preserved as many quality trees as possible, but still more than 100 bit the dust, including several that were 70 feet or taller. Each weekend I'd get another few yards further up the hillside.

I was about 450 feet in when I reached the first of my prospective sites. This time the gods left no doubt as to their wishes. "This will do," they told me.

There were other trials and tribulations. Getting the engineering work and permit to install a culvert to cross our tiny creek took more than a year. (Yes, we needed a culvert permit, as well as a sanitation permit, driveway permit, land-use permit, building permit and address-sign permit, all with their own separate fees.) We had to deal with an array of regulators, contractors and inspectors. And I managed to have an accident with a chain saw that sliced my ear in half.

In search of inspiration, I checked out a model Amish cabin on Highway 14 just east of Richland Center. Two thoughts occurred to me. The first: This is gorgeous. The second: This is *way* out of my league.

I contacted Harvey Schmucker, the builder of those cabins, who lives on a beautiful spread a few miles from our land. He has a sawmill on his property, and 11 – er, make that 12 – kids to help him with his business.

Harvey's cabins – he reckons he's completed more than 300 in all – are made with rectangular grooved logs stacked on top of one another, joined with wooden pegs and huge screws. He uses freshly milled logs (his yard contains some of the thickest pine trees I've ever seen) that dry after the cabin is assembled.

Harvey gave me template drawings of building plans – including front, back and side views – and some advice. Then it was up to me to produce the building plans. After a few frustrating hours with a ruler and bottle of white-out, I scanned the drawings and imported them into Photoshop, then tailored them to our cabin's dimensions: 28 by 16 feet, with a loft on one side and an eight-foot front porch.

Building this cabin, start to finish, took Harvey's crew nine days in the middle of December. It snowed several of those days, but the crew's hired driver plowed the driveway, and "the boys" kept warm with scrap-wood fires. I saw them finish the job on the last day, Dec. 20. It was like they were all part of a single organism, none charged with any particular task but all constantly doing something that needed to be done.

And then we wrote the final checks and Harvey handed us the keys.

EARLIER, I HAD WORRIED THAT NOT ACTUALLY BUILDING THE CABIN MIGHT deprive me of a sense of contribution. I was wrong. When Harvey's crew finished, my work had just begun.

I installed a wood stove and built a bathroom. I painstakingly cut 10 holes into the log walls, for electric outlets, using a plunge router powered by a cheap generator to reach the vertical holes the Amish had drilled through the three lowest rungs. In early spring, I crawled under the cabin, through mud and puddles, tacking up the electric wiring. I sanded and sealed the floors, installed cabinets and built bookshelves. I gathered rocks on the property, rolling them down hillsides, to construct a 30-foot-long retaining wall. I built a two-cord woodshed using trees for its support, with a giant birch going literally right through the roof.

The electric didn't get hooked up until August, in part because the ground was soaked all summer from the spring rains. Then we plugged in our composting toilet, which vents up though the loft and out the roof. I rigged up a vanity to draw water from a five-gallon jug on the other side of the wall, inside the bathroom.

As fall arrived, there was grass seed to plant and wood to split, from piles I'd stacked the year before. And it was around this time – after a lifetime of want and three years of work; after I'd spent dozens of weekends working morning to night, returning with bags of clothes soaked in sweat and socks so dirty they had to be thrown out; after the umpteenth time I worked until my hands and forearms locked up in painful cramps; after I stumbled upon a hornet's nest whose occupants greeted me more than 30 times – it dawned on me: I've earned the right to be here.

In mid-October, we had a cookout at the cabin and invited all the neighbors. They brought their children and their dogs, and we had more food than necessary. People enjoyed each others' company and hiked the trails we'd made.

Our cabin feels, if not like home, then at least a place where we belong. I think about it often, whether I'm there or not, planning projects, envisioning what it will become. The hardest part for me is to remember that it's about more than just work. Sometimes, I make myself put down my tools even though there's more to do, and sit for a while on my cabin's porch, listening to the not-so-distant burble of the creek.

SEPTEMBER 2009

This is a slightly longer version of an essay that appeared in Wisconsin Trails *magazine.*

About the Author

BILL LUEDERS, A NATIVE OF MILWAUKEE, IS THE NEWS EDITOR of *Isthmus,* Madison's alternative weekly newspaper, and the elected president of the Wisconsin Freedom of Information Council, a statewide group that works to protect public access to government meetings and records. He is the editor of a 1982 anthology of Milwaukee poets and a co-founder of *The Crazy Shepherd,* now the successful city weekly, *Shepherd Express.* Lueders (pronounced "leaders") has worked at *Isthmus* since 1986, receiving national awards for editorial writing and reporting on animal issues, and state awards for investigative reporting, legal reporting, interpretative reporting, business reporting and column writing. He is the author of the books *An Enemy of the State: The Life of Erwin Knoll* and *Cry Rape: The True Story of One Woman's Harrowing Quest for Justice.* He lives on Madison's north side with his wife, Linda Falkenstein, and two much-loved dogs.